ENGLISH FILE

Pre-intermediate Student's Book

Paul Seligson and Clive Oxenden are the original co-authors of
English File 1 and *English File 2*

Contents

		Grammar	Vocabulary	Pronunciation
	1			
4	**A** Where are you from?	word order in questions	common verb phrases, spelling and numbers	vowel sounds, the alphabet
6	**B** Charlotte's choice	present simple	describing people: appearance and personality	final -s / -es
8	**C** Mr and Mrs Clark and Percy	present continuous	clothes, prepositions of place	/ə/ and /ɜː/
10	**PRACTICAL ENGLISH** Episode 1 Hotel problems			
	2			
12	**A** Right place, wrong person	past simple: regular and irregular verbs	holidays	regular verbs: -ed endings
14	**B** The story behind the photo	past continuous	prepositions of time and place: at, in, on	sentence stress
16	**C** One dark October evening	time sequencers and connectors	verb phrases	word stress
18	**REVISE AND CHECK 1&2**			
	3			
20	**A** Plans and dreams	be going to (plans and predictions)	airports	sentence stress and fast speech
22	**B** Let's meet again	present continuous (future arrangements)	verbs + prepositions e.g. arrive in	sounding friendly
24	**C** What's the word?	defining relative clauses	expressions for paraphrasing: like, for, example, etc.	pronunciation in a dictionary
26	**PRACTICAL ENGLISH** Episode 2 Restaurant problems			
	4			
28	**A** Parents and teenagers	present perfect + yet, just, already	housework, make or do?	/j/ and /dʒ/
30	**B** Fashion and shopping	present perfect or past simple? (1)	shopping	c and ch
32	**C** Lost weekend	something, anything, nothing, etc.	adjectives ending -ed and -ing	/e/, /əʊ/, and /ʌ/
34	**REVISE AND CHECK 3&4**			
	5			
36	**A** No time for anything	comparative adjectives and adverbs, as…as	time expressions: spend time, etc.	sentence stress
38	**B** Superlative cities	superlatives (+ ever + present perfect)	describing a town or city	word and sentence stress
40	**C** How much is too much?	quantifiers, too, not enough	health and the body	/ʌ/, /uː/, /aɪ/, and /e/
42	**PRACTICAL ENGLISH** Episode 3 The wrong shoes			
	6			
44	**A** Are you a pessimist?	will / won't (predictions)	opposite verbs	'll, won't
46	**B** I'll never forget you	will / won't (decisions, offers, promises)	verb + back	word stress: two-syllable verbs
48	**C** The meaning of dreaming	review of verb forms: present, past, and future	adjectives + prepositions	the letters ow
50	**REVISE AND CHECK 5&6**			

		Grammar	Vocabulary	Pronunciation
	7			
52	**A** How to...	uses of the infinitive with *to*	verbs + infinitive: *try to*, *forget to*, etc.	weak form of *to*, linking
54	**B** Being happy	uses of the gerund (verb + *-ing*)	verbs + gerund	the letter *i*
56	**C** Learn a language in a month!	*have to*, *don't have to*, *must*, *mustn't*	modifiers: *a bit*, *really*, etc.	*must*, *mustn't*
58	**PRACTICAL ENGLISH** Episode 4 At the pharmacy			
	8			
60	**A** I don't know what to do!	*should*	*get*	/ʊ/ and /uː/, sentence stress
62	**B** If something can go wrong,…	*if* + present, *will* + infinitive (first conditional)	confusing verbs	linking
64	**C** You must be mine	possessive pronouns	adverbs of manner	sentence rhythm
66	**REVISE AND CHECK 7&8**			
	9			
68	**A** What would you do?	*if* + past, *would* + infinitive (second conditional)	animals	word stress
70	**B** I've been afraid of it for years	present perfect + *for* and *since*	phobias and words related to fear	sentence stress
72	**C** Born to sing	present perfect or past simple? (2)	biographies	word stress, /ɔː/
74	**PRACTICAL ENGLISH** Episode 5 Getting around			
	10			
76	**A** The mothers of invention	passive	verbs: *invent*, *discover*, etc.	/ʃ/, *-ed*, sentence stress
78	**B** Could do better	*used to*	school subjects	*used to* / *didn't use to*
80	**C** Mr Indecisive	*might*	word building: noun formation	diphthongs
82	**REVISE AND CHECK 9&10**			
	11			
84	**A** Bad losers	expressing movement	sports, expressing movement	sports
86	**B** Are you a morning person?	word order of phrasal verbs	phrasal verbs	linking
88	**C** What a coincidence!	*so*, *neither* + auxiliaries	similarities	sentence stress, /ð/ and /θ/
90	**PRACTICAL ENGLISH** Episode 6 Time to go home			
	12			
92	**A** Strange but true!	past perfect	verb phrases	contractions: *had* / *hadn't*
94	**B** Gossip is good for you	reported speech	*say* or *tell*?	double consonants
96	**C** The *English File* quiz	questions without auxiliaries	revision	revision
98	**REVISE AND CHECK 11&12**			

100	Communication		126	Grammar Bank	164	Irregular verbs
111	Writing		150	Vocabulary Bank	166	Sound Bank
118	Listening					

G word order in questions
V common verb phrases, spelling and numbers
P vowel sounds, the alphabet

1A Where are you from?

What do you do?
I'm at university.

1 VOCABULARY & SPEAKING common verb phrases

1 HOME AND FAMILY
- Where _____ you from?
- Where _____ you born?
- Where do you _____?
- Do you _____ in a house or flat?
- Do you _____ any brothers and sisters?
- Do you _____ any pets?

2 JOB / STUDIES
- What do you _____?
- Where do you _____?
- Do you _____ your job?
- What school / university do you _____ to?
- What year _____ you in?
- Can you _____ any other languages? Which?
- Where did you _____ English before?

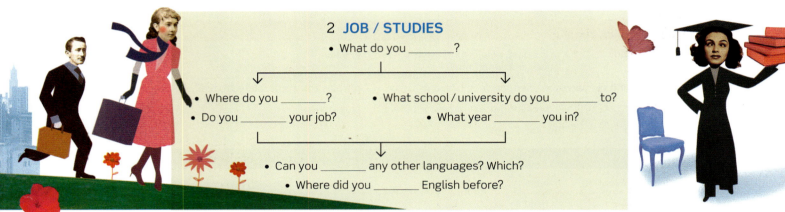

3 FREE TIME
- What kind of music do you _____ to?
- Do you _____ a musical instrument? Which?
- What TV programmes do you _____?
- Do you _____ any sport or exercise? What?
- What kind of books or magazines do you _____?
- How often do you _____ to the cinema?
- What did you _____ last weekend?

a Complete the questions with a verb.

b  2))) Listen and repeat the Free Time questions. Copy the rhythm.

> **Sentence stress**
> Remember that we usually stress the important words in a sentence (the ones that carry important information), and say the other words less strongly, e.g. **Where** are you **from**? **What** do you **do**?

c In pairs, ask and answer the questions. Can you find at least **one** thing from each section which you have in common?

We live in the city centre.

2 GRAMMAR word order in questions

a Re-order the words to make questions.
1 born where your parents were ?
2 where from teacher our is ?
3 name your how you do spell ?
4 did last you go night out ?

b ▶ p.126 **Grammar Bank 1A.** Learn more about word order in questions and practise it.

c Stand up and ask different students the first question until somebody says *yes*. Then ask the follow-up question. Continue with the other questions, asking different students.

Do you drink a lot of coffee?   *Yes, I do.*
How many cups of coffee do you drink?   *Five cups a day.*

Present
/ drink a lot of coffee (or tea)? How many cups…?
/ go to bed early during the week? What time…?
/ spend a long time on Facebook every day? How long…?

Past
/ have a big breakfast today? What…?
/ go somewhere nice on Saturday? Where…?
/ see a good film last week? What film…?

3 PRONUNCIATION
vowel sounds, the alphabet

a **1 5))** Look at the sound pictures. What are the words and vowel sounds? Listen and check.

train

b ▶ p.166 **Sound Bank.** Look at the typical spellings of these sounds.

c Add these letters to the circles.

E   G   H   J   M   O   R   W   X   Y

d **1 6))** Listen and check. Practise saying the letters in each circle.

e Ask and answer with a partner.
- Do you normally get in touch with your friends by phone, email, or Facebook?
- Do you have an iPod or MP3 player? What kind?
- Do you often watch DVDs? What kind?
- Do you watch the BBC, CNN, or MTV?
- Do you have any friends from the UK or the USA?

4 SPELLING & NUMBERS

a **1 7))** Listen and write six first names.

b ▶ **Communication** *What's his name? How do you spell it?* **A** *p.100* **B** *p.106*.

c How do you say these numbers?

| 13 | 30 | 76 | 100 | 150 | 375 | 600 | 1,500 | 2,000 | 10,500 |

d **1 8))** Listen and write the numbers.
1 Gate _____   3 Tel: _____   5 £_____
2 _____ miles   4 Population: _____

e Interview your partner and complete the form.

Student information	
first name	
surname	
address	
phone number	
email	

G present simple
V describing people: appearance and personality
P final -s / -es

1B Charlotte's choice

> I like good books.
> He doesn't like sport.

1 VOCABULARY describing people

a ►)) 1 9 Listen to a man describing his girlfriend and tick (✓) her picture.

b Listen again. What two questions does Luke's friend ask him? How does Luke answer the second question?

> **What does she look like? What is she like?**
> *What does she look like?* = Tell me about her appearance (Is she tall / short? What colour hair does she have?).
> *What is she like?* = Tell me what kind of person she is (Is she friendly? Is she shy?).

c ▶ p.150 **Vocabulary Bank** *Describing people.*

2 READING

a Who do you think knows you better, your mother (or father) or your best friend? Why?

b Read the introduction and the first paragraph of the article.
1 What is the idea of the experiment?
2 Who is Charlotte?
3 Who are Alice and Katie?
4 What do Alice and Katie have to do? Then what happens?

c Now read what Charlotte says. With a partner guess the meaning of the highlighted words and phrases.

d Cover the text. Can you remember?
1 What does Charlotte like doing?
2 What's she like?
3 What kind of men does / doesn't she like?
4 Who does she think is going to choose better? Why?

Who knows you better –

your mother or your best friend?

In our weekly experiment, single people who are looking for a partner ask their mother and their best friend to help.

This week's single person is Charlotte Ramirez, a 25-year-old web designer. Her father is Spanish and her mother is English. She lives in Brighton and she doesn't have a partner at the moment. Her mother, Alice, chooses a man she thinks is perfect for her daughter and her best friend, Katie, chooses another. Then Charlotte goes on a date with each man. Which one does she prefer?

' I love going to the cinema, but I often feel like staying at home with a good book,' says Charlotte. 'I'm quite friendly and sociable and I get on well with most people. I think I have a good sense of humour.'

'What kind of men do I like? Well, I like interesting men who can make me laugh. Physically, I prefer men with a really nice smile who are taller than me. And I don't usually like men with beards! I like men who are into literature and art, and classical music.'

'I'm not sure who is going to choose better for me. Both my mum and my best friend know me very well. Perhaps Katie could find me a guy who is physically more compatible, but my mother has known me for longer!'

3 GRAMMAR present simple

a From memory, try to complete the sentences using the present simple.
   1 She _____ have a partner at the moment.
   2 She _____ on a date with each man.
   3 Which one _____ she prefer?
   4 What kind of men _____ I like?
   5 I _____ usually like men with beards.

b In pairs, answer the questions.
   1 Which letter do you add to most verbs with *he*, *she*, and *it*?
   2 How do the verbs below change with *he*, *she*, and *it*?
      watch / study / go / have
   3 What auxiliary verbs do you use to make questions and negatives with…?
      a I / you / we / they   b he / she / it

c ▶ **p.126 Grammar Bank 1B.** Learn more about the present simple and practise it.

d Can you remember the kind of men Charlotte likes and doesn't like?

e Look at the photos of Alexander and Oliver. Find out about them. ▶ **Communication** *Alexander and Oliver* **A** *p.100* **B** *p.106*.

f Which man do you think is better for Charlotte? Why?

4 LISTENING

a (1 14)) Listen to Charlotte talking about what happened when she met Alexander. What did she think of him? Does she want to see him again?

b Listen again and write down any adjectives or expressions that Charlotte uses to describe his appearance and personality.

c (1 15)) Now repeat for Oliver.

d What does Charlotte decide in the end? Do you agree with her?

5 PRONUNCIATION final -s / -es

a (1 16)) Listen and repeat.

/s/	snake	She likes cats. He works with his parents.
/z/	zebra	He has brown eyes. She wears jeans.
/ɪz/		She relaxes with boxes of chocolates. He uses glasses to read.

> **Pronunciation of final -s / -es: verbs and nouns**
> The final **-s** is pronounced /s/ or /z/. The difference is quite small.
> The final **-es** is pronounced /ɪz/ after *ch*, *c*, *g*, *sh*, *s*, *z*, and *x*.

b (1 17)) How do you say the *he / she / it* form of these verbs and the plural of these nouns? Listen and check.

verbs: choose cook go live stop teach
nouns: boy class date friend language parent

6 SPEAKING & WRITING

a Look at the form below and prepare to give this information about your friend.

Do you have a friend who is looking for a partner? Help him / her to find one!

Name
Relationship: Single / Divorced / Separated
Age
Job
Appearance
Personality
Likes
Doesn't like
Search

b Work in pairs. Ask and answer about your people. Compare the information. Do you think the two people are compatible?

   What's his (her) name?

c ▶ **p.111 Writing** *Describing a person*. Write a description of a person you know.

7 (1 18)) SONG ♪ Ugly ♫

G present continuous
V clothes, prepositions of place
P /ə/ and /ɜː/

> What's the woman doing?
> She's standing in front of the window.

1C Mr and Mrs Clark and Percy

1 VOCABULARY clothes

a Look at the pictures. What are the models wearing? Match the words and clothes.

- [ ] boots
- [ ] shirt
- [ ] shoes
- [ ] skirt
- [ ] top
- [ ] trousers

b ▶ p.151 **Vocabulary Bank** *Things you wear.*

2 PRONUNCIATION /ə/ and /ɜː/

a ◯ 20))) Listen to these words and sounds. Practise saying them.

1	computer	tr**ou**sers tr**ai**ners
		s**a**ndals sw**ea**ter
		c**a**rdigan
2	bird	sh**i**rt sk**i**rt T-sh**i**rt

b Underline the stressed syllable in the words below. Which sound do they have, 1 or 2?

act**o**r	cin**e**ma	f**i**rst	paint**e**r	th**i**rd
arrive	fash**io**n	w**o**rld	univ**e**rsity	
pict**u**re	w**o**rking	pref**e**r		

c ◯ 21))) Listen and check.

d ▶ p.166 **Sound Bank.** Look at the typical spellings for these sounds.

e Ask and answer the questions with a partner.

What clothes do you usually wear…?
- at work / university / school
- when you go out at night
- when you want to relax at the weekend

3 GRAMMAR present continuous

a Look at the painting on p.9 by the British artist David Hockney (1937–). In pairs, describe the man and the woman.
- What do they look like?
- What are they wearing?
- What are they doing?

b Underline the correct form of the verb, present continuous or present simple.
1 In the painting the man *isn't wearing | doesn't wear* shoes.
2 In the UK women often *wear | are wearing* big hats at weddings.
3 In the painting a white cat *sits | is sitting* on the man's knee.
4 My son usually *sits | is sitting* at the back of the class so that the teacher can't see him.

c ▶ p.126 **Grammar Bank 1C.** Learn more about the present continuous and practise it.

d Look at the pictures on page 4. What are the people wearing? What are they doing?

4 LISTENING

a ◯ 24))) Look at the painting of *Mr and Mrs Clark and Percy* on p.9 and listen to the audio guide. Focus on the people and things in the painting as they are mentioned.

b Listen again. Mark the sentences **T** (true) or **F** (false).
1 Percy is the name of the cat.
2 Mr and Mrs Clark made clothes for famous people.
3 The painting shows their living room.
4 The painting is quite small.
5 Celia is pregnant in the painting.
6 Ossie is putting his feet into the carpet because he is cold.
7 The position of the couple in the painting is unusual.
8 The open window is a symbol of the love between them.
9 The cat is a symbol of infidelity.
10 Celia and Ossie later got divorced.
11 Celia doesn't like the painting.
12 Ossie Clark died in 1995.

Celia today.

Mr and Mrs Clark and Percy (1970–71) by David Hockney in the Tate Gallery, London

5 VOCABULARY prepositions of place

a Look at some sentences which describe the painting. Complete them with a word or phrase from the list.

| in (x2)   on (x2)   under   in front of   behind   between |
| next to   on the right   on the left   in the middle |

1 There are two people _____ the room.
2 The woman is standing _____ , and the man is sitting _____ .
3 _____ of the painting, _____ the man and the woman, there's an open window.
4 A white cat is sitting _____ the man.
5 There's a carpet _____ the man's chair.
6 There's a telephone _____ the floor _____ the man's chair.
7 _____ the telephone there's a lamp.
8 _____ the woman there's a table, and a vase with flowers _____ it.

b **1 25))** Listen and check. Then cover the sentences and look at the painting. Say where the things and people are.

6 SPEAKING

> **Describing a picture (a painting or photo)**
> When we describe a picture we normally use:
> - *There is / There are* to say what is in the picture, e.g. *There is a table and a vase with flowers in it. There are two people.*
> - The present continuous to say what the people are doing, e.g. *The woman is standing and the man is sitting.*
> - Sometimes we combine *There is* and the present continuous, e.g. *There is a woman standing near the window.*

a ▶ **Communication** *Describe and draw* **A** p.100 **B** p.106. Describe your picture for your partner to draw.

b In small groups, ask and answer the questions.
1 Which of the three paintings in this lesson do you prefer? Why?
2 What pictures or posters do you have on the wall in your bedroom or living room?
3 Do you have a favourite painting? What? Can you describe it?
4 Do you have a favourite painter? Who?
5 Do you (or did you) paint or draw? What kind of things?

Practical English Hotel problems

EPISODE 1

1 ◼ INTRODUCTION

a Look at the photos. Describe Jenny and Rob.

b ◉ 1 26))) Watch or listen to Jenny. Number the pictures 1–6 in the order she mentions them.

c Watch or listen again and answer the questions.
1 What does Jenny do?
2 Where did she go a few months ago?
3 Who's Rob Walker?
4 What did they do together?
5 What does she think of Rob?
6 What's Rob's one negative quality?
7 How long is Rob going to be in New York?

A 1

B

C

D

E

F

2 CALLING RECEPTION

a **1 27)))** Cover the dialogue and watch or listen. Who does Rob call? Why?

b Watch or listen again. Complete the **You Hear** phrases.

))) You Hear	You Say 💬
Hello, reception.	Hello. This is room 613.
How can I _____ you?	There's a problem with the air conditioning. It isn't working, and it's very hot in my room.
I'm sorry, sir. I'll _____ somebody up to look at it right now.	Thank you.
Good _____, reception.	Hello. I'm sorry to bother you again. This is room 613.
How can I help you?	I have a problem with the Wi-fi. I can't get a signal.
I'm sorry sir. I'll _____ you through to IT.	Thanks.

c **1 28)))** Watch or listen and repeat the **You Say** phrases. Copy the rhythm.

> 🔍 *I'll*
> A There's a problem with the air conditioning.
> B I'll send somebody to look at it.
>
> *I'll* = I will. We use *I'll* + verb to offer to do something.

d Practise the dialogue in **2b** with a partner.

e 👥 In pairs, roleplay the dialogue.

  A (book open) You are the receptionist. **B** (book closed) You are a guest. You have two problems with your room (think about what they are). **A** Offer to do something about **B**'s problems. You begin with *Hello, reception*.

f Swap roles.

3 JENNY AND ROB MEET AGAIN

a **1 29)))** That evening Jenny goes to the hotel to meet Rob and they go out for a drink. Watch or listen and mark the sentences **T** or **F**.
1 Rob says he doesn't like the hotel.
2 Jenny is going to show him round the city tomorrow.
3 Barbara is Jenny's boss.
4 Rob is hungry.
5 It's four in the morning for Rob.
6 They're going to meet at eleven.
7 Jenny thinks that Rob is going to get lost.

b Watch or listen again. Say why the **F** sentences are false.

c Look at the **Social English phrases**. Can you remember any of the missing words?

> **Social English phrases**
> **Jenny** Here you _____ at last.
> **Rob** It's _____ to be here.
> **Jenny** Do you have a _____ view?
> **Jenny** Barbara's _____ forward to meeting you.
> **Jenny** You _____ be really tired.
> **Rob** I guess you're _____.
> **Rob** By the _____ ...
> **Jenny** It's _____ to see you too.

d **1 30)))** Watch or listen and complete the phrases.

e Watch or listen again and repeat the phrases. How do you say them in your language?

> 👤 **Can you...?**
> ☐ tell somebody about a problem (e.g. in a hotel)
> ☐ offer to do something
> ☐ greet a friend who you haven't seen for a long time

G past simple: regular and irregular verbs
V holidays
P regular verbs: -ed endings

"Where did you go on holiday?" "I went to Venice with some friends."

2A Right place, wrong person

1 VOCABULARY holidays

a In one minute, write down five things you like doing when you're on holiday, e.g. *relaxing, going to museums*. Then compare with a partner.

b ➤ p.152 **Vocabulary Bank** *Holidays*.

c In pairs, interview your partner with the holiday questionnaire. Ask *Why?*

My perfect summer holiday

Which do you prefer...?

going abroad **or** going on holiday in your country
going by car, bus, plane **or** train
going to the beach **or** going to a city
staying in a hotel (or apartment) **or** going camping
sunbathing, going sightseeing **or** going for walks
hot, sunny weather **or** cool, cloudy weather
going with friends **or** going with your family

2 READING & SPEAKING

a Work in pairs. **A** read about **Joe's** holiday. **B** read about **Laura's** holiday. Find the answers to questions 1–5.

1 Where did he / she go on holiday?
2 Who did he / she go with?
3 Where did he / she stay?
4 What was the weather like?
5 Why didn't he / she enjoy the holiday?

b Now tell your partner about the holiday you read. Use questions 1–5 to help you.

c Read your partner's text. In pairs, guess the meaning of the highlighted words and phrases. Whose holiday do you think was worse? Why?

d Have you ever had a holiday that you didn't enjoy very much? What happened?

The place is perfect, the weather is wonderful,
but if you're with the wrong person, a holiday can be a disaster...

Joe 28, a flight attendant

Last October I went on holiday to Thailand for two weeks with my girlfriend, Mia.

The holiday began well. We spent two days in Bangkok and saw the Floating Market and the Royal Palace. But things went wrong when we left Bangkok. I wanted to stay in hostels, which were basic but clean, but Mia said they were too uncomfortable and so we stayed in quite expensive hotels. I wanted to experience the local atmosphere but Mia just wanted to go shopping. I thought I knew Mia very well, but you don't know a person until you travel with them. It was awful! We argued about everything.

For our last four days we went to Ko Chang, a beautiful island. It was like being in paradise. The weather was lovely and the beaches were wonderful, but we just sunbathed without speaking. We spent our last night back in Bangkok and we went for a drink with some Australians. They were really friendly and Mia started flirting with one of the boys. That was the end.

'you don't know a person until you travel with them'

When we arrived at Heathrow airport the next day we decided to break up.

I took hundreds of photos, but when I got home I didn't show them to anyone.

Laura 26, a nurse

Last spring my best friend Isabelle and I booked a holiday in Venice. We rented a small apartment for a week with a fantastic view of the canals. At the last moment another friend, Linda, asked if she could come too. We felt sorry for her because she had problems with her boyfriend, so we said yes.

'I'd love to go back to Venice one day... but without Linda.'

Venice was magical and the weather was perfect, but the holiday was a disaster for one simple reason: Linda was so mean! She has a good job so she's not poor, but she just didn't want to pay for anything. When we went sightseeing she didn't want to go to any museums or galleries that cost money. When we went on a gondola she complained that it was very expensive. When we went to have lunch or dinner she always wanted to go to cheap restaurants or she bought pizzas and ate them in the flat. But the night I invited her and Isabelle out on my birthday she chose the most expensive things on the menu! The worst thing was that although Isabelle and I paid for the apartment, Linda never once bought us a coffee or a drink.

I'd love to go back to Venice one day...but without Linda.

3 LISTENING

a 1 34)) You are going to listen to Mia and Linda talking about the holidays. First listen to Mia. Does she agree with Joe about the holiday?

b Listen again. What does Mia say about…?

1. her relationship with Joe before they went
2. the places where they stayed
3. talking to other travellers
4. photos
5. going on holiday with a boyfriend

c 1 35)) Now listen to Linda. What's her opinion of the holiday? Then listen again. What does she say about…?

1. Venice
2. what they did there
3. the cost of her holiday
4. her next holiday

d Who do you sympathize with most, Joe or Mia? Laura or Linda?

4 GRAMMAR past simple: regular and irregular verbs

a What is the past simple of these verbs? Are they regular or irregular? Check your answers in **Joe's** text.

go _____   begin _____
spend _____   leave _____
want _____   be _____ / _____
stay _____   think _____
know _____   argue _____
sunbathe _____   take _____

b Now underline the past simple + verbs in **Laura's** text. What are the infinitives?

c Find and underline two past simple − verbs in the two texts. How do you make − and ? in the past simple…?
- with normal verbs
- with *was* / *were*
- with *could*

d ▶ p.128 **Grammar Bank 2A.** Learn more about the past simple and practise it.

5 PRONUNCIATION regular verbs: -ed endings

a 1 37)) Listen and repeat the sentences.

t ie	We book**ed** a holiday. We walk**ed** around the town.
d og	We sunbath**ed** on the beach. We argu**ed** about everything.
/ɪd/	We rent**ed** a flat. We decid**ed** to break up.

b Say the past simple of these verbs. In which ones is *-ed* pronounced /ɪd/?

arrive   ask   end   invite   like   love   need   park   start   stay

c 1 38)) Listen and check.

> **Regular past simple verbs**
> Remember that we don't normally pronounce the *e* in *-ed*. The *-ed* ending is usually pronounced /t/ or /d/. The difference between these endings is very small.
> We <u>only</u> pronounce the *e* in *-ed* when there is a **t** or a **d** before it, e.g. wan**t**ed, en**d**ed. With these verbs *-ed* = /ɪd/.

6 SPEAKING

a Look at **Your last holiday** below. What are the questions?

b Think about your answers to the questions.

YOUR LAST HOLIDAY
1. Where / go?
2. When / go?
3. Who / go with?
4. Where / stay?
5. What / the food like?
6. What / the weather like?
7. What / do during the day?
8. What / do at night?
9. / have a good time?
10. / have any problems?

c Work in pairs. Ask your partner about his / her holiday. Show interest in what he / she says, and ask for more information. Then swap roles.

> **Useful language for showing interest**
> + *Really? Wow! Fantastic! Great!* etc.
> − *Oh no! How awful!* etc.
> ? *Was it expensive? Why? What happened?* etc.

G past continuous
V prepositions of time and place: *at, in, on*
P sentence stress

2B The story behind the photo

What was happening?
People were waiting for the results.

1 READING

a Look at a photo which news photographer Tom Pilston took in 2008. What do you think is happening?

b Read Tom's description of what happened on the night he took the photo. Were you right?

c Read it again and answer the questions.
  1 Why did Tom Pilston go to Chicago?
  2 Why couldn't he take a photograph of Obama?
  3 What was the weather like?
  4 Where did he take this photo?
  5 Where could the people see the election results?
  6 Was he sorry that he couldn't go inside the center?
  7 What happened when Obama won?

d Why do you think the photographer thought his photo was better than a photo of Obama himself? Do you agree?

A moment in history

On 4th November I arrived in Chicago late in the evening. I wanted to photograph Barack Obama and his family in the Convention Center, but when I got there I discovered that I didn't have my press pass and I couldn't go inside. I walked around the park outside the center. Although it was November, it was a warm night. The atmosphere was wonderful. When I took this photo everybody was looking at the TV screens waiting for the election results. Some people were quietly holding hands and smiling – others were tense and nervous. They felt that it was their moment. Suddenly I realized that this was a better place to be than inside. I was watching Obama's victory through the faces of all these people, African, Hispanic, Chinese, white. At about 11 o'clock the results were announced, and everybody went mad. People started laughing, shouting, and crying. But when Obama made his speech they all became quiet and emotional. There was only one place to be on the planet that night – and I was there.

Adapted from a British newspaper

2 GRAMMAR past continuous

a Look at the highlighted verbs in an extract from the text. Do they describe actions that happened…?
  a after he took the photo
  b at the same time as he took the photo

> When I took this photo everybody was looking at the TV screens waiting for the election results. Some people were quietly holding hands and smiling – others were tense and nervous.

b ▶ p.128 Grammar Bank 2B. Learn more about the past continuous and practise it.

c 1 41))) In pairs, listen to the sounds and make a sentence using the past continuous and the past simple.

> They were playing tennis when it started to rain.

3 VOCABULARY *at, in, on*

a Which preposition do you use before…?
  1 a date (e.g. 4th November) _____
  2 a time (e.g. 11 o'clock) _____
  3 the morning, the afternoon, etc. _____
  4 a room or building (e.g. the Convention Center) _____

b Check your answers to a in the text. What preposition do you use with…?
  1 a month (e.g. January) _____   3 home, work, school _____
  2 the weekend _____

c ▶ p.153 Vocabulary Bank *Prepositions*. Do part 1.

d ▶ Communication *at, in, on* A p.100 B p.106. Answer the questions with a preposition and a time or place.

14

4 PRONUNCIATION sentence stress

a **1 43))** Listen and repeat the dialogue. Copy the rhythm.

> A **Where** were you at **six o'clock** in the **evening**?
> B I was at **work**.
> A **What** were you **doing**?
> B I was **having** a **meeting** with the **boss**.

b In pairs, take turns to answer the questions about yesterday.

| 6.30 a.m. | 11.00 a.m. | lunchtime | 4.00 p.m. |
| 6.00 p.m. | 10.00 p.m. | midnight | |

Where were you at 6.30 in the morning? — *I was at home.*

What were you doing?

5 LISTENING

a Look at a famous photo which was on the cover of many magazines around the world in the 1960s. Where do you think the people are? What do you think is happening?

b Read the beginning of a newspaper article. Why do you think it is called '*The image that cost a fortune*'?

c **1 44))** Now listen to the woman in the photo talking about it. Were you right?

d Listen again. Choose a, b, or c.

1 In 1968 she ____.
  a wasn't interested in politics
  b was a communist
  c was an anarchist
2 She loved the atmosphere because all the students were fighting for ____.
  a peace b democracy c freedom
3 She was sitting on a friend's shoulders ____.
  a because she was tired
  b to take photos
  c so that she could see better
4 She was carrying the flag because ____.
  a she was a leader in the demonstration
  b somebody gave it to her
  c she brought it with her
5 Her grandfather died six ____ later.
  a days b weeks c months

e Do you think she is sorry that she was in that photo?

6 SPEAKING & WRITING

a Talk to a partner. Give more information if you can.

1 Do you have a photo you really like? Who took it? What was happening at the time?
2 Do you upload photos onto Facebook or other internet sites? What was the last photo you uploaded?
3 Do you have a photo as the screen saver on your computer or phone? What is it of?
4 Do you have a favourite photo of yourself as a child? Who took it? What was happening when they took it? What were you wearing?
5 Do you have any photos in your bedroom or living room? What are they of?
6 Do you know any other famous historical photos? Who or what are they of?

b ▶ p.112 **Writing** *My favourite photo*. Write a description of your favourite photo.

The image that cost a fortune

Caroline de Bendern was born in 1940. She was the granddaughter of Count Maurice de Bendern, a rich aristocrat who owned a lot of property in Paris and Monaco. Although he had other grandchildren, the Count decided to leave all his money to Caroline. 'I never knew why,' says Caroline. 'Perhaps because I was pretty.' He paid for her to go to very expensive schools in England, and he hoped that she would marry well, perhaps a member of a European royal family. But Caroline was a rebel. She went to New York and worked there for a short time as a model. Then, in 1968 when she was 28 years old she returned to Paris…

Adapted from a British newspaper

G time sequencers and connectors
V verb phrases
P word stress

2C One dark October evening

Why was she was going very fast? *Because she was in a hurry.*

1 GRAMMAR
time sequencers and connectors

a ▶ 1 45)) Read the story once. Then complete it with a word or phrase from the box. Listen to the story and check.

| After that | Next day | One evening in October |
| Suddenly | ~~Two minutes later~~ | When |

b With a partner, answer the questions.
1 Why did Hannah go and speak to Jamie?
2 Why did Jamie play *Blue As Your Eyes*?
3 What happened when Hannah left the club?
4 What was the restaurant like?
5 Where did they go every evening after that?
6 What was the weather like that evening?
7 Why was Hannah driving fast?
8 Why didn't she see the man?

c From memory complete these sentences from the story with *so*, *because*, or *although*. Then check with the story.
1 She was going very fast _because_ she was in a hurry.
2 _Although_ the food wasn't very good, they had a wonderful time.
3 He was wearing a dark coat, _so_ Hannah didn't see him at first.

d ▶ p.128 **Grammar Bank 2C.** Learn more about time sequencers and connectors and practise them.

e Complete the sentences in your own words. Then compare with a partner.
1 They fell in love on their first date. Two months later…
2 I went to bed early last night because…
3 The weather was beautiful, so we decided…
4 It was really cold that night, and when I woke up next morning…
5 Although we didn't play well in the final…
6 I was driving along the motorway listening to the radio. Suddenly…

Hannah met Jamie in the summer of 2010. It was Hannah's 21st birthday and she and her friends went to a club. They wanted to dance, but they didn't like the music, so Hannah went to speak to the DJ. 'This music is awful,' she said. 'Could you play something else?' The DJ looked at her and said, 'Don't worry, I have the perfect song for you.'

¹ _Two minutes later_ he said, 'The next song is by Scouting For Girls. It's called *Blue As Your Eyes* and it's for a beautiful girl who's dancing over there.' Hannah knew that the song was for her. ² _When_ Hannah and her friends left the club, the DJ was waiting for her at the door. 'Hi, I'm Jamie,' he said to Hannah. 'Can I see you again?' So Hannah gave him her phone number.

³ _Next day_ Jamie phoned Hannah and invited her to dinner. He took her to a very romantic French restaurant and they talked all evening. Although the food wasn't very good, they had a wonderful time. ⁴ _After that_ Jamie and Hannah saw each other every day. Every evening when Hannah finished work they met at 5.30 in a coffee bar in the high street. They were madly in love.

⁵ _One evening in October_, Hannah was at work. As usual she was going to meet Jamie at 5.30. It was dark and it was raining. She looked at her watch. It was 5.20! She was going to be late! She ran to her car and got in. At 5.25 she was driving along the high street.

She was going very fast because she was in a hurry. ⁶ _Suddenly_, a man ran across the road. He was wearing a dark coat, so Hannah didn't see him at first. Quickly, she put her foot on the brake…

2 PRONUNCIATION word stress

> **Stress in two-syllable words**
> Approximately 80% of two-syllable words are stressed on the first syllable.
>
> Most two-syllable nouns and adjectives are stressed on the first syllable, e.g. _mother_, _happy_. However, many two-syllable verbs and prepositions or connectors are stressed on the second syllable, e.g. _arrive_, _behind_, _before_.

a Under<u>line</u> the stressed syllable in these words from the story.

a|cross	af|ter	a|gain	a|long
al|though	aw|ful	be|cause	birth|day
eve|ning	in|vite	per|fect	se|cond

b (1 49)) Listen and check.

3 VOCABULARY verb phrases

a Make verb phrases with a verb from box 1 and a phrase from box 2. All the phrases are from the story.

invite somebody to dinner

1
~~invite~~
have
drive
meet
give
take
wait
be
play
leave
run

2
along the high street
somebody your email / phone number
a song
across the road
in a hurry
in a coffee bar
for somebody
the club very late
~~somebody to dinner~~
somebody to a restaurant
a wonderful time

b Cover box 1. Try to remember the verb for each phrase.

4 SPEAKING & LISTENING

a Read the story of Hannah and Jamie in **1** again.

b In pairs, use pictures 1–5 to re-tell the story. Try to use connectors and the verb phrases in **3**.

c There are two different endings to the story. Have a class vote. Do you want to listen to the **happy ending** or the **sad ending**?

d (1 50, 51)) What do you think is going to happen in the ending you have chosen? Listen once and check.

e Listen again. If you chose the happy ending, answer the questions in ▶ **Communication** _Happy ending p.101_. If you chose the sad ending, answer the questions in ▶ **Communication** _Sad ending p.109_.

5 (1 52)) SONG _Blue As Your Eyes_ ♪

1&2 Revise and Check

GRAMMAR

Circle a, b, or c.

1 _____ any brothers or sisters?
   a Have you   b Do you   c Do you have
2 _____ last night?
   a Where you went
   b Where did you go
   c Where you did go
3 My brother _____ football.
   a doesn't like   b don't like   c doesn't likes
4 Her parents _____ a small business.
   a has   b haves   c have
5 I _____ to music when I'm working.
   a never listen   b don't never listen   c listen never
6 In the picture the woman _____ a blue dress.
   a wears   b wearing   c is wearing
7 A What _____?   B I'm looking for my keys.
   a you are doing   b do you do   c are you doing
8 She's at university. She _____ history.
   a 's studing   b 's studying   c studying
9 We _____ to Malta last August.
   a were   b went   c did go
10 I saw the film, but I _____ it.
   a didn't liked   b don't liked   c didn't like
11 When I got home my parents _____ on the sofa.
   a were sitting   b was sitting   c were siting
12 What _____ at 11 p.m.? You didn't answer my call.
   a you were doing   b you was doing   c were you doing
13 She couldn't see him because she _____ her glasses.
   a wasn't wearing   b didn't wear   c didn't wearing
14 We went to the cinema. _____ we decided to go for a walk.
   a After   b Then   c When
15 We had a great time, _____ the weather wasn't very good.
   a so   b because   c although

VOCABULARY

a Complete the phrases with a verb from the list.

book	do	drive	invite	leave
look	play	stay	take	wear

1 A What do you _____?   B I'm a doctor.
2 A What does she _____ like?   B She's tall and slim.
3 She doesn't usually _____ jewellery, only her wedding ring.
4 A Did you _____ any photos?   B No, I didn't.
5 A Where did you _____?   B In a small hotel.
6 Did you _____ your flights online?
7 A Let's _____ your parent to dinner.   B Good idea.
8 A Are you going to _____ there?
   B No, we're going to get the train.
9 A Go on! Ask the DJ to _____ our song!   B OK.
10 A What time do we need to _____ home tomorrow?
   B About 7.00. Our flight is at 9.00.

b Complete with *at*, *in*, or *on*.

1 The meeting is _____ March 13th.
2 A Where's Mum?   B She's _____ the kitchen.
3 He was born _____ 1989.
4 A Where's the dictionary?
   B It's _____ the shelf in my room.
5 Mark's not back yet – he's still _____ school.
6 It's a very quiet town, especially _____ night.
7 We went _____ holiday to Malta last year.

c **Circle** the word that is different.

1 straight	long	blonde	beard
2 clever	lazy	generous	funny
3 friendly	mean	stupid	unkind
4 dress	skirt	tights	tie
5 socks	gloves	trainers	sandals
6 necklace	bracelet	ring	scarf
7 windy	foggy	dirty	sunny
8 basic	dirty	uncomfortable	luxurious

PRONUNCIATION

a **Circle** the word with a different sound.

1 E   G   J   V
2 shirt   shorts   work   curly
3 /ɪz/   chooses   languages   lives   glasses
4 weight   height   kind   night
5 painter   trainers   university   trousers

b Under<u>line</u> the stressed syllable.

1 tal|ka|tive   3 pre|fer   5 com|for|ta|ble
2 mou|stache   4 dis|gu|sting

18

CAN YOU UNDERSTAND THIS TEXT?

a Read the newspaper article once. Does the journalist think that taking photos in museums is a good thing or a bad thing?

b Read the article again. Mark the sentences **T** (true) or **F** (false).
1 The journalist saw tourists taking photographs of works of art in Rome and New York.
2 When he first saw people taking photos in the MOMA he didn't understand what they were really doing.
3 Then he realised that the photographers were not looking at the paintings.
4 They were taking photos because they wanted to look at the paintings later.
5 Later a couple asked him to take a photo of them in front of a painting.
6 He suggests two possible ways of solving the problem.

c Look at the highlighted words in the text. Guess their meaning from the context. Check with your teacher or with a dictionary.

We were there!

The first time I noticed this phenomenon was a few years ago, in St Peter's Basilica in Rome – a crowd of people standing round Michelangelo's Pietà, taking photos with their cameras and mobile phones. Then last week I saw it again at the Museum of Modern Art (the MOMA) in New York. At first, I wasn't too worried when I saw people photographing the paintings. It was a bit irritating, but that was all. It didn't make me angry. Then the sad truth hit me. Most of the people were taking photos without looking at the paintings themselves. People were pushing me, not because they were trying to get a better view of the art, but because they wanted to make sure that no one blocked their photo. Was it possible that perhaps they were taking the photos so that they could admire the paintings better when they got home? This was very improbable. They were not there to see the paintings, but to take photos to prove that they had been there.

Then it got worse. Now people were taking photos of their partners or friends who were posing next to, or in front of some of the most famous paintings. Neither the photographers nor the person they were photographing had looked at the art itself, although I saw that sometimes they read the label, to make sure that the artist really was famous. At least nobody asked me to take a picture of them together, smiling in front of a Picasso!

I think that photography in museums should be banned, but I also have a less drastic solution. I think that people who want to take a photo of an exhibit should be forced to look at it first, for at least one minute.

Adapted from Marcel Berlin's article in The Guardian

CAN YOU UNDERSTAND THESE PEOPLE?

1 53)) **In the street** Watch or listen to five people and answer the questions.

Justin   Joanna   Sarah Jane   David   Andy

1 Justin _____.
  a looks like his mother
  b looks like his father
  c doesn't look like his father or his mother
2 Joanna's favourite painting is of _____.
  a a landscape   b a person   c an animal
3 Sarah Jane's last holiday was a _____ holiday.
  a beach   b walking   c sightseeing
4 David _____.
  a takes a lot of photos
  b is in a lot of photos
  c has a lot of photos on his phone
5 Andy says _____.
  a he enjoys crying at the end of a film
  b he thinks films with a sad ending are more realistic
  c most of his favourite films have a sad ending

CAN YOU SAY THIS IN ENGLISH?

Do the tasks with a partner. Tick (✓) the box if you can do them.

Can you…?
1 ☐ ask and answer six questions about work / studies, family, and free time activities
2 ☐ describe the appearance and personality of a person you know well
3 ☐ describe a picture in this book and say what is happening, what the people are wearing, etc.
4 ☐ ask and answer three questions about a recent holiday
5 ☐ describe a favourite photo and say what was happening when you took it
6 ☐ say three true sentences using the connectors *so*, *because*, and *although*

Short films A photographer
Watch and enjoy a film on iTutor.

G be going to (plans and predictions)
V airports
P sentence stress and fast speech

3A Plans and dreams

What are you going to do there?
I'm going to teach English

1 VOCABULARY airports

a When was the last time you were at an airport? Was it to travel somewhere (where?) or to meet someone (who?)?

b Look at the airport signs and match them to the words and phrases below.

- [ ] Arrivals
- [✓] Baggage drop-off
- [ ] Baggage reclaim
- [ ] Check-in
- [ ] Customs
- [ ] Departures
- [ ] Gates
- [ ] Lifts
- [ ] Passport control
- [ ] Terminal
- [ ] Toilets
- [ ] Trolley

c ◁)) 1.54 Listen and check. Then cover the words and look at the symbols. Remember the words and phrases.

2 LISTENING

a Look at the three travellers in the picture. Who do you think is…?
- going to work abroad for an NGO (= non-governmental organization)
- going to see an ex-partner
- going to do a photo shoot in an exotic place

We spent a morning in Departures last week asking people about their travel plans.

b ◁)) 1.55 Listen and check your answers to **a**. Then listen again and complete the chart.

	Where to?	Why?	Other information
Olivia			
Matthew			
Lily			

3 GRAMMAR
be going to (plans and predictions)

a ▶1 56))) Look at these sentences from the airport interviews and complete the gaps with a form of *be going to* + verb. Then listen and check.

1 _____ English to young children.
2 How long _____ there for?
3 It's winter in Australia now, so _____ quite cold.
4 _____ you at the airport?
5 I'm sure _____ a great time.

b In pairs decide if sentences 1–5 are plans or predictions about the future. Write **PL** (plan) or **PR** (prediction).

c ▶ p.130 **Grammar Bank 3A.** Learn more about *be going to* and practise it.

4 PRONUNCIATION & SPEAKING
sentence stress and fast speech

a ▶1 58))) Listen and repeat the sentences. Copy the rhythm.

1 **What** are you **going** to **do tonight**?
2 **Are** you **going** to **see** a **film**?
3 I'm **going** to **cook** a **meal** for you.
4 I **think** it's **going** to **rain**.
5 We **aren't going** to **have** a **holiday** this year.

> 🔍 **Fast speech:** *gonna*
> When people speak fast they often pronounce *going to* as *gonna* /ˈɡənə/, e.g. *What are you going to do?* sounds like *What are you gonna do?*

b ▶1 59))) Listen and write six sentences.

c ▶ **Communication** *What are your plans?* **A** p.101 **B** p.107. Interview each other about your plans.

5 READING

a What is your nearest airport? What's it like? What can you do there while you're waiting for a flight?

b Read an article about the top airports in the world. Which is the best airport(s) if you…?

1 have a medical problem
2 would like to see a film
3 want to do some sport or exercise
4 need to leave your dog for the weekend
5 are worried about getting lost
6 want to sleep between flights
7 would like to see the city between flights

Singapore airport orchid garden

Top airports
in the world

For many people airports are a nightmare – long queues when you check in and go through **security** and an even longer wait if your flight is **delayed**. But there are some airports where you can actually enjoy yourself. All good airports have excellent **facilities** for business people and children, free Wi-fi, restaurants, cafés, and shops. But the best airports have much more…

SINGAPORE AIRPORT is paradise for flower lovers, as it has an indoor orchid garden! It also has a rooftop swimming pool and a free sight-seeing tour for people who have at least five hours to wait for their **connecting flight**.

If you like computer games, you'll never be bored at **HONG KONG INTERNATIONAL AIRPORT** – there are dozens of free Playstations all over the terminals! It's also good for people with no sense of direction – there are 'Airport Ambassadors' in red coats, who help you to get from one place to another.

SEOUL AIRPORT is the place to relax. You can go to the hairdresser and have beauty treatments or a massage. Sports fans can also play golf at their 72-hole golf course!

MUNICH AIRPORT helps to keep **passengers** entertained with a 60-seat cinema and non-stop films. There is also free coffee and tea near all the seating areas, and lots of free magazines and newspapers.

If you worry about your health and like to be near medical services at all times, **OSAKA AIRPORT** in Japan is the perfect place to wait, as it has a dentist and doctor's surgery. And for people with animals, there is even a pet hotel!

If you have a long wait between flights at **ZURICH AIRPORT** in Switzerland, you can rent day rooms with their own bathroom and kitchen and wake-up call service. So you can have a shower and then sleep peacefully until you have to **board** your flight.

c Look at the highlighted words and phrases related to airports and guess their meaning.

d Roleplay with a partner.

A imagine you are at one of these airports and your flight is delayed for three hours. **B** calls you on your mobile. Tell **B** where you are and what you are going to do. Then swap roles. Do the same with other airports.

6 ▶1 60))) SONG *This is the Life* 🎵

G present continuous (future arrangements)
V verbs + prepositions, e.g. *arrive in*
P sounding friendly

When are you leaving? On Monday, and I'm coming back on Friday.

3B Let's meet again

1 READING & LISTENING

a ⏵ 1 61 How do you say these dates? Listen and check.

3rd May   12th August 2012   31st December
22/6   5/2   20th July 1998

b Ben and Lily are old friends from university. Read their Facebook messages and number them in order.

Search   Home   Profile

Lily Varnell
☐ Great. I'm going to book my tickets tomorrow, and then I can let you know my flight times.

Ben West
☐ OK. Why don't you phone me nearer the time, at the end of April? Then we can **fix** a day and a time to meet. I know a great restaurant…

Lily Varnell
[1] Hi Ben! No news from you **for ages**. How are things? Are you still working at Budapest University? I have a conference there next month and I thought **perhaps** we could meet. I'd love to see you again! Lily.

Ben West
☐ It depends on the day. I'm going to Vienna one day that week, but it's not very far – I'm coming back the same day. I'm sure we can find a time that's good for **both** of us.

Lily Varnell
☐ It's from 3rd to 7th May, but I don't know my travel **arrangements** yet. What are you doing that week? Are you free any time?

Ben West
☐ Lily! Great to hear from you. Yes, **I'm still** at the university here and it's going very well – Budapest is a wonderful city to live in. When exactly is the conference?

Lily Varnell
☐ Fantastic. I can't wait!

---

c Read the messages again in the right order. Why does Lily get in touch with Ben? What are they planning to do?

d Match the highlighted words and phrases to their meaning.

1 _____ for a long time
2 _____ definite plans for the future
3 _____ I continue to be
4 _____ maybe
5 _____ the two
6 _____ to decide sth (e.g. a day / date)

e ⏵ 1 62 Lily phones Ben and leaves him a message. Listen and complete her flight details.

Thank you for booking with easyJet

YOUR RESERVATION NUMBER IS: **I5CS2L**

Going out: Flight EZY4587   Date: _____
  Depart   London Gatwick at 11.10.
  Arrive   Budapest at _____.

Going back: Flight EZY4588   Date: _____
  Depart   Budapest at _____.
  Arrive   London Gatwick at 18.10.

Hotel reservations:
  Six nights at Hotel _____.

2 GRAMMAR present continuous (future arrangements)

a In pairs, underline five present continuous verbs in the Facebook messages. Which two are about now? What time period do the other three refer to?

b 1 63)) Look at three extracts from the message Lily leaves Ben. Can you remember the missing verbs? Listen and check.

1 I'm _____ from Gatwick with Easyjet.
2 I'm _____ at Budapest airport at 14.40.
3 I'm _____ at a lovely old hotel.

c ▶ p.130 Grammar Bank 3B. Learn more about the present continuous for future arrangements and practise it.

d 1 65)) Lily phones Ben when she arrives at the hotel. Listen to the conversation. What day do they arrange to meet?

e Listen again. Complete Ben's diary for the week.

Sunday 2	seeing Paul
Monday 3	
Tuesday 4	
Wednesday 5	
Thursday 6	
Friday 7	

f Cover the diary. Work with a partner and test your memory.

What's Ben doing on Sunday? — *He's seeing Paul. What's he doing on Monday?*

g 1 66)) Listen. What happens when Ben and Lily meet?

3 PRONUNCIATION & SPEAKING
sounding friendly

a 1 67)) Listen to another dialogue. Then listen again and repeat it sentence by sentence. Try to copy the speakers' intonation.

A Would you like to go out for dinner?
B I'd love to.
A Are you free on Thursday?
B Sorry, I'm going to the cinema.
A What about Friday? What are you doing then?
B Nothing. Friday's fine.
A OK. Let's go to the new Italian place.
B Great.

b Practise the dialogue with a partner. Try to sound friendly.

c Complete your diary with different activities for three evenings.

Monday	Wednesday	Friday	Sunday

Tuesday	Thursday	Saturday

d Talk to other students. Try to find days when you are both free and suggest doing something. Write it in your diary. Try to make an arrangement with a different person for every night.

Are you free on Friday evening? — *Yes, I am.*
Would you like to go to the cinema? — *Yes, I'd love to.*

4 VOCABULARY verbs + prepositions

a Look at things Lily and Ben say. What are the missing prepositions?

1 It depends ____ the day.
2 I'm arriving ____ Budapest at 14.40.
3 Paul invited me ____ dinner ages ago.

b ▶ p.153 Vocabulary Bank *Prepositions*. Do part 2 (Verbs + prepositions).

c Complete the questions with a preposition. Then ask and answer with a partner.

1 What do you usually ask ____ if you go to a café with friends?
2 Who do you think should pay ____ the meal on a first date?
3 Who do you normally speak ____ when you're worried ____ something?
4 Do you spend more money ____ clothes or ____ gadgets?
5 Do you think it's possible to fall ____ love ____ somebody without meeting them face-to-face?

5 WRITING

▶ p.113 Writing *An informal email*. Write an email about travel arrangements.

G defining relative clauses
V expressions for paraphrasing: *like, for example*, etc.
P pronunciation in a dictionary

3C What's the word?

> What's a surgery? It's a place where you can see a doctor or dentist.

1 LISTENING

a Do you like playing word games like *Scrabble* or doing crosswords? Look at the *Scrabble* letters on the page. How many words of four or more letters can you make in three minutes?

b 2 2))) Listen to the introduction to a TV game show, *What's the word?* How do you play the game?

c 2 3))) Now listen to the show. Write down the six words.

1 _____
2 _____
3 _____
4 _____
5 _____
6 _____

d 2 4))) Listen and check your answers.

2 GRAMMAR
defining relative clauses

a Look at three sentences from *What's the word?* and complete them with *who, which,* or *where.*

1 It's something _____ people use to speak to another person.
2 It's a place _____ people go when they want to go shopping.
3 It's somebody _____ works in a hospital.

b Read sentences 1–3 again. When do we use *who, which,* and *where?*

c ▶ **p.130 Grammar Bank 3C.** Learn more about defining relative clauses and practise them.

3 VOCABULARY paraphrasing

a What do you usually do if you're talking to someone in English and you don't know a word that you need?
  a Look up the translation on your phone.
  b Try to mime the word.
  c Try to explain what you mean using other words you know.

b 2 6))) Complete the useful expressions with these words. Then listen and check.

example   kind   like   opposite   similar
somebody   something   somewhere

Useful expressions for explaining a word that you don't know:

1 It's _____ / a person who works in a hospital.
2 It's _____ / a thing which we use for everything nowadays.
3 It's _____ / a place where people go when they want to buy something.
4 It's a _____ of gadget.
5 It's the _____ of dark.
6 It's _____ light, but you use it to describe hair.
7 It's _____ to intelligent.
8 For _____ , you do this to the TV.

c Complete the definitions for these words.

1 **a DJ** It's somebody…
2 **an art gallery** It's somewhere…
3 **a camera** It's something…
4 **a lift** It's a kind of…
5 **sunbathe** For example, you do this…
6 **curly** It's the opposite…

4 SPEAKING

▶ **Communication** *What's the word?* **A** p.101 **B** p.107. Play a game and define words for your partner to guess.

5 READING

a Read the article. How many ways does it mention of creating new words? What are they?

b Look at the highlighted new words. What do you think they mean? Match them to the definitions below.

1 _____ *n* a young man who is going out with a much older woman
2 _____ *v* to send a message using a mobile phone
3 _____ *n* a person who works in a coffee bar
4 _____ *n* feeling angry because of the traffic or another person's driving
5 _____ *n* coffee with hot milk
6 _____ *n* a pub where you can also have very good food

c Can you explain the meaning of these other words from the text.

| emoticon | to tweet | iPod | to google |
| Wi-fi | ringtone | smartphone | |

6 PRONUNCIATION
pronunciation in a dictionary

a Look at two dictionary extracts. What do the abbreviations mean?

search /sɜːtʃ/ *v* look carefully because you are trying to find sb or sth

busy /ˈbɪzi/ *adj* occupé

1 *v* _____   3 *sb* _____
2 *adj* _____   4 *sth* _____

b Look at the phonetic transcriptions in **a**. How do you pronounce the words?

> 🔍 **Checking pronunciation in a dictionary**
> This symbol (ˈ) shows stress. The stressed syllable is the one <u>after</u> the symbol.
> The **Sound Bank** on *p.166* can help you to check the pronunciation of new words.

c 🔊 2 7 Look carefully at the pronunciation of the words below. Practise saying them correctly. Listen and check. Do you know what they mean?

1 YouTube /ˈjuːtjuːb/   4 gadget /ˈɡædʒɪt/
2 keyboard /ˈkiːbɔːd/   5 message /ˈmesɪdʒ/
3 zoom /zuːm/   6 hacker /ˈhækə/

900 new words in 3 months

Everyone knows the English language is changing. Every three months, the OED (Oxford English Dictionary) publishes updates to its online dictionary. One recent update contained 900 new words, new expressions, or new meanings for existing words. But where do they all come from?

New words are created in many different ways. We can make a new word by combining two words, like **gastropub** (gastronomy + pub) or **emoticon** (emotion + icon). Sometimes we put two words together in a new way, for example **road rage** or **toy boy**.

We also find that nouns can change into verbs. Take the word **text**. Text was always a noun (from about 1369, according to the OED), but it is now very common as a verb, **to text** somebody. Other new words already existed but with a different meaning. For example, **tweet** was the noise that a bird makes, but now we use it more often (as a verb or a noun) for a message that people put on the social networking site Twitter.

Another way in which we make new words is by 'adopting' words from foreign languages, like **barista** or **latte** (imported from Italian when coffee bars became really popular in the UK in the 1990s).

A lot of new words come from the names of brands or companies, for example we play music on an **iPod** and we **google** information. We also need more general words to describe new technology or new gadgets: **Wi-fi**, **ringtone**, and **smartphone** are some recent examples.

The invention of new words is not a new phenomenon. The word **brunch** (breakfast + lunch) first appeared in 1896, **newspaper** (news + paper) in 1667, and English speakers started to use the word **café** (from French) in the late 19th century. The difference now is how quickly new words and expressions enter the language and how quickly we start to use and understand them.

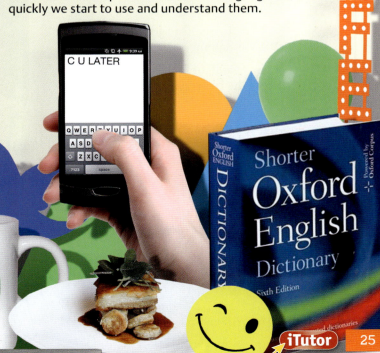

Practical English Restaurant problems

EPISODE 2

1 🖥 IN THE NEW YORK OFFICE

a **2 8))** Watch or listen. Mark the sentences **T** (true) or **F** (false).

1 The New York office is smaller than the London office.
2 Barbara is the designer of the magazine.
3 Rob has never been to New York before.
4 Barbara is going to have lunch with Rob and Jenny.
5 Holly is going to work with Rob.
6 Holly wants to go to the restaurant because she's hungry.

b Watch or listen again. Say why the **F** sentences are false.

2 VOCABULARY restaurants

Do the restaurant quiz with a partner.

RESTAURANT QUIZ

What do you call...?
1 the book or list which tells you what food there is
2 the three parts of a meal
3 the person who serves you
4 the piece of paper with the price of the meal
5 extra money you leave if you are happy with your meal or with the service

What do you say...?
1 if you want a table for four people
2 when the waiter asks you what you want
3 when you are ready to pay

3 🖥 AT THE RESTAURANT

a **2 9))** Cover the dialogue and watch or listen. Answer the questions.

1 What do they order?
2 What problems do they have?

b Watch or listen again. Complete the **You Hear** phrases.

🔊 You Hear	You Say 💬
Are you ready to _____?	Yes, please.
Can I get you something to _____ with?	No, thank you. I'd like the tuna with a green salad.
And for you, sir?	I'll have the steak, please.
Would you like that with fries or a baked _____?	Fries, please.
How would you like your steak? Rare, _____, or well done?	Well done.
	Nothing for me.
OK. And to _____?	Water, please.
_____ or sparkling?	Sparkling.
The tuna for you ma'am, and the steak for you, _____.	I'm sorry, but I asked for a green salad, not fries.
No problem. I'll _____ it.	Excuse me.
Yes, sir?	Sorry, I asked for my steak well done and this is rare.
I'm really sorry. I'll _____ it back to the kitchen.	

> 🔍 **British and American English**
> (*French*) fries = American English
> chips = British English

c  Watch or listen and repeat the **You Say** phrases. <u>Copy</u> the <u>rhy</u>thm.

d Practise the dialogue with a partner.

e 👥 In pairs, roleplay the dialogue.
  A You are in the restaurant. Order a steak or tuna.
  B You are the waiter/waitress. Offer **A** fries, a baked potato, or salad with the steak or tuna. You begin with *Are you ready to order*?
  A There is a problem with your order. Explain it to the waiter/waitress.
  B Apologize, and try to solve the problem.

f Swap roles.

4 🎬 HOLLY AND ROB MAKE FRIENDS

a 🔊 2 11 Watch or listen to Rob, Holly, and Jenny. Do they enjoy the lunch?

b Watch or listen again and answer the questions.
  1 What's Rob going to write about?
  2 How does Holly offer to help him with interviews?
  3 What does she say they could do one evening?
  4 What's the problem with the check?
  5 Why does Jenny say it's time to go?
  6 Do you think Jenny wanted Holly to come to lunch?

> 🔍 **British and American English**
> check = American English
> bill = British English

c Look at the **Social English phrases**. Can you remember any of the missing words?

Social English phrases
Holly _____ tell me, Rob…
Rob Well, to _____ with…
Rob Do you have any _____?
Rob That would _____ great.
Jenny _____ we have the check (bill), please?
Jenny Excuse me, I think there's a _____.
Jenny OK, _____ to go.

d 🔊 2 12 Watch or listen and complete the phrases.

e Watch or listen again and repeat the phrases. How do you say them in your language?

> 👤 **Can you…?**
> ☐ order food in a restaurant
> ☐ explain when there is a problem with your food, the bill, etc.
> ☐ ask what somebody is going to do today

G present perfect + *yet, just, already*
V housework, *make* or *do*?
P /j/ and /dʒ/

Have you tidied your room yet?

Yes, I've just done it.

4A Parents and teenagers

1 READING

a Look at the definition of *teenager*. How do you pronounce it? Do you have a similar word in your language to describe a person of that age?

> **teenager** /ˈtiːneɪdʒə/ a person who is between 13 and 19 years old

b Read the article about some annoying habits. Write **P** if you think the comment is a parent talking about teenagers, or **T** if you think it is a teenager talking about his / her parents.

Teenagers have annoying habits – but so do their parents!
#itreallyannoysme

1. **Simon Fry** @simonfry — 15m
They come into my room <mark>without knocking</mark> and then are surprised to see things they don't really want to know about.

2. **Rachel Black** @blackr — 16m
They <mark>carry on texting</mark> when I'm telling them something really important and they say "Yeah, yeah I heard you". Of course they didn't.

3. **Anthony Smith** @tonysmith — 20m
They always pick up the remote and <mark>change the channel</mark> when I'm watching something really interesting.

4. **Isla May** @ibmay — 1h
They leave their room in a terrible mess and then roll their eyes when I ask them <mark>to tidy it</mark>.

5. **Sarah Vine** @sarahvine — 1h
They never <mark>pick up dirty clothes</mark> or wet towels from the floor. They think some elves come later and pick them up!

6. **James Bright** @brightone — 2h
They say no before I've even finished explaining what I want to do.

7. **Ed Scott** @edwardthescott — 4h
They tell me to <mark>do the washing-up</mark> and then <mark>complain</mark> that I put things in the wrong place in the dishwasher.

8. **Sam James** @sujames — 6h
Whenever I need to call them their mobile is either switched off or the battery is dead.

c Compare with a partner. Do you agree?

d Look at the <mark>highlighted</mark> verbs and verb phrases. With a partner, say what you think they mean.

e Do any of the parents' or teenagers' habits annoy *you*? Which ones?

2 VOCABULARY
housework, *make* or *do*?

a Look again at the <mark>highlighted</mark> phrases from the text. Which three are connected with housework?

b ▶ p.154 **Vocabulary Bank** *Housework, make or do?*

3 GRAMMAR
present perfect + *yet, just, already*

a **2 15))** Look at the pictures. What do you think the people are arguing about? Listen and check.

28

b Listen again and complete the dialogues with a past participle from the list.

cleaned done dried
finished looked ~~seen~~

1 A Have you *seen* my yellow jumper? I can't find it.
   B No, I haven't. Have you _____ in your wardrobe?
   A Of course I have. What's that under your bed?
   B Oh, yes. I remember now. I borrowed it.

2 A Why aren't you doing your homework?
   B I've already _____ it.
   A Really? When?
   B I did it on the bus this evening.

3 A Have you _____ yet?
   B Nearly.
   A I need the bathroom now.
   B But I haven't _____ my hair yet.
   A Well, hurry up then.

4 A Can you get a plate for that sandwich? I've just _____ the floor.
   B OK. Oops – too late. Sorry!

c Look at the first two questions in dialogue 1. Are they about…?
  a a specific time in the past
  b a non-specific time (i.e. sometime between the past and now)

d Underline the sentences with *just*, *yet*, and *already* in dialogues 2–4. What do you think they mean?

e ▶ **p.132 Grammar Bank 4A.** Learn more about the present perfect and practise it.

f 2 18))) Listen and make the ⊕ sentences negative and the ⊖ sentences positive.

))) I've finished.   (I haven't finished.
))) It hasn't rained.   (It's rained.

4 PRONUNCIATION & SPEAKING /j/ and /dʒ/

a 2 19))) Listen and repeat the picture words and sounds.

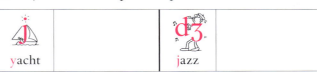

yacht   jazz

b 2 20))) Put the words in the right column. Listen and check. Then listen and repeat the words.

just yet jumper yellow change teenager
new uniform year student enjoy
beautiful jacket young bridge argue

c Practise saying these sentences.

I've just bought Jane a jumper and a jacket.
Have you worn your new uniform yet?

d ▶ **Communication** *Has he done it yet?* p.101.

e 2 21))) Listen. Say what's just happened.

5 LISTENING

a 2 22))) Listen to the first part of a radio programme about teenage carers. Answer the questions.

1 What reputation do teenagers have?
2 What do thousands of teenagers have to do?
3 How many hours do they have to help a week?

b 2 23))) Now listen to the rest of the programme. In what way are the two teenagers unusual? Do they feel positive or negative about their lives?

c Listen again and answer with **A** (Alice), **D** (Daniel), or **B** (both of them).

Who…?
1 looks after their mother
2 looks after their brother and sister
3 does a lot of housework
4 can't cook
5 doesn't live with their father
6 gives their mother a massage
7 is sometimes angry with their friends
8 never goes out without their phone

d Do you know any teenagers like Alice and Daniel? What do they do?

G present perfect or past simple? (1)
V shopping
P c and ch

4B Fashion and shopping

> Have you ever been to that shop?

> Yes. I bought this shirt there.

1 READING

a With a partner, write down the names of three fashion designers. What nationality are they? Do they design more for men or for women? What kind of things does their company make?

b Read the introduction to an interview and look at the photos. Do you like the clothes?

c Read the interview. Complete the gaps with A–F.

A I absolutely hated dressing as a man.
B I really understand how women want to feel.
C My boyfriend at that time was very lucky.
D My feet were killing me!
E The only things I enjoyed there were art and sewing.
F They are so chic, and their sense of colour is so natural to them.

d Look at the highlighted words and phrases related to fashion and shopping, and guess their meaning.

THE STYLE INTERVIEW

LINDKA CIERACH is a fashion designer. She makes very exclusive clothes for women. She has made clothes for many celebrities including members of the British royal family, for example Kate Middleton and Sarah Ferguson, whose wedding dress she designed, and actresses like Helen Mirren.

DID YOU ALWAYS WANT TO BE A DESIGNER?
Not at all! When I was at school I had problems reading, and later I was diagnosed as dyslexic. ¹ __E__ After school I did a secretarial course and then I got a job at Vogue magazine. I loved it, and there I realized that what I wanted to do was design clothes.

WHY DO YOU THINK PEOPLE LIKE YOUR CLOTHES?
Being a female designer has many advantages. ² __B__ My customers leave the studio feeling a million dollars!

WHAT NATIONALITY DO YOU THINK HAS THE BEST FASHION SENSE?
Probably the Italians. ³ __F__

HAVE YOU EVER BEEN TO A FANCY DRESS PARTY?
I hate fancy dress parties. But I can remember one, when I was ten.

WHAT DID YOU GO AS?
My mother made me and my younger sister dress as a bride and bridegroom – I was the bridegroom! ⁴ __A__

HAVE YOU EVER MET SOMEONE WHO WAS WEARING EXACTLY THE SAME AS YOU?
Never, thank goodness! I'm lucky because I can choose from a large selection of our Collection each season!

HAVE YOU EVER FALLEN OVER BECAUSE YOU WERE WEARING VERY HIGH HEELS?
I've never fallen over, but once I had to take off my shoes in the middle of a reception at the House of Lords! ⁵ __D__

WHAT DID YOU DO?
I walked out into the street in bare feet and jumped into a taxi!

HAVE YOU EVER DESIGNED CLOTHES FOR A MAN?
Yes, I have.

WHEN WAS IT?
It was when I was studying at the London College of Fashion. I designed my first Men's Wear collection – shirts, trousers and leather jackets. ⁶ __C__ He didn't need to buy any clothes that year!

Glossary
bride / bridegroom a woman / man on the day of her / his wedding
The House of Lords the second house of the British Parliament

2 GRAMMAR
present perfect or past simple? (1)

a Look at the last four questions in the interview. Answer with a partner.
1 Which questions are about experiences sometime in Lindka's life?
2 Which questions are about a specific moment in Lindka's past?
3 What does *ever* mean in the questions that begin *Have you ever…*?

b ▶ **p.132 Grammar Bank 4B.** Learn more about the present perfect and past simple and practise them.

3 LISTENING

a 2 26))) Listen to four people answering the question *Have you ever bought something that you've never worn?* What did they buy? Write 1–4 in the boxes. (There is one item you don't need.)

☐ a coat ☐ some sports clothes ☐ a skirt
☐ some trousers ☐ a shirt

b Listen again. What was the problem with the clothes? Write 1–4 in the boxes.

This person…
☐ bought something online, but didn't like the clothes when they arrived.
☐ bought the clothes too quickly and later didn't like them.
☐ wanted to look like a famous singer, but looked like another.
☐ suddenly didn't need the new clothes any more.

c Have you ever bought something that you've never worn? What was it?

4 VOCABULARY shopping

a 2 27))) Listen to some sentences from the listening. Complete the gaps with one word. With a partner, say what the highlighted phrases mean.
1 I remember when I was in the _____ room I thought they looked fantastic.
2 I _____ it on eBay.
3 I hate clothes shopping and I never _____ things on.
4 I didn't have the receipt, so I couldn't _____ it back.
5 Well, I bought it _____ from a website that has cheap offers.

b ▶ **p.155 Vocabulary Bank** *Shopping*.

5 PRONUNCIATION c and ch

a How is *c* pronounced in these words? Put them in the right row.

account auction cinema city click
clothes credit card customer proceed
receipt shopping centre

k	key
s	snake

b 2 30))) Listen and check. When is *c* pronounced /s/?

c 2 31))) How is *ch* usually pronounced? Listen and circle the two words where *ch* is pronounced differently. How is it pronounced in these words?

changing rooms cheap checkout
chemist's chic choose

d Practise saying the words in **a** and **c**.

6 SPEAKING

a Complete the questions with the past participle of the verb.

1 **Have you ever** _____ (*buy*) or _____ (*sell*) anything on eBay? What? Did you pay or get a good price?
2 **Have you ever** _____ (*buy*) something online and had a problem with it? What was it? What did you do?
3 **Have you ever** _____ (*have*) an argument with a shop assistant? What was it about?
4 **Have you ever** _____ (*try*) to change something without the receipt? Were you successful?
5 **Have you ever** accidentally _____ (*take*) something from a shop without paying? What did you take? What happened?
6 **Have you ever** _____ (*buy*) shoes without trying them on? Did they fit?
7 **Have you ever** _____ (*get*) to the supermarket checkout and then found you didn't have enough money? What did you do?
8 **Have you ever** _____ (*lose*) your credit card? Where did you lose it? Did you get it back?

b Ask other students question **1**. Try to find somebody who says *Yes, I have*. Then ask them the past simple questions. Do the same for questions **2–8**.

G *something, anything, nothing,* etc.
V adjectives ending *-ed* and *-ing*
P /e/, /əʊ/, and /ʌ/

Did you do anything at the weekend? No, nothing. I didn't do anything.

4C Lost weekend

1 LISTENING

a 2 32))) Listen to a news story about Sven. How did he spend his weekend?

b Listen again and answer the questions.

1 What does Sven do?
2 What floor was his office on?
3 What happened when he first pressed the lift button?
4 How did he try to get help?
5 Where did Sven's wife think he was?
6 How did Sven get out of the lift on Monday morning? How did he feel?
7 What is Sven going to do every day now?

c Have you (or has anyone you know) ever had a similar experience? What happened?

2 GRAMMAR
something, anything, nothing, etc.

a 2 33))) Look at three sentences from the story. Can you remember the missing words? Listen and check.

1 I pressed the button again, but _____ happened.
2 The police couldn't find him _____.
3 They phoned the emergency number and _____ came and repaired the lift.

b Complete the rule with **people**, **places**, or **things**.

1 Use *something, anything,* and *nothing* for _____.
2 Use *somebody, anybody,* and *nobody* for _____.
3 Use *somewhere, anywhere,* and *nowhere* for _____.

c ▶ p.132 **Grammar Bank 4C.** Learn more about *something, anything, nothing,* etc. and practise them.

3 PRONUNCIATION /e/, /əʊ/, and /ʌ/

a	b	c
egg	phone	up

a What sound do the **pink** letters make? Write **a**, **b**, or **c**.

1 ☐ N**o**body kn**o**ws where he g**o**es.
2 ☐ S**o**mebody's c**o**ming to l**u**nch.
3 ☐ I n**e**ver s**ai**d **a**nything.
4 ☐ I've d**o**ne n**o**thing since S**u**nday.
5 ☐ Don't t**e**ll **a**nybody about the m**e**ssage.
6 ☐ There's n**o**where to g**o** except h**o**me.

b 2 35))) Listen and check. Practise saying the sentences.

c 2 36))) Listen and answer the questions.

))) What did you buy? ⎰ Nothing. I didn't buy anything.

4 READING

a Read the article once. What is the best summary?
 a People in the UK have boring weekends.
 b People who use Facebook have more exciting weekends.
 c People sometimes don't tell the truth about their weekend.

b Read the article again. With a partner, choose a, b, or c.

1 The survey has shown that 25% of people…
 a have very exciting weekends.
 b lie about their weekend.
 c go out on a Saturday night.
2 30% of the people they interviewed…
 a needed to go to work at the weekend.
 b had a very tiring week.
 c didn't want to go out at the weekend.
3 Some people don't tell the truth about their weekend because…
 a their real weekend is very boring.
 b they don't want to make their friends jealous.
 c they forget what they have done.
4 Social networking sites make people…
 a spend more time on the computer.
 b try to make their lives seem more exciting.
 c be more truthful about their lives.

c Do you think a survey in your country would have similar results?

WHAT DID YOU REALLY DO AT THE WEEKEND?

The next time a friend or colleague tells you about their fantastic weekend, wait a moment before you start feeling jealous – maybe they are inventing it all!

A survey of 5,000 adults in the UK has shown that one person in four invents details about their weekend because they want to impress their friends. When they are asked, 'Did you have a good weekend?' they don't like to
5 say that they just stayed at home and watched TV, because it sounds boring. So they invent the details. The most common lie that people told was 'I went out on Saturday night', when really they didn't go anywhere. Other common lies were 'I had a romantic meal', 'I went to a party', and 'I went away for the
10 weekend'.

In fact, in the survey, 30% of people who answered the questions said that they spent their weekend sleeping or resting because they were so tired at the end of the week.

Another 30% said that they needed to work or study at
15 the weekend. Psychologist Corinne Sweet says that people often don't tell the truth about their weekend 'because we don't want to feel that everyone else is having a better time than us, if we have had a boring weekend doing housework, paperwork, or just resting after a tiring week at work'. She also
20 believes that networking sites such as Facebook and Twitter may be encouraging us to invent details about our social lives. 'People can create an illusion of who they want to be and the life they want to live,' says Corinne, 'and of course they want that life to seem exciting.'

5 SPEAKING

a Look at the questions in **b**. Plan your answers. Answer them truthfully, but **invent one answer** to make your weekend sound more exciting.

b Interview each other with the questions. Try to guess which answer your partner invented.

LAST WEEKEND
Friday
- Did you go anywhere exciting on Friday night?

Saturday
- Did you do anything in the house (cleaning, etc.) on Saturday morning?
- Did you work or study at all?
- What did you do on Saturday night?

Sunday
- Did you go anywhere nice on Sunday?
- What did you have for lunch?
- Did you do anything relaxing in the afternoon?

6 VOCABULARY
adjectives ending *-ed* and *-ing*

a Look at these two adjectives in the text: *tired* in line 13 and *tiring* in line 19. Which one describes how you feel? Which one describes things and situations?

b 2 37)) Circle the right adjective in questions 1–10. Listen and check. How do you say the adjectives?

1 Do you think Sundays are usually *bored / boring*?
2 Are you *bored / boring* with your job or studies?
3 What kind of weather makes you feel *depressed / depressing*?
4 Why do you think the news is often *depressed / depressing*?
5 What activity do you find most *relaxed / relaxing*?
6 Do you usually feel *relaxed / relaxing* at the end of the weekend? Why (not)?
7 What is the most *interested / interesting* book you've read recently?
8 What sports are you *interested / interesting* in?
9 Are you *excited / exciting* about your next holiday?
10 What's the most *excited / exciting* sports match you've ever watched?

c Ask and answer the questions with a partner. Give more information if you can.

7 2 38)) SONG
If You Love Somebody Set Them Free ♫

3&4 Revise and Check

GRAMMAR

Circle a, b, or c.

1 How long _____ to stay in Italy?
   a do you go   b are you going   c you are going
2 I think _____ rain tonight.
   a it's going   b it goes to   c it's going to
3 They _____ to get married until next year.
   a aren't going   b don't go   c not going
4 I _____ to the cinema after class this evening.
   a go   b am going   c going go
5 A What time _____ tomorrow?   B At 8.00.
   a you leave   b do you leaving   c are you leaving
6 He's the man _____ lives next door to Alice.
   a who   b which   c where
7 Is that the shop _____ sells Italian food?
   a who   b which   c where
8 A _____ your bed?   B No, I'm going to do it now.
   a Have you made
   b Have you make
   c Has you made
9 A Has Anne arrived _____?
   B No, but she's on her way.
   a yet   b just   c already
10 _____ already seen this film! Let's change channels.
   a We're   b We haven't   c We've
11 A _____ been to Africa?   B No, never.
   a Have you ever   b Did you ever   c Were you ever
12 A When _____ those shoes?   B Last week.
   a do you buy   b have you bought   c did you buy
13 I've never _____ this coat. It's too small.
   a wear   b worn   c wore
14 There's _____ at the door. Can you go and open it please?
   a something   b someone   c somewhere
15 I don't want _____ to eat, thanks. I'm not hungry.
   a nothing   b anything   c something

VOCABULARY

a Complete with a preposition.

1 We arrived _____ Prague at 7.15.
2 I'm coming! Wait _____ me.
3 What did you ask _____, meat or fish?
4 A Are you going to buy the flat?
   B I don't know. It depends _____ the price.
5 How much did you pay _____ those shoes?

b Complete with *make* or *do*.

1 _____ the washing-up
2 _____ a mistake
3 _____ an exam
4 _____ exercise
5 _____ a noise

c Complete the missing words.

1 Dinner's ready. Please could you l_____ the table.
2 I'll cook if you do the w_____-up.
3 Where are the changing rooms? I want to tr_____ o_____ this sweater.
4 If you want to take something back to a shop, you need to have the r_____.
5 These shoes don't f_____ me. They're too small.
6 The flight to Berlin is now leaving from G_____ 12.
7 If you have a lot of luggage, you can find a tr_____ over there.
8 First you need to go to the ch_____-i_____ desk where you get your boarding pass.
9 International flights depart from T_____ 2.
10 There are l_____ to the first and second floors.

d Circle the right adjective.

1 This exercise is really *bored* / *boring*.
2 I never feel *relaxed* / *relaxing* the day before I go on holiday.
3 It was a very *excited* / *exciting* match.
4 Jack is a bit *depressed* / *depressing*. He lost his job.
5 Are you *interested* / *interesting* in art?

PRONUNCIATION

a Circle the word with a different sound.

1 j**u**st   M**o**nday   s**o**mething   tr**o**lley
2 n**o**where   cl**o**thes   w**o**rry   g**o**
3 sear**ch**   **ch**emist   **ch**eap   **ch**oose
4 **c**ustomer   **c**entre   **c**inema   ni**c**e
5 **j**acket   chan**g**e   en**j**oy   **y**et

b Underline the stressed syllable.

1 A|rri|vals   3 tee|na|ger   5 a|rrange|ment
2 o|ppo|site   4 de|li|ve|ry

CAN YOU UNDERSTAND THIS TEXT?

a Read the article. What were thieves stealing in a) Sweden b) Denmark? Answer the questions below.

1 Where did the first robbery take place?
2 Who were the thieves and what did they steal?
3 Who helped the police to solve the crime?
4 How long does it take to get from Malmö to Copenhagen?
5 Why were robberies taking place in both cities?
6 Did the police catch the thieves?
7 Why is it easier to steal from many stores these days?
8 Why is it not a solution to ask Danish shoe shops to display the left shoe?

b Look at the highlighted words or phrases in the text. Guess their meaning from the context. Check with your teacher or with a dictionary.

Shoe shops discover matching crimes

Swedish fictional detectives like Wallander and Lisbeth Salander are famous worldwide. But recently real-life Swedish police were completely puzzled by a mysterious crime. Somebody was stealing expensive designer shoes from shoe shops in Sweden – but not pairs of shoes, only the left shoes, the ones which were on display.

The first robbery took place in a shopping mall in Malmö, Sweden's third-largest city. Staff at a shoe shop saw two men stealing at their boutique. They escaped with seven left shoes which – if paired with the right shoes – were worth £900.

In the end it was shop assistants who pointed the police in the right direction – to Denmark, where shops traditionally display the right shoe in their shop windows. "We noticed that left shoes were disappearing in the past, but we never caught the thieves," said a shop assistant. "Since we know that Danish stores display the right shoes, we thought that the matching shoes were probably disappearing as well in stores in Denmark." Malmö, home to 125 shoe shops, is only a 30-minute train ride away from Copenhagen, which has several hundred shops, and many brands are sold in both cities.

Yesterday police finally announced that they had arrested the men responsible for the robberies. But Ms Johansson, a Swedish shoe shop owner, fears that shoe shop robberies will increase this year. "Shoes are attractive to steal – they are easy to move and easy to sell and they have become very expensive lately. Also many stores have cut the number of shop assistants they employ."

Police in Malmo have thought of asking Danish shoe shops to also display the left shoe. But this won't work. All the thieves will have to do is move to Germany – where they also display the right shoe…

Adapted from a British newspaper

CAN YOU UNDERSTAND THESE PEOPLE?

2 39)) **In the street** Watch or listen to five people and answer the questions.

Paul   Gurjot   Ellie   Alise   Anya

1 Paul went to the airport _____.
   a to get a plane to London
   b to get a plane to Frankfurt
   c to meet a friend from Frankfurt
2 Tonight Gurjot is _____.
   a seeing a film
   b going to a Chinese restaurant
   c meeting an old friend
3 Ellie _____ ironing.
   a hates   b doesn't mind   c likes
4 The shoes Alise bought online _____.
   a were the wrong size
   b never arrived
   c were a beautiful colour
5 Last weekend Anya _____.
   a went to a friend's birthday party
   b had dinner with a friend
   c bought something for a friend's birthday

CAN YOU SAY THIS IN ENGLISH?

Do the tasks with a partner. Tick (✓) the box if you can do them.

Can you…?

1 ☐ talk about three plans you have for next month using *going to*, and make three predictions
2 ☐ say three arrangements you have for tomorrow using the present continuous
3 ☐ explain what the following three words mean, using expressions for paraphrasing:
     a a thief   b a shopping mall   c a shoe
4 ☐ say three things you have already done or haven't done yet today
5 ☐ ask a partner three questions about his/her experiences using *ever*. Answer your partner's questions
6 ☐ say three sentences using *something*, *anywhere*, and *nobody*

Short films Shopping in the UK
Watch and enjoy a film on iTutor.

5A No time for anything

G comparative adjectives and adverbs, as...as
V time expressions: spend time, etc.
P sentence stress

"Are we living faster?"
"Yes, we need to slow down."

1 READING & VOCABULARY time expressions

a Read an article about living faster and match the headings to the paragraphs.

☐ No time for Snow White
☐ No time to write
☐ No time to wait
☐ More time on the road
☐ No time for Van Gogh
☐ No time to stop

b Read the article again. One paragraph contains an invented piece of information. Which one is it?

c Look at the highlighted time expressions and guess their meaning.

d In pairs, cover the text and look at the paragraph headings in **a**. Can you remember the information in the text? Have you noticed any of these things happening where you live?

e Look at a questionnaire about living faster. In pairs, ask and answer the questions. Answer with *often*, *sometimes*, or *never* and give more information.

We're living **faster**, but are we living **better**?

1
People in cities around the world walk 10% more quickly than they did twenty years ago. Singapore, a world business centre, is top of the list for fast walkers.

2
In the USA there is a book called One-Minute Bedtime Stories for children. These are shorter versions of traditional stories, especially written for busy parents who need to save time.

3
People aren't as patient as they were in the past. If the lift takes more than 15 seconds to arrive, people get very impatient because they think they're wasting time. It's exactly the same when an Internet page does not open immediately.

4
Written communication on the internet is getting shorter and shorter and using more and more abbreviations, like BFN (bye for now) or NP (no problem). Twitter only allows you to use 140 characters, and now a new social networking site has a limit of just ten words.

5
Even in our free time we do things in a hurry. Twenty years ago when people went to art galleries they spent ten seconds looking at each picture. Today they spend much less time – just three seconds!

6
Our cars are faster, but the traffic is worse, so we drive more slowly. The average speed of cars in New York City is 15 km/h. We spend more time than ever sitting in our cars, feeling stressed because we aren't going to arrive on time.

QUESTIONNAIRE
How fast is **your** life?

1 Do people tell you that you talk too quickly?
2 Do you get impatient when other people are talking?
3 Are you the first person to finish at mealtimes?
4 When you are walking along a street, do you feel frustrated when you are behind people who are walking more slowly?
5 Do you get irritable if you sit for an hour without doing anything, e.g. waiting for the doctor?
6 Do you walk out of shops and restaurants if there is a queue?

f ▶ **Communication** *How fast is your life?* p.101. Read the results. Do you agree?

2 GRAMMAR comparative adjectives and adverbs, as...as

a Look at the following words from the text. Are they adjectives, adverbs, or both?

> quickly   fast   busy   patient
> bad   slowly   stressed

b Circle the right form. Tick (✓) if both are correct.

1 Life is *faster | more fast* than before.
2 Traffic in cities is *more bad | worse* than it was.
3 Everybody is *busyer | busier* than they were five years ago.
4 We are *more stressed | stresseder* than our grandparents were.
5 We do everything *more quickly | faster*.
6 People aren't *as patient as | as patient than* they were before.

c ▶ p.134 **Grammar Bank 5A.** Learn more about comparatives and *as…as* and practise them.

3 PRONUNCIATION sentence stress

> 🔍 **The /ə/ sound**
> Remember! *-er*, and unstressed words like *a*, *as*, and *than* have the sound /ə/.

a ⟨2 41⟩)) Listen and repeat the sentences. Copy the rhythm and try to get the /ə/ sound right.

1 I'm **busi**er than a **year** ago.
2 My **life** is **more stress**ful than in the **past**.
3 I **work hard**er than **before**.
4 I **walk** and **talk fast**er.
5 I'm **not** as **relaxed** as I **was** a **few years ago**.

b Are any of the sentences true for you?

4 SPEAKING

a Think about how your life has changed over the last 3–5 years. Read the questions below and think about your answers.

> 1 Do you spend more or less time on these things? Say why.
>
> working or studying   sleeping
> getting to work / school   cooking
> sitting in traffic   shopping
> talking to friends   eating
> meeting friends   using your phone
> being online   using your computer
>
> 2 Do you have more or less free time? Why?
> 3 What *don't* you have time for nowadays? What would you like to have more time for?

b Answer the questions with a partner. Whose life has changed more?

5 LISTENING

a You're going to listen to an expert talking about how to live your life more slowly. Look at her five main tips (= good ideas). Guess what the missing words are.

1 Whatever you are doing, just try to _____ _____ and enjoy it.
   Example: _____
2 Make a list of three things which are _____ _____ for you.
   Example: _____
3 Don't try to do _____ _____ at the same time.
   Example: _____
4 Sit down and do _____ for half an hour every day.
   Example: _____
5 Be near _____ .
   Example: _____

b ⟨2 42⟩)) Listen and check. Then listen again and write one example for each tip.

c Are there any tips that you think you might use? Why (not)?

G superlatives (+ *ever* + present perfect)
V describing a town or city
P word and sentence stress

5B Superlative cities

What did you think of Rio? It's the most beautiful city I've ever been to.

1 GRAMMAR superlatives (+ *ever* + present perfect)

a Match the photos and cities. Which European countries are the cities in? What do you know about them? Have you been to any of them?

☐ Barcelona ☐ Copenhagen ☐ Dublin ☐ Paris ☐ Venice

b Read the article and complete it with the cities in **a**.

Travel survey gives its verdict on European cities

London is **the dirtiest** city in Europe says a new survey by travel website TripAdvisor, but it has **the best** public parks and the best nightlife. According to the survey of almost 2,400 travellers…

1 _____ is **the most romantic** city.
2 _____ is **the cleanest** city.
3 _____ has **the best-dressed** people.
4 _____ has **the best** architecture.
5 _____ is **the friendliest** city.

'Europe's big cities all have their highs and lows, but they offer travellers a huge variety of culture and sights within very short distances,' said a TripAdvisor spokesman.

c Look at 1–5 in the survey in **b**. Think about your country or continent. Which cities would *you* choose?

d Look at the **bold** superlative adjectives in the survey. How do you make the superlative of…?

1 a one-syllable adjective
2 a two-syllable adjective that ends in *-y*
3 a three-syllable adjective
4 *good* and *bad*

e ▶ p.134 **Grammar Bank 5B**. Learn more about superlatives and practise them.

2 PRONUNCIATION word and sentence stress

a Under<u>line</u> the stressed syllable in the **bold** adjectives.

1 What's the most **beautiful** city you've ever been to?
2 What's the most **expensive** thing you've ever bought?
3 Who's the most **impatient** person you know?
4 Who's the most **generous** person in your family?
5 What's the most **frightening** film you've ever seen?
6 What's the most **exciting** sport you've ever done?
7 What's the most **interesting** book you've read recently?
8 What's the most **romantic** restaurant you've ever been to?

b 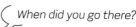 Listen and check. Listen again and repeat the questions. <u>Copy</u> the <u>rhythm</u>. Which words are stressed?

c Work with a partner. **A** answer question 1 with a sentence. **B** ask for more information. Swap roles for question 2, etc.

The most beautiful city I've ever been to is Rio de Janeiro.   *When did you go there?*

3 READING & SPEAKING

a Read the article. In pairs, answer the questions.
1 What are the three tests?
2 Do you think they are good ones?
3 Which city do you think will be the friendliest / most unfriendly?

All capital cities are unfriendly – or are they?

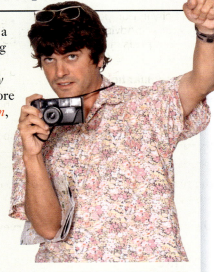

Big cities often have a reputation for being rude, unfriendly places for tourists. *Sunday Times* journalist Tim Moore went to four cities, *London*, *Rome*, *Paris*, and *New York*, to find out if this is true. He went dressed as a foreign tourist and did three (not very scientific!) tests to see which city had the friendliest and most polite inhabitants. The three tests were:

1 The photo test

Tim asked people in the street to take his photo (not just one photo, but several – with his hat, without his hat, etc.). Did he find someone to do it?

2 The shopping test

Tim bought something in a shop and gave the shop assistant too much money. Did the shop assistant give back the extra money?

3 The accident test

Tim pretended to fall over in the street. Did anybody come and help him?

b ▶ **Communication** *The friendliest city* **A** p.102 **B** p.107 **C** p.110. Read about what happened in New York, Paris, and Rome.

4 LISTENING

a ⏵ 2 45))) Now listen to Tim Moore talking about what happened in London. How well does London do in each test?

b Listen again and answer the questions.

The photo test
1 Who did he ask first?
2 What did the person say?
3 Who did he ask next? What happened?

The shopping test
4 Where was the tourist shop?
5 How much did the bus and key ring cost?
6 How much did he give the man?
7 Did he get the right change?

The accident test
8 Where did he do the accident test?
9 Did anyone help him?
10 What did the man say?

c Think about the nearest big city to where you live. Imagine you did the three tests there. What do you think would happen? Is it a friendly city?

5 VOCABULARY describing a town or city

a Think about how to answer these questions about where you live. Compare with a partner.

- Do you live in a village, a town, or a city?
- Where is it?
- How big is it?
- What's the population?
- What's it like?

b ▶ p.156 **Vocabulary Bank** *Describing a town or city.*

6 WRITING

▶ p.114 **Writing** *Describing where you live.* Write a description of the place where you live.

7 ⏵ 2 49))) SONG *Nobody Does It Better* ♫

G quantifiers, *too, not enough*
V health and the body
P /ʌ/, /uː/, /aɪ/, and /e/

5C How much is too much?

I watch too much TV.

I don't spend enough time in the sun.

1 SPEAKING

a With a partner, answer the questions below.

DIET & LIFESTYLE QUESTIONNAIRE

1 Do you drink coffee? How many cups do you drink a day? What kind of coffee? What time do you drink your last cup of the day?

2 How much time do you spend a day in the sun…?
  a in the winter
  b in the summer
  c when you're on holiday
  Do you always wear sunscreen?

3 Do you play a lot of video or computer games? What are your favourite games? How much time do you spend a week playing them?

4 How often do you eat chocolate? What kind of chocolate do you prefer – milk, white, or dark?

5 How many hours a day do you watch TV…?
  a during the week
  b at weekends
  What kind of programmes do you watch regularly?

b Do you think any of your habits are unhealthy?

2 READING & LISTENING

a Read the article once. Does it change what you think about your answers to the questionnaire?

b Read the article again. Look at the highlighted words related to health and the body. Match them to a picture or definition.

1 _____
2 _____
3 _____

4 *noun* it covers the outside of a person's body
5 *verb* to stop sth from happening
6 *noun* sth which makes you unwell
7 *adj* feeling worried or nervous

Everything BAD is GOOD for you

COFFEE We all know that a cup of coffee helps to wake you up in the morning, but several studies show that drinking coffee helps to prevent some illnesses like diabetes and Parkinson's disease. Experts say that you can safely drink three cups of espresso during the day, but if you drink too much coffee it can make you feel anxious or keep you awake at night.

SUNLIGHT Spending a long time in the sun is dangerous and can give you skin cancer. But on the other hand, not spending enough time in the sun is also bad for you, as sunlight helps us to produce vitamin D. This vitamin is important for strong bones and a healthy immune system, and it also makes people feel happier. Nowadays many people don't get enough sunlight because they wear sunscreen all the time, especially on their faces. However, don't spend too long in the sun – 15 minutes a day without sunscreen is a healthy amount, and not at midday.

COMPUTER GAMES You probably worry about how much time you or your children waste playing computer games. But in fact some studies show that these games can help us learn important skills. It seems that computer games stimulate the brain and that people who often play them are probably better at solving problems and making quick decisions. But don't spend too many hours in front of the computer – not more than about two hours a day.

c **2 50))** Listen and check. Practise saying the words.

d Now cover the text. Can you remember…?
1 what is good about coffee, sunlight, and computer games
2 what you need to be careful about

e **2 51))** With a partner, decide in what ways you think chocolate and watching TV could be good for you. Listen to a radio programme and check your answers.

f Listen again. Answer the questions.
1 What does chocolate have in common with red wine?
2 What kind of chocolate is a) good for you b) not good for you?
3 How are TV series different from the ones 20 years ago? Why is this good for us?
4 What can we learn from reality TV shows?

g Do the article and the radio programme make you feel happier about your lifestyle?

3 GRAMMAR quantifiers, *too, not enough*

a Can you remember how to use *much, many*, etc? In pairs, choose the correct word or phrase for each sentence. Say why the other one is wrong.
1 How *much | many* cups of coffee do you drink a day?
2 I don't spend *much | many* time in the sun.
3 I eat *a lot of | many* chocolate.
4 Drinking *a few | a little* red wine can be good for you.
5 I only have *a few | a little* computer games.
6 My parents read *a lot | a lot of*.

b Look at some sentences from the reading and listening. Match the **bold** phrases in 1 and 2 to meanings **A** and **B**.
1 Don't eat **too much** chocolate or **too many** sweets if you don't want to put on weight.
Don't spend **too** long in the sun.
2 Nowadays many people **don't** get **enough** sunlight.
We are **not** active **enough**.
A less than you need or than is good for you
B more than you need or than is good for you

c Look again at the sentences with *enough*. What's the position of *enough* a) with a noun b) with an adjective?

d ▶ **p.134 Grammar Bank 5C.** Learn more about quantifiers, *too*, and *not enough* and practise them.

4 PRONUNCIATION & SPEAKING
/ʌ/, /uː/, /aɪ/, and /e/

a Cross out the word with a different pronunciation.

ʌ	up	en**ou**gh m**u**ch n**o**ne b**u**sy
uː	b**oo**t	f**ew** c**u**ps t**oo** f**oo**d
aɪ	b**i**ke	qu**i**te d**ie**t l**i**ttle l**i**ke
e	**e**gg	m**a**ny **a**ny h**ea**lthy w**a**ter

b **2 54))** Listen and check. Practise saying the words.

c Ask and answer the questions with a partner. Say why.

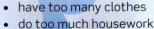

Do you think you read enough?

Not really. I only read school textbooks, not for pleasure.

Do you think you…?
- read enough
- eat enough fruit and vegetables
- do enough sport or exercise
- drink enough water
- have enough free time
- eat too much fast food
- spend too much time online
- spend too much money on things you don't need
- work or study too many hours
- have too many clothes
- do too much housework
- get too much homework

Practical English The wrong shoes

EPISODE 3

1 ROB HAS A PROBLEM

a (2 55))) Watch or listen to Rob and Holly and answer the questions.

1. What reason does Rob give for why he isn't in shape?
2. Why does he find it difficult to eat less?
3. How does he keep fit in London?
4. Why doesn't he do the same in New York?
5. How does Jenny keep fit?
6. What does Holly think about this?
7. What does Holly suggest that Rob could do?
8. What does Rob need to do first?

> **British and American English**
> *sneakers* = American English; *trainers* = British English
> *store* = American English; *shop* = British English

b (2 56))) Look at the box on making suggestions. Listen and repeat the phrases.

> **Making suggestions with *Why don't you...?***
> **A** Why don't you get a bike?
> **B** That's a good idea, but I'm only here for a month.
> **A** Why don't you come and play basketball?
> **B** That's a great idea!

c Practise making suggestions with a partner.

A You have problems remembering English vocabulary. Tell **B**.
B Make two suggestions.
A Respond. If you don't think it's a good idea, say why.

d Swap roles.

B You are a foreigner in **A**'s country. You have problems meeting new people.

2 VOCABULARY shopping

Do the quiz with a partner.

SHOPPING QUIZ
1. What four letters do you often see in clothes which tell you the size?
2. What do the letters mean?
3. What's the name of the room where you can try on clothes?
4. What's the name of the piece of paper a shop assistant gives you when you buy something?
5. How do you say these prices?
   £25.99   75p $45   15c   €12.50

3 TAKING SOMETHING BACK TO A SHOP

a (2 57))) Cover the dialogue and watch or listen. Answer the questions.

1. What's the problem with Rob's trainers?
2. What does he do in the end?

b Watch or listen again. Complete the **You Hear** phrases.

🔊 You Hear	You Say 💬
Can I help you, sir?	Yes. Do you have these in an eight?
Just a _____, I'll go and check.	
Here you are, these are an eight. Do you want to _____ them on?	No, thanks. I'm sure they'll be fine. How much are they?
They're $83.94.	Oh, it says $72.99.
Yes, but there's an added sales tax of _____%.	Oh, OK. Do you take MasterCard?
Sure.	
Can I help you?	Yes, I bought these about half an hour ago.
Yes, I remember. Is there a _____?	Yes, I'm afraid they're too small.
What _____ are they?	They're an eight. But I take a UK eight.
Oh right. Yes, a UK eight is a US nine.	Do you have a pair?
I'll go and check. Just a minute.	
I'm _____, but we don't have these in a nine. But we do have these and they're the _____ price. Or you can have a refund.	Erm…I'll take this pair then, please.
No problem. Do you have the _____?	Yes, here you are.
Brilliant.	

> 🔍 **A pair**
> We often use *a pair* to talk about plural clothes, e.g. *a pair of shoes*, *trainers*, *boots*, *jeans*, *trousers*, etc.

c 🔊 2 58)) Watch or listen and repeat the **You Say** phrases. <u>C</u>opy the <u>r</u>hythm.

d Practise the dialogue with a partner.

e 👥 In pairs, roleplay the dialogue.

  A You're a customer. You bought some jeans yesterday. They're too big.

  B You're a shop assistant. You don't have the same jeans in **A**'s size. Offer **A** a different pair or a refund. You begin with *Can I help you, sir / madam?*

f Swap roles.

  B You're a customer. You bought some boots yesterday. They're too small.

  A You're a shop assistant. You don't have the same boots in **B**'s size. Offer **B** a different pair or a refund. You begin with *Can I help you, sir / madam?*

4 🖥 ROB DECIDES TO DO SOME EXERCISE

a 🔊 2 59)) Watch or listen and (circle) the right answer.

1. Rob went to *Boston* / *Brooklyn*.
2. He *shows* / *doesn't show* Jenny his new trainers.
3. Jenny goes running every *morning* / *evening* in Central Park.
4. She wants to go running with him at *6.45* / *7.45*.
5. Rob thinks it's too *early* / *late*.
6. They agree to meet at *6.45* / *7.15*.
7. Holly thinks Rob *has* / *doesn't have* a lot of energy.

b Look at the **Social English phrases**. Can you remember any of the missing words?

> **Social English phrases**
> **Rob** Have you _____ a good day?
> **Jenny** Oh, you _____. Meetings!
> **Jenny** Why _____ you come with me?
> **Rob** Can we _____ it a bit later?
> **Rob** _____, seven forty-five?
> **Jenny** _____ make it seven fifteen.

c 🔊 2 60)) Watch or listen and complete the phrases.

d Watch or listen again and repeat the phrases. How do you say them in your language?

> 👤 **Can you…?**
> ☐ make suggestions to do something
> ☐ take something you have bought back to the shop
> ☐ arrange a time to meet somebody

G will / won't (predictions)
V opposite verbs
P 'll, won't

> I'm doing my driving test today.
>
> You'll fail.

6A Are you a pessimist?

1 VOCABULARY opposite verbs

a With a partner, write the opposites of these verbs.

| win _____ | buy _____ | remember _____ |
| turn on _____ | start _____ / _____ |

b ▶ p.157 **Vocabulary Bank** *Opposite verbs.*

2 GRAMMAR will / won't (predictions)

a Look at the cartoon. Which fish is an optimist? Why? Are you an optimist or a pessimist?

b Look at the phrase book app. Read the **You Say** phrases, then write the **A Pessimist Says** responses.

> He won't pay you back.   They'll be late.   You won't pass.
> It'll rain.   They'll lose.   You won't understand a word.
> You won't find a parking space.   You'll break your leg.

c 3 3))) Listen and check. Repeat the responses.

d Practise in pairs. **A** (book open) read the **You Say** phrases. **B** (book closed) say the **A Pessimist Says** responses. Then swap roles.

e Look at the **A Pessimist Says** phrases again. Do they refer to the present or the future?

f ▶ p.136 **Grammar Bank 6A.** Learn more about *will / won't* and practise them.

g Imagine now that you are an optimist. With a partner make positive predictions to respond to the **You Say** sentences in the phrase book.

> 1 *It'll be a great evening.*

3 PRONUNCIATION 'll, won't

a 3 5))) Listen and repeat the contractions. Copy the rhythm.

I'll	I'll be late	I'll be late for work.
You'll	You'll break	You'll break your leg.
She'll	She'll miss	She'll miss the train.
It'll	It'll rain	It'll rain tomorrow.
They'll	They'll fail	They'll fail the exam.

b 3 6))) Listen. Can you hear the difference?

| clock | want | I want to pass. |
| phone | won't | I won't pass. |

c 3 7))) Listen and write six sentences.

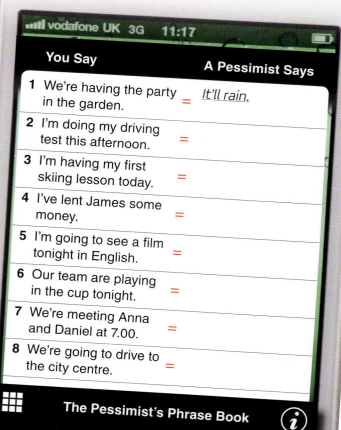

The Pessimist's Phrase Book

	You Say		A Pessimist Says
1	We're having the party in the garden.	=	It'll rain.
2	I'm doing my driving test this afternoon.	=	
3	I'm having my first skiing lesson today.	=	
4	I've lent James some money.	=	
5	I'm going to see a film tonight in English.	=	
6	Our team are playing in the cup tonight.	=	
7	We're meeting Anna and Daniel at 7.00.	=	
8	We're going to drive to the city centre.	=	

4 READING

a Read an article about the actor Hugh Laurie. What two things do Hugh Laurie and Dr House have in common?

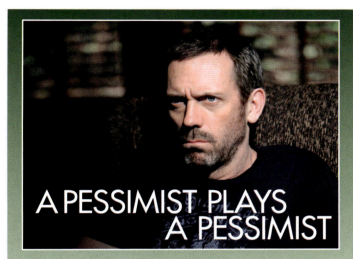

A PESSIMIST PLAYS A PESSIMIST

DR GREGORY HOUSE, the main character in the hit TV series *House M.D.*, is famous for being a pessimist. But it is not only Dr House who is a pessimist. Hugh Laurie, the actor who plays him, is a pessimist too.

Laurie never thought that *House M.D.* was going to be a success. Even after seven series he still feels pessimistic about it. He said in a recent interview, "If we do a bad show next week, they'll say, 'That's it. No more.' It'll just stop. I am of course someone who is constantly expecting a plane to drop on my head, if not today then tomorrow."

Like Dr House, Laurie is also a talented musician and is passionate about the blues. He recently went to New Orleans to record an album in which he plays 15 of his favourite songs. But of course he doesn't think that people will like it.

When he was asked on a TV show why he was so pessimistic about life, Laurie said it was because he is Scottish. 'I definitely think that's where it comes from.'

Because of his reputation as a pessimist, people always talk to him about positive thinking. He says that complete strangers come up to him in the street and say 'Cheer up, mate, it'll never happen!'

b Read the article again. Mark the sentences **T** (true) or **F** (false). Say why.

1. Hugh Laurie always thinks the worst will happen.
2. He thinks they will make many more series of *House M.D.*
3. He doesn't think his album will be successful.
4. He thinks that Scottish people are optimistic.
5. People often try to make him feel happier.

c Have you seen any episodes of *House M.D.*? Do you like…?
   a the character   b the actor

5 LISTENING & SPEAKING

a 3 8))) Listen to the introduction to a radio programme. Why is positive thinking good for you?

b Try to guess the missing words in these callers' tips.

Caller 1   Live in the _____, not in the _____.
Caller 2   Think _____ thoughts, not negative ones.
Caller 3   Don't spend a lot of time reading the _____ or watching the _____ on TV.
Caller 4   Every week make a list of all the _____ _____ that happened to you.
Caller 5   Try to use _____ _____ when you speak to other people.

c 3 9))) Listen and check.

d Listen again. Write down any extra information you hear. Which tips do you think are useful? Do you have any tips of your own?

e Ask and answer with a partner. Use a phrase from the box and say why. Which of you is more optimistic?

ARE YOU A POSITIVE THINKER?
Do you think…
+ you'll have a nice weekend?
+ you'll pass your next English exam?
+ you'll get a good (or better) job in the future?
+ you'll get an interesting email or message from someone tonight?
+ you'll meet some new friends on your next holiday?
+ you'll live to be 100?
+ you'll get to the end of this book?

> **Responding to predictions**
> I hope so. / I hope not.
> I think so. / I don't think so.
> I doubt it.
> M<u>a</u>ybe. / Perh<u>a</u>ps.
> Pr<u>o</u>bably (not).
> D<u>e</u>finitely (not).

Do you think you'll have a nice weekend?
I hope so. I think the weather will be good and…

G will / won't (decisions, offers, promises)
V verb + back
P word stress: two-syllable verbs

6B I'll never forget you

1 GRAMMAR
will / won't (decisions, offers, promises)

a Look at the cartoons. What do you think the missing phrases are?

b ▶ 3 10))) Listen and complete the gaps.

c Look at the cartoons again. In which one does somebody…?

- [ ] promise to do something
- [ ] decide to have something
- [ ] offer to do something

d ▶ **p.136 Grammar Bank 6B.** Learn more about making offers, promises, and decisions and practise them.

e ▶ **Communication** *I'll / Shall I?* game p.102. Play the game.

2 PRONUNCIATION
word stress: two-syllable verbs

> 🔍 **Stress in two-syllable verbs**
> Remember that most two-syllable verbs are stressed on the second syllable.

a Look at the two-syllable verbs below. Which syllable are they stressed on? Put them in the right column.

a|gree	a|rrive	bo|rrow	com|plain	de|cide	de|pend
for|get	ha|ppen	im|press	in|vent	in|vite	o|ffer
prac|tise	pre|fer	pro|mise	re|ceive	re|pair	sun|bathe

1st syllable	2nd syllable

b ▶ 3 12))) Listen and check.

1 **A** That's two burgers, a double portion of chips, and two ice cream sundaes. Anything else?
  B Yes, _____, please.

2 **A** Do I want to go back to the previous version? Do I press Yes or No?
  B I need to do my homework now. _____ when I finish.

3 **A** _____ ! I promise!
  B Well, hurry up. I can't wait much longer.
  A Just one more kiss…

It's a secret.
OK, I won't tell anyone.

3 SPEAKING & LISTENING

a Look at the sentences. Talk to a partner.
1 When do you think people say them?
2 What do you think they all have in common?

I'll pay you back.
This won't hurt.
I'll come back and finish the job tomorrow.
I'll text you when I get there.
I won't tell anyone.
I'll do it later.
We'll build new schools and hospitals.

b Look at the title of a newspaper article. Do you think it's another promise that people often break?

I'll never forget you

THEN   NOW

Steve Smith from Devon in the UK met Carmen Ruiz-Perez from Spain 17 years ago when they were both in their 20s. Carmen was studying English at a language school in Steve's town, Torbay.

They fell in love and got engaged. But a year later Carmen moved to France to work, and the long-distance relationship first cooled and then ended.

A few years later Steve tried to get in touch with Carmen again, but she had changed her address in Paris. So he sent her a letter to her mother's address in Spain. In the letter he asked her if she was married and if she ever thought of him. He gave her his telephone number and asked her to get in touch. But Carmen's mother didn't send the letter to her daughter and it fell down behind the fireplace, where it stayed for ten years...

Adapted from a British newspaper

c Read the article and answer the questions.
1 What were Carmen and Steve doing in Torbay?
2 Why didn't they get married?
3 Why didn't Steve's letter get to Carmen?

d 3 13))) Now listen to part of a news programme and answer the questions.

What happened…?
1 when the builders found the letter
2 when Carmen got the letter
3 when Carmen called Steve
4 when they met in Paris
5 last week

4 VOCABULARY verb + *back*

a Look at the sentences. What's the difference between *go* and *go back*?

I'm **going** to work.   I'm **going back** to work.

b Complete the dialogues with a phrase from the list.

call you back   come back   give it back
pay me back   send it back   take it back

1 **A** The shirt you bought me is too small.
   B Don't worry. I'll _____ to the shop and change it. I still have the receipt.

2 **A** Hi, Jack. It's me, Karen.
   B I can't talk now, I'm driving – I'll _____ in 15 minutes.

3 **A** Could I see the manager?
   B She's at lunch now. Could you _____ in about half an hour?

4 **A** That's my pen you're using! _____!
   B No, it's not. It's mine.

5 **A** Can you lend me 50 euros, Nick?
   B It depends. When can you _____?

6 **A** I bought this jacket on the internet, but it's too big.
   B Can't you _____?

c 3 14))) Listen and check. In pairs, practise the dialogues.

d Ask and answer in groups. Ask for more information.
1 When someone leaves you a message on your phone do you usually **call** them **back** immediately?
2 If you buy something online that is not exactly what you wanted, do you always **send** it **back**?
3 Have you ever lent somebody money and they didn't **pay** you **back**?
4 When you **come back** after a holiday do you usually feel better or worse than before?
5 When you borrow a book or a DVD from a friend do you usually remember to **give** it **back**? What about if you lend something to your friends?
6 If you buy something to wear from a shop and then decide you don't like it, do you usually **take** it **back**?

5 3 15))) SONG
Reach Out I'll Be There ♫

G review of verb forms: present, past, and future
V adjectives + prepositions
P the letters *ow*

> I dreamt about a road.

> That means you're going to travel.

6C The meaning of dreaming

1 READING & LISTENING

a Do you often remember your dreams? Do you think dreams can tell us anything about the future?

b 3 16)) Listen to a psychoanalyst talking to a patient about his dreams. Number the pictures 1–6 in the correct order.

c Listen again and complete the gaps with a verb in the right form.

Dr Allen So, tell me, what did you dream about?
Patient I was at a party. There were a lot of people.
Dr What were they ¹_____?
P They were drinking and ²_____.
Dr Were you drinking?
P Yes, I was ³_____ champagne.
Dr And then what happened?
P Then, suddenly I was in a garden. There ⁴_____ a lot of flowers...
Dr Flowers, yes... what kind of flowers?
P I ⁵_____ really see – it was dark. And I could hear music – somebody was ⁶_____ the violin.
Dr The violin? Go on.
P And then I ⁷_____ an owl, a big owl in a tree...
Dr How did you ⁸_____? Were you frightened of it?
P No, not frightened really, no, but I ⁹_____ I felt very cold. Especially my feet – they were freezing. And then I ¹⁰_____.
Dr Your feet? Mmm, very interesting, very interesting indeed. Were you ¹¹_____ any shoes?
P No, no, I wasn't.
Dr Tell me. Have you ever ¹²_____ this dream before?
P No, never. So what does it ¹³_____, Doctor?

d What do you think the patient's dream means? Match five of the things in his dream with interpretations 1–5.

Understanding your dreams

You dream...
☐ that you are at a party.
☐ that you are drinking champagne.
☐ about flowers.
☐ that somebody is playing the violin.
☐ about an owl.

This means...
1 you are going to be very busy.
2 you're feeling positive about the future.
3 you want some romance in your life.
4 you need to ask an older person for help.
5 you'll be successful in the future.

e 3 17)) Listen to Dr Allen interpreting the patient's dream. Check your answers to **d**.

f 3 18)) Dr Allen is now going to explain what picture 6 means. What do you think the meaning could be? Listen and find out.

2 GRAMMAR review of verb forms

a Look at the sentences below. Which one is the present perfect? Mark it **PP**. Then look at the other sentences. What time do they refer to? Mark them **P** (the past), **PR** (the present) or **F** (the future).

1. ☐ I was drinking champagne.
2. ☐ Maybe you'll have a meeting with your boss.
3. ☐ I saw an owl.
4. ☐ You are feeling positive.
5. ☐ You're going to meet a lot of people.
6. ☐ You work in an office.
7. ☐ I'm meeting her tonight.
8. ☐ Have you ever had this dream before?

b ▶ **p.136 Grammar bank 6C.** Revise all the verb forms you've studied in Files 1–6 and practise them.

3 SPEAKING

a ▶ **Communication** *Dreams* **A** *p.103* **B** *p.108*. Roleplay interpreting your partner's dream.

b Interview a partner with the questionnaire. Choose two questions from each group. Ask for more information.

REVISION QUESTIONNAIRE

- Where do you usually buy your clothes?
- What do you like doing at the weekend?
- Are you watching any TV series at the moment?
- Are you studying for an exam at the moment?

- Where did you go on holiday last year?
- Did you do anything exciting last Saturday night?
- Where were you at 10 o'clock last night? What were you doing?
- Were you sleeping when the alarm clock rang this morning?

- Have you ever had the same dream again and again?
- Have you ever dreamed about something that then happened?

- Are you going to learn a new foreign language next year?
- Are you going to do anything exciting next weekend?
- Do you think it will be sunny tomorrow?
- Do you think your country will win the next football World Cup?
- What are you doing tonight?

4 PRONUNCIATION the letters *ow*

> **Pronunciation of *ow***
> Be careful: *ow* can be pronounced /aʊ/, e.g. *flower* or /əʊ/, e.g. *window*.

a **3 20** 🔊 Listen and repeat the two words and sounds.

/aʊ/	/əʊ/
owl	phone

b Write the words in the list in the right columns.

blow borrow brown crowded	
down how know low	
now show shower snow	
throw towel town	

c **3 21** 🔊 Listen and check.

d Practise saying the sentences.

Show me the flowers.
The town is very crowded now.
Don't throw snow at the windows.
How do you know?
Can I borrow a towel for the shower?

5 VOCABULARY adjectives + prepositions

> **Adjectives + prepositions**
> Some adjectives are usually followed by certain prepositions, e.g. *Were you **frightened of** the owl?* It's useful to learn the prepositions with the adjectives.

a Complete the gaps with a preposition.

1. Are you afraid ___ the dark?
2. Do you think chocolate is good ___ you?
3. Is your town full ___ tourists in the summer?
4. What is your country famous ___?
5. At school, what subjects were you bad ___?
6. Are you good ___ dancing?
7. Do you often get angry ___ your family? What ___?
8. Are people in your country very different ___ the English?
9. Are people in your country nice ___ tourists?
10. Are you interested ___ politics?

b Ask and answer the questions with a partner. Say why.

5&6 Revise and Check

GRAMMAR

Circle a, b, or c.

1 She drives _____ than her brother.
  a faster   b more fast   c more fastly
2 His new book isn't as good _____ his last one.
  a than   b that   c as
3 Women spend _____ time cooking than in the past.
  a less   b little   c fewer
4 Friday is _____ day of the week.
  a the busier   b the busiest   c the most busy
5 It's the _____ road in the world.
  a more dangerous
  b dangerousest
  c most dangerous
6 It's the hottest country I've _____ been to.
  a never   b always   c ever
7 My sister drinks _____ coffee.
  a too   b too much   c too many
8 These jeans are _____ small. Do you have them one size bigger?
  a too   b too much   c too many
9 You haven't spent _____ on your homework.
  a time enough
  b enough time
  c many time
10 They're playing really badly. They _____ the match.
  a want win   b won't win   c won't to win
11 A My exam is today.
   B Don't worry. _____.
   a You'll pass   b You pass   c You're passing
12 A It's cold in here.   B _____ the window.
   a I close   b I'm closing   c I'll close
13 They met for the first time when they _____ in Madrid.
   a were living   b are living   c was living
14 A Have you been to the USA?
   B Yes, I _____ to New York last year.
   a 've been   b went   c was going
15 A _____ today?   B No, she's on holiday.
   a Does she work
   b Is she working
   c Will she work

VOCABULARY

a Circle the right verb or phrase.
  1 I *waste* / *lose* a lot of time playing games on my phone.
  2 We *spend* / *take* a lot of time sitting in our cars every day.
  3 Can you *borrow* / *lend* me 50 euros?
  4 I'm leaving tonight and I'm *coming* / *coming back* on Friday.
  5 This is Ben. He's *teaching* / *learning* me to play the piano.

b Write the opposite verb.
  1 buy _____   3 remember _____   5 teach _____
  2 push _____   4 pass _____

c Write words for the definitions.
  1 cr_____ (adj) full of people or things
  2 s_____ (adj) opposite of *dangerous*
  3 n_____ (adj) opposite of *quiet* (for a place)
  4 s_____ (adj, noun) opposite of *north*
  5 m_____ (noun) a building where you can see old things
  6 p_____ (noun) the place where a king or queen lives
  7 m_____ (noun) a religious building for Muslims
  8 b_____ (noun) you have 206 of these in your body
  9 br_____ (noun) the organ we use to think
  10 sk_____ (noun) it covers the outside of your body

d Complete the sentences with a preposition.
  1 My husband's always late. He's never _____ time for anything.
  2 Are you interested _____ this TV programme?
  3 When I was a child I was afraid _____ dogs.
  4 I'd really like to be good _____ dancing.
  5 Eating too many sweets and biscuits is bad _____ you.

PRONUNCIATION

a Circle the word with a different sound.
  1 too   lose   polluted   much
  2 eat   many   healthy   mend
  3 lot   won't   borrow   offer
  4 shower   now   snow   towel
  5 receive   castle   mosque   active

b Underline the stressed syllable.
  1 im|pa|tient   2 in|teres|ting   3 in|vent   4 prac|tise   5 de|cide

CAN YOU UNDERSTAND THIS TEXT?

a Read the text once. Does the journalist think music made him run faster?

b Read the text again and mark the sentences **T** (true) or **F** (false).
1 The psychologist says that all kinds of music can help us exercise better.
2 He says that exercise is more fun with music.
3 Men and women prefer different music when they exercise.
4 Music helped Haile Gebreselassie break a record.
5 Most top athletes use music when they run.
6 Music can help amateur runners to run faster.
7 The journalist chose his music for the marathon.
8 All the songs helped him run faster.

c Look at the highlighted words or phrases in the text. Guess their meaning from the context. Check with your teacher or with a dictionary.

Can music really make you run faster?

Costas Karageorghis, a sports psychologist at Brunel University in the UK, calls music 'sport's legal drug'. He says that exercising with music can improve athletic performance by 15%. The music must be carefully chosen so that the tempo or 'beat' is synchronised with the exercise you are doing. According to Professor Karageorghis, music also makes you feel less pain and makes an exercise session less boring and more enjoyable.

The UK's biggest gym chain, *Fitness First*, recognizes the importance of music to workouts, and plays music in all its clubs. The most popular song for male gym members is Survivor's *Eye of the Tiger*, while women love Abba's *Dancing Queen*.

Music works well with weightlifting, and other repetitive actions, but it can also help with running. The best example of this is Haile Gebreselassie, perhaps the world's greatest distance runner, who used the techno-pop song *Scatman* as a metronome when he broke the world 2,000m record. But if music was so important to Gebreselassie, why do other top runners never race with headphones?

Karageorghis says 'Research has shown that for most top athletes music is less effective. Elite athletes focus more on their bodies, and less on outside stimuli like music.' So although music can help amateur runners run faster and further, most top athletes prefer silence.

I decided to try running with music myself. I was going to run a half marathon, and a sports doctor gave me the perfect playlist of songs for running. When I did the race, I found that some of the tracks, like Von Kleet's *Walking on Me*, made running easier. Others made me want to throw away the mp3 player. When I crossed the line, I had beaten my previous personal best by one minute, but was it because of the music? To be honest, I felt it was probably because of the extra training.

Warren Pole in The Times

CAN YOU UNDERSTAND THESE PEOPLE?

3 22))) In the street Watch or listen to five people and answer the questions.

Ian   Yvonne   Ben   Joanna   Anya

1 Three years ago Ian _____.
  a retired
  b had more free time
  c was working part time
2 When Yvonne talks about why she loves Rome, she *doesn't* mention _____.
  a the scenery   b the food   c the buildings
3 Ben eats _____ sugar.
  a too much   b a lot of   c a little
4 Joanna says her friends _____.
  a are mostly pessimists
  b think she is a pessimist
  c think she is an optimist
5 Anya often has bad dreams _____.
  a when she's having problems at work
  b after she's had a big meal
  c when she's having problems with her partner

CAN YOU SAY THIS IN ENGLISH?

Do the tasks with a partner. Tick (✓) the box if you can do them.

Can you…?
1 ☐ compare two members of your family using adjectives and adverbs
2 ☐ talk about your town using four superlatives (*the biggest*, *the best*, etc.)
3 ☐ talk about your diet using (*not*) *enough* and *too much / too many*
4 ☐ make three predictions about the future using *will / won't*
5 ☐ make a promise, an offer, and a decision using *will / won't*

Short films Chicago
Watch and enjoy a film on iTutor.

G uses of the infinitive with *to*
V verbs + infinitive: *try to, forget to*, etc.
P weak form of *to*, linking

> What do I need to do?
> It's important not to be late.

7A How to...

1 READING & LISTENING

a Look at the poster of a well-known film. Do you know what it's about? Have you seen it?

b With a partner, think of two pieces of advice for somebody who is going to meet their partner's parents for the first time.

c Now read an article adapted from the website *wikiHow*. Is your advice there?

d Read the article again and complete the gaps with the verbs in the list.

| to answer | not to be | to do (x2) | to have | to know |
| to make | to say | to show | not to talk | |

e 3 23)) Listen to Nigel meeting his girlfriend's parents for the first time. Does the meeting start well or badly? How does it end?

f Listen again and answer the questions.
1 What does he do wrong?
2 What does he do right?

g Do you think the advice in the article would be good for people in your country? Why (not)? Do you think the advice would be the same for a girl meeting her boyfriend's parents for the first time?

How to... Survive Meeting Your Girlfriend's Parents for the First Time

It's stressful, but these top tips can help you to get it right…

Tips

1 **You need** _to do_ **some 'homework'** before you go. Ask your girlfriend about her parents. Where does her mother work? Does her father like football? Do you have any common interests? If you do this, it will be easy _____ a conversation with them.

2 **Make sure you dress** _____ the right impression. Don't wear a suit, but don't just wear your old jeans and the Che Guevara T-shirt you bought in the market.

3 **Be punctual.** It's very important _____ late at a first meeting.

4 **When they greet you at the door** shake the father's hand firmly (no father likes a weak handshake!). Ask your girlfriend what kind of greeting her mum will prefer.

5 **Call her parents Mr and Mrs** (Smith) until they ask you to call them 'Dave' and 'Sharon'.

6 **Be ready** _____ questions about yourself! Her parents will want _____ everything about you and your ambitions. Make a good impression!

7 **If you are invited for a meal,** eat everything they give you and say something positive about the meal, like 'This is absolutely delicious!'. Offer _____ the washing-up after the meal (_____ them that you are a 'new man').

8 **Be yourself,** and don't be a 'yes' man. If they ask you for your opinion, be honest. However, try _____ about controversial subjects – this isn't the moment to give your views on religion and politics!

9 **If the conversation is dying** and you can't think what _____, ask them what your partner was like as a child. This is a brilliant tactic! All parents love talking about their children and it shows you have a deep interest in their daughter.

Adapted from wikiHow

52

2 GRAMMAR
uses of the infinitive with *to*

a Match sentences a–d from the article with rules 1–4.

- a ☐ If you do this, it will be easy **to have** a conversation with them.
- b ☐ Offer to do the washing-up after the meal (**to show** them that you are a 'new man').
- c ☐ If the conversation is dying and you can't think what **to say**, ask them what your partner was like as a child.
- d ☐ You need **to do** some 'homework' before you go.

Use the infinitive with *to*...
1 after some verbs, e.g. *need, want*, etc.
2 after adjectives
3 to give a reason for doing something
4 after a question word, e.g. *who, what, how*

b Look at the other infinitives you used to complete the article. Which rules are they?

c ▶ **p.138 Grammar Bank 7A.** Learn more about uses of the infinitive and practise them.

3 VOCABULARY verbs + infinitive

a Without looking back at the article try to remember the missing verbs.
1 You _____ to do some homework before you go.
2 Her parents will _____ to know everything about you and your ambitions.
3 _____ to do the washing-up after the meal…
4 However, _____ not to talk about controversial subjects…

b ▶ **p.158 Vocabulary Bank** *Verb forms*. Do part 1 (Verbs + infinitive).

4 PRONUNCIATION & SPEAKING
weak form of *to*, linking

a ⏵ 3 26 Listen to two sentences. Is *to* stressed? How is it pronounced?

> I want to come.
> He decided to leave.

> 🔍 **Linking words with the same consonant sound**
> When a word ends in a consonant sound and the next word begins with the same or a very similar sound, we often link the words together and only make the consonant sound once. This happens when a verb ends in /t/ or /d/ before *to*, so *want to* is pronounced /ˈwɒntə/ and *decided to* is pronounced /dɪˈsaɪdɪtə/.

b ⏵ 3 27 Listen and write six sentences. Then practise saying them.

c Work in pairs. **A** ask **B** the first six questions. **B** give as much information as you can. Swap roles for the last six questions.

- Have you ever offered to look after somebody's dog (or other pet)?
- Do you think it is difficult to stay friends with an ex-boyfriend/girlfriend?
- Have you ever tried to learn something new and failed?
- Do you think it is important to learn to cook at school?
- How long do you usually spend deciding what to wear in the morning?
- Do you know how to change a wheel on a car?

- Do you think it's possible to learn a foreign language studying on your own at home?
- Are you planning to go anywhere next weekend?
- Would you like to work or study in another country?
- Have you ever pretended to be ill (when you weren't)?
- Have you ever forgotten to turn off your mobile phone during a class or concert?
- What do you think is the most interesting thing to do for a visitor to your town?

d ▶ **Communication** *How to...* **A** *p.103* **B** *p.107.* Read and re-tell two more *How to…* articles.

5 WRITING

With a partner, write a 'How to…' article. Choose one of the titles below, and try to think of at least four tips.

How to…
- make a good impression on your first day in your English class.
- make a good impression at a job interview.

7B Being happy

G uses of the gerund (verb + -ing)
V verbs + gerund
P the letter *i*

> What's your idea of happiness?
> Making soup.

1 GRAMMAR uses of the gerund

a Talk to a partner. Is there a book, a film, or a song that makes you feel happy whenever you read, watch, or listen to it? What is it? Why does it make you feel happy?

b Read a magazine article where different people on the magazine's staff say what happiness is for them. Who do you think said what? Match the people to the paragraphs.

Erin, fashion editor

Harriet, health editor

Sebastian, music editor

Kate, cinema editor

Marco, food editor

Andrew, travel editor

c Read the article again. Is there anybody you really agree/don't agree with? Compare with a partner.

d Look at the highlighted phrases in the first paragraph. Find an example of a gerund (verb + -*ing*):
1 after another verb _____
2 after a preposition _____
3 used as a noun _____

e ▶ p.138 **Grammar Bank 7B.** Learn more about the uses of the gerund and practise them.

f Write your own continuation for *Happiness is…*

g Work in groups of four. Read the other students' texts. Do you agree with their ideas of happiness?

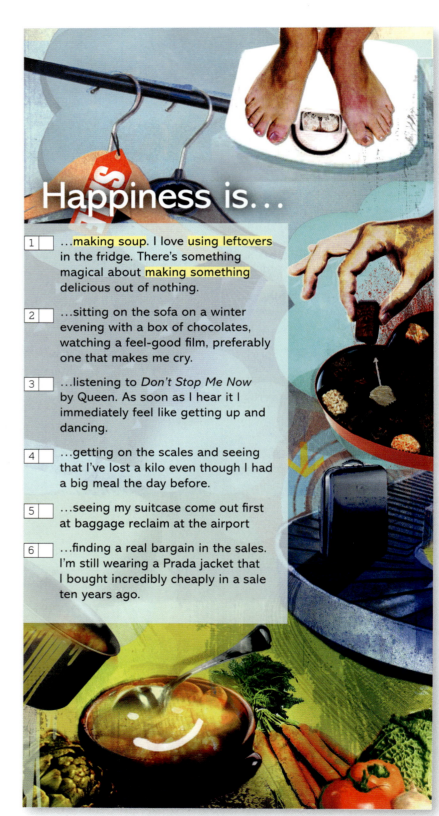

Happiness is…

1 …making soup. I love using leftovers in the fridge. There's something magical about making something delicious out of nothing.

2 …sitting on the sofa on a winter evening with a box of chocolates, watching a feel-good film, preferably one that makes me cry.

3 …listening to *Don't Stop Me Now* by Queen. As soon as I hear it I immediately feel like getting up and dancing.

4 …getting on the scales and seeing that I've lost a kilo even though I had a big meal the day before.

5 …seeing my suitcase come out first at baggage reclaim at the airport

6 …finding a real bargain in the sales. I'm still wearing a Prada jacket that I bought incredibly cheaply in a sale ten years ago.

2 VOCABULARY & SPEAKING
verbs + gerund

a ▶ p.158 Vocabulary Bank *Verb forms*. Do part 2 (Verbs + gerund).

b Choose five things to talk about from the list below.

> Something…
> - you **don't mind doing** in the house
> - you **like doing** with your family
> - you **love doing** in the summer
> - you **don't feel like doing** at weekends
> - you **spend too much time doing**
> - you **dream of doing**
> - you **hate doing** at work / school
> - you **don't like doing** alone
> - you are **thinking of doing** this weekend
> - you think you are **very good (or very bad) at doing**

c Works in pairs. **A** tell **B** about the five things. Say why. **B** ask for more information. Then swap roles.

3 PRONUNCIATION the letter *i*

a Put the one-syllable words below into the right column.

find	give	high	hire	kind	like
mind	miss	night	right	skin	slim
thin	time	which	win	with	

fish	bike

b 3 30)) Listen and check. Then look at the words in each column. What rules can you see for the pronunciation of…

- *i* + consonant + *e* (but which word is an exception?)
- *ind* and *igh*
- *i* between other consonants

c 3 31)) Now listen to some two-syllable words. Is the *i* pronounced /ɪ/ or /aɪ/? Listen and check.

arrive	decide	engine	invite
online	practise	promise	
revise	service	surprise	

d What's the difference in the stress between the verbs in **c** where *i* is pronounced /ɪ/ and where *i* is pronounced /aɪ/?

4 SPEAKING & LISTENING

a Ask and answer with a partner.
1 When you are happy do you sometimes feel like singing?
2 Do you ever sing…?
 - in the shower
 - karaoke
 - in the car
 - in a choir or band
 - while you're listening to music, e.g. on an iPod
3 Is there a particular singer whose songs you like singing? Do you have a favourite song?

b In pairs, say if you think sentences 1–7 are **T** (true) or **F** (false).
1 Singing is good for your health.
2 If you want to sing well, you need to learn to breathe correctly.
3 People who sing are usually fatter than people who don't.
4 Not everybody can learn to sing.
5 You need to know how to read music to be able to sing well.
6 If you make a surprised face, you can sing high notes better.
7 It takes years to learn to sing better.

c 3 32)) Now listen to an interview with the director of a singing school and a student who did a course there. Were you right?

d Listen again. Choose the right answer.
1 When you are learning to sing you need to ____ correctly.
 a stand b dress c eat
2 Singing well is 95% ____.
 a repeating b listening c breathing
3 Gemma's course lasted ____.
 a one day b one week c one month
4 Gemma has always ____.
 a been good at singing b been in a choir c liked singing
5 At first the students learnt to ____.
 a breathe and sing b listen and breathe c listen and sing
6 At the end of the day they could sing ____.
 a perfectly b much better c a bit better

e Would you like to learn to sing (better)? Are there any tips from the listening that you could use?

5 3 33)) SONG *Don't Stop Me Now* ♪

G *have to, don't have to, must, mustn't*
V modifiers: *a bit, really,* etc.
P *must, mustn't*

> You have to come to all the classes. You don't have to do an exam.

7C Learn a language in a month!

1 GRAMMAR
have to, don't have to, must, mustn't

a Match the notices to the rules.

1. ☐ You have to pay before the end of the month.
2. ☐ You don't have to pay to see this.
3. ☐ You mustn't eat here.
4. ☐ You must turn off your phone before you come in.

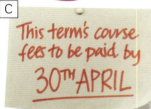

b Look at the highlighted expressions and answer the questions.

1. Which two phrases mean…?
   It is a ⊞ rule. There's an obligation to do this. _____ _____
2. Which phrase means…?
   a It isn't permitted. It is against the rules.
   _____
   b It isn't obligatory or it isn't necessary.
   _____

c ▶ p.138 **Grammar Bank 7C.** Learn more about *have to*, *don't have to*, *must*, and *mustn't*, and practise them.

d With a partner, complete four sentences about the school where you are learning English.

We have to…   We don't have to…
We must…   We mustn't…

e Compare your rules with another pair. Which rule do you think is the most important?

2 PRONUNCIATION *must, mustn't*

a ◉ 3 36))) Listen to these sentences. Which letter is <u>not</u> pronounced in *mustn't*? Listen again and repeat.

> You must use a dictionary.   You mustn't use a dictionary.

b ◉ 3 37))) Listen and write five sentences.

3 READING & LISTENING

a Do you think people from your country are good at learning languages? Why (not)? Are British people good at learning your language?

b Read about Max, a British journalist who did an intensive Spanish course. Then cover the article and answer the questions.

1. What reputation do the British have?
2. What experiment did Max's newspaper want to do?
3. Why did Max choose to learn Spanish?
4. Where did he do the course? How long was it?
5. What did he find easy and difficult about Spanish?
6. What were the four tests? What were the rules?

c ◉ 3 38))) Which test do you think was the easiest for Max? Which do you think was the most difficult? Listen to Max doing the tests in Madrid and check your answers.

d Listen again. Mark the sentences **T** (true) or **F** (false). Correct the false information.

1. The waiter didn't understand Max.
2. The bill was six euros.
3. The chemist's was the first street on the right.
4. The driver understood the name of the stadium.
5. Max made a grammar mistake when he left the voicemail message.
6. Max's final mark was eight.
7. Max says you can learn Spanish in a month.

I will survive (in Spanish)... or will I?

The British have a reputation for being bad at learning languages, but is it really true? I work for a newspaper which was doing a series of articles about this. As an experiment, they asked me to try and learn a completely new language for one month. Then I had to go to the country and do some 'tests' to see if I could 'survive' in different situations. I decided to learn Spanish because I would like to visit Spain and Latin America in the future. If I go, I don't want to be the typical Brit who expects everyone else to speak English.

I did a one-month intensive course in Spanish at a language school in London. I was a complete beginner but I soon found that some Spanish words are very similar to English ones. For example, *hola* isn't very different from 'hello' and *inglés* is very similar to 'English'. But other things were more difficult, for example the verbs in Spanish change for each person and that means you have to learn a lot of different endings. My biggest problem was the pronunciation. I found it very difficult to pronounce some letters in Spanish, especially *r* and *j*. I downloaded sentences in Spanish onto my phone and I listened and repeated them again and again.

When my course finished I went to Madrid for the weekend to do my tests. A Spanish teacher called Paula came with me and gave me a mark out of 10 for each test and then a final mark for everything.

These were the tests and the rules:

TESTS
You have to...
1 order a drink and a sandwich in a bar, ask how much it is, and understand the price.
2 ask for directions in the street (and follow them).
3 get a taxi to a famous place in Madrid.
4 leave a message on somebody's voicemail.

RULES
– you mustn't use a dictionary or phrase book
– you mustn't speak English at any time
– you mustn't use your hands or mime or write anything down

4 VOCABULARY modifiers

My pronunciation of the stadium wasn't **very** good.
I was feeling **a bit** nervous at this point.

a Complete the chart with the words in the box.

| a bit | incredibly | not very | quite | really | very |

Spanish is _____ very _____ difficult.
_____
not very

 a bit
We only use *a bit* before negative adjectives and adverbs, e.g. *a bit difficult, a bit slowly*.

b Complete the sentences with one of the words or phrases so that it makes a true sentence. Compare with a partner.
1 I'm _____ good at learning languages.
2 I'm _____ motivated to improve my English.
3 English pronunciation is _____ difficult.
4 English grammar is _____ complicated.
5 I'm _____ worried about the next English exam.
6 English is _____ important for my work / studies.

5 SPEAKING

a How well do you think you could do Max's four tests in English? Why?

I think I could order a drink and a sandwich quite well...

b Talk to a partner.

HAVE YOU EVER...
- spoken to a tourist in English? When? Why?
- had to speak in English on the phone? Who to? What about?
- seen a film or video clip in English? Which? Did it have subtitles? How much did you understand?
- read a book or magazine in English? Which one(s)?
- asked for directions in English in a foreign city? Where? What happened?
- used an app or website to improve your English? Which one?
- learnt another foreign language? How well can you speak it?

6 WRITING

▶ p.115 Writing *A formal email*. Write an email asking for information.

Practical English   At the pharmacy

EPISODE 4

1 RUNNING IN CENTRAL PARK

a **3 39))** Watch or listen to Rob and Jenny. Are they enjoying their run?

b Watch or listen again and answer the questions.
1 How does Rob say he feels?
2 What does Jenny say about Central Park?
3 Is Rob happy he came to New York?
4 What is Rob tired of doing?
5 What does Jenny invite him to do?
6 How many more times are they going to run round the park?

2 VOCABULARY feeling ill

a Match the phrases and pictures.

What's the matter?

☐ I have a <u>head</u>ache. /ˈhedeɪk/
☐ I have a <u>tem</u>perature. /ˈtemprətʃə/
☐ I have a <u>cough</u>. /kɒf/
☐ I have a bad <u>sto</u>mach. /ˈstʌmək/
☐ I have flu. /fluː/
☐ I have a cold.

b **3 40))** Listen and check. Cover the phrases and practise with a partner.

What's the matter?   *I have a headache.*

3 GOING TO A PHARMACY

a **3 41))** Cover the dialogue and watch or listen. (Circle) the correct answer.
1 Rob thinks he has *a cold* / *flu*.
2 The pharmacist gives Rob *ibuprofen* / *penicillin*.
3 He has to take the medicine every *four hours* / *eight hours*.
4 They cost *$16.99* / *$6.99*.

b Watch or listen again. Complete the **You Hear** phrases.

))) You Hear	You Say)
Good morning. Can I help you?	I'm not feeling very well. I think I have flu.
What are your symptoms?	I have a headache and a cough.
Do you have a _____?	No, I don't think so.
Are you allergic to any drugs?	I'm allergic to penicillin.
No _____. This is buprofen. It'll make you feel _____.	How many do I have to take?
_____ every four hours.	Sorry? How often?
_____ every four hours. If you don't feel better in _____ hours, you should see a doctor.	OK, thanks. How much is that?
That's $6.99, please.	Thank you.
You're _____.	

> **British and American English**
> *pharmacy* = American English (and sometimes British English)
> *chemist's* = British English
> *drugs* = *medicine* in American English
> *drugs* = *illegal substances* in British and American English

c 3 42))) Watch or listen and repeat the **You Say** phrases. Copy the rhythm.

d Practise the dialogue with a partner.

e In pairs, roleplay the dialogue.
  A (book closed) You don't feel very well. Decide what symptoms you have. Are you allergic to anything?
  B (book open) You are the pharmacist. You begin *Can I help you?*

f Swap roles.

4 **DINNER AT JENNY'S APARTMENT**

a 3 43))) Watch or listen to Rob and Jenny. Mark the sentences **T** (true) or **F** (false).
  1 Rob broke up with his girlfriend a year before he met Jenny.
  2 Jenny hasn't had much time for relationships.
  3 Jenny knew that Rob wasn't feeling well in the morning.
  4 Rob wants to go back to his hotel because he's tired.
  5 Jenny is going to call a taxi.

b Watch or listen again. Say why the **F** sentences are false.

c 3 44))) Read the information box about *have got*. Listen and repeat the phrases.

> **have got**
> We sometimes use *have got* instead of *have* to talk about possession.
> **I've got** a busy day tomorrow.
> **Have you got** any children?   Yes, I have. **I've got** a girl and a boy.
>   No, I haven't. **I haven't got** children.
>
> ➤ See **appendix** p.165.

d Ask and answer with a partner. Use *Have you got…? Yes, I have. / No, I haven't.* Give more information if you can.
  A any pets   a bike or motorbike   a garden
  B any brothers and sisters   a car   a laptop

  Have you got any pets?   *Yes I have. I've got two dogs.*

e Look at the **Social English phrases**. Can you remember any of the missing words?

Social English phrases	
Rob That was a lovely _____.	**Jenny** I'm _____ you're feeling better.
Rob That isn't very _____ for you.	**Rob** Thanks again for a _____ evening.
Rob I'm _____ I'll be fine.	**Jenny** _____ time.
Rob I think I _____ get back to the hotel now.	

f 3 46))) Watch or listen and complete the phrases.

g Watch or listen again and repeat the phrases. How do you say them in your language?

> **Can you…?**
> ☐ describe symptoms when you feel ill
> ☐ get medicine at a pharmacy
> ☐ talk about possessions with *have got*

G *should*
V *get*
P /ʊ/ and /uː/, sentence stress

> What should I do?
> You should talk to her.

8A I don't know what to do!

1 READING

a Talk to a partner.
   1 If you have a problem that you need to talk about, do you talk to a friend or to a member of your family? Why?
   2 Do you think that men find it more difficult than women to talk about their problems? Why (not)?

b Read three problems from a weekly article in a British newspaper. Match two pieces of advice to each problem.

c Read the problems and advice again. Look at the highlighted verb phrases and guess their meaning.

d Talk to a partner. Which piece of advice do you agree with most for each problem? Do you have any other suggestions?

Too macho to talk?

Are you a man who finds it difficult to talk about feelings and problems with your friends and family?
Send us your problem and you will **get advice** from our readers.

Problem A
Three weeks ago I asked my girlfriend to marry me – we have been together for 18 months. It was an impulse, but now **I am having second thoughts**. I am deeply in love with her, but is this too soon? Please help.

Problem B
My wife is running her first marathon in London and she really wants me to go and watch her. However, there is a business conference in New York the same weekend and my boss would like me to attend. What should I do?

Problem C
My girlfriend wants us to spend two weeks in France in the summer with her family, but I find her sister really **difficult to get on with**. Should I go and risk having arguments all the time or should I suggest separate holidays this year?

Our readers' advice!

1 ☐ *This seems an easy one – go, but try to* **avoid her** *where possible, and if you can't avoid her, then just smile and don't get into a conversation.*

2 ☐ *In my opinion, I don't think* **it's worth** *making problems at work. Why don't you suggest that she asks a girlfriend or a family member to go with her instead?*

3 ☐ *You should tell your girlfriend how you feel. Be polite and, above all, be honest. You do not have to like her sister. If she really is difficult, everyone else will already know.*

4 ☐ *You felt it was right at the time, but for some reason now you are not sure. You clearly love this girl and I think you should* **go for it**. *I got married after four months of dating, and we celebrated 30 years this year.*

5 ☐ *You should be there. Maybe this is a once in a lifetime moment for her. You can always* **keep in touch** *with colleagues on your phone.*

6 ☐ *You shouldn't do anything in a hurry. Fix a date 18 months from now which will give you time to be sure you're doing the right thing. And don't plan too much. If you start booking restaurants and getting clothes for the big day, it will make things worse if you then* **change your mind**.

Adapted from a British newspaper

2 GRAMMAR should

a Find and underline seven examples of *should | shouldn't* in the problems and advice in **1**. Answer with a partner:

1 What do we use *should* for?
2 How do you make negatives and questions with *should*?

b ▶ **p.140 Grammar Bank 8A.** Learn more about *should* and practise it.

3 PRONUNCIATION

/ʊ/ and /uː/, sentence stress

a (3 48)) Listen and repeat the words and sounds. What's the difference between the two sounds?

| ʊ | b**u**ll | g**oo**d | p**u**t | sh**ou**ld | w**ou**ld |
| uː | b**oo**t | d**o** | s**oo**n | tr**u**e | y**ou** |

b (3 49)) Are the pink letters in these words sound 1 (/ʊ/) or sound 2 (/uː/)? Listen and check. Which consonant isn't pronounced in *should*, *would*, and *could*?

| b**oo**k | c**ou**ld | fl**e**w | f**oo**d | f**oo**t | l**oo**k | sch**oo**l |

c (3 50)) Listen and write six sentences.

d Listen again and repeat the sentences. Copy the r**h**ythm.

e ▶ **Communication** *What should I do?*
A *p.103* **B** *p.108*. Listen to your partner's problems and give advice.

4 LISTENING & SPEAKING

a (3 51)) Listen to someone phoning a radio programme called *What's the Problem?* What is the problem about? Make notes in the chart.

	problem	expert's advice
caller 1		
caller 2		

b Compare your notes with a partner. What do *you* think the man should do?

c (3 52)) Now listen to an expert giving advice and make notes in the chart. Is it the same as yours? Is it good advice? Why (not)?

d (3 53, 54)) Now repeat for caller 2.

5 VOCABULARY get

a Look at three sentences from the lesson. Match the examples of *get* with meanings a–c.

a buy / obtain **b** receive **c** become

1 ☐ Send us your problem and you will **get** advice…
2 ☐ If you start booking restaurants and **getting** clothes for the big day…
3 ☐ I'm **getting** really stressed about it.

b ▶ **p.159 Vocabulary Bank** *get.*

c In pairs, ask and answer the questions with *get*.

1 When was the last time you **got a present**? What was it? Who was it from?
2 Would you like to **get fitter**? What do you think you should do?
3 What website do you use if you want to **get tickets** a) to travel b) for the cinema / theatre / concerts?
4 Who do you **get on with** best in your family? Is there anybody you don't get on with?
5 How do you **get to work** / school? How long does it usually take you?
6 What's the first thing you do when you **get home** from work / school?
7 Do you have a good sense of direction, or do you often **get lost**?
8 How many **emails** or **text messages** do you **get** a day? Are they mostly from friends? Do you usually reply immediately?

6 WRITING

a Read two problems on a website. Write a response to one of them giving advice.

Goodadvice.com
Post your problems here and you'll get advice from all over the world.

My best friend wants to borrow some money to help her buy a car. I have the money, and she says she'll pay me back next year. But I'm worried that it's not a good idea to lend money to friends. What should I do?

My friend Anna has gone away on holiday for two weeks and I'm looking after her cat. Yesterday I couldn't find the cat anywhere. My friend is coming home in three days. I'm desperate. Should I phone her now and tell her? What should I do?

🔍 **Language for giving advice**
(I think / don't think) you should… Why don't you…?
You shouldn't… You could…

b In groups of four read your responses. Whose advice is the best?

7 (3 56)) SONG *Why Do I Feel So Sad?* 🎵

G *if* + present, *will* + infinitive (first conditional)
V confusing verbs
P linking

8B If something can go wrong,...

If we change queues, this one will move quicker.
Yes, that always happens!

1 READING

a If you are waiting to check in at the airport and you change queues, what will usually happen?

b Read the first two paragraphs of the article and check. Who was Murphy? What is his 'Law'?

c Now look at the eight examples of Murphy's Law in the article and match them with sentences A–H.

   A your flight will be delayed.
   B you will spill wine or coffee on it.
   C you will find a parking space right in front of it.
   D all the traffic lights will be red.
   E will have a problem with their credit card.
   F they will already have a partner.
   G there will be a hyperactive five-year-old in the seat behind you.
   H it will work when the shop assistant tries it.

d Do any of these things or things like this often happen to you?

2 GRAMMAR *if* + present, *will* + infinitive

a In pairs, cover A–H and look at 1–8 in the text. How many of the Laws can you remember?

b Look at the sentences again. What tense is the verb after *if*? What form is the other verb?

c ▶ p.140 **Grammar Bank 8B.** Learn more about the first conditional and practise it.

d In pairs, complete these Murphy's Laws.
   1 If you find something in a shop that you really like,…
   2 If you stop waiting for a bus and start walking,…
   3 If you call a telephone company helpline,…
   4 If you leave your mobile phone at home,…
   5 If you lose a glove and buy a new pair,…

e Compare your laws with other students. Do you have the same (or similar)?

IT ALWAYS HAPPENS!

If you are in a check-in queue and you change to another queue which is moving more quickly, what will happen? The queue you were in before will suddenly start moving faster. What will happen if you take your umbrella because you think it's going to rain later? It won't rain, of course. It will only rain if you forget to take your umbrella. These are examples of Murphy's Law, which says, 'If there is something that can go wrong, it will go wrong'.

Murphy's Law took its name from Captain Edward Murphy, an American aerospace engineer from the 1940s. He was trying to improve safety for pilots flying military planes. Not surprisingly, he got a reputation for always thinking of the worst thing that could happen in every situation. Here are some more examples of Murphy's Law.

AIR TRAVEL
1 ☐ If you get to the airport early,…
2 ☐ If you want to sleep on the plane,…

SHOPPING
3 ☐ If you are in a hurry, the person in front of you…
4 ☐ If you take something that doesn't work back to a shop,…

DRIVING
5 ☐ If you're late for something important,…
6 ☐ If you park a long way from a restaurant,…

SOCIAL LIFE
7 ☐ If you are single and you meet somebody at a party who you really like,…
8 ☐ If you wear a new white shirt or dress,…

3 PRONUNCIATION linking

> **Sound linking**
> Remember that if a word finishes with a consonant and the next word begins with a vowel, we usually link the words together, e.g. we'll‿eat‿in‿a pub

a ◁4 3))) Listen and repeat the sentences. Try to link the marked words.
1 If‿I see her‿I'll tell her.
2 We'll go if‿it doesn't rain.
3 If‿I get there‿early, I'll‿order the food.
4 They'll‿arrive‿at‿eight‿if their flight's‿on time.
5 If you aren't‿in‿a hurry, we can walk.

b ◁4 4))) Listen and write five more sentences.

4 VOCABULARY & SPEAKING
confusing verbs

a What's the difference between *know* and *meet*, and *wear* and *carry*?

b ▶ p.160 **Vocabulary Bank** *Confusing verbs*.

c (Circle) the right verb. Then ask and answer with a partner.
1 Who do you *look* / *look like* in your family?
2 How many classes have you *missed* / *lost* this year?
3 What gadgets do you always *bring* / *take* with you when you go on holiday?
4 Do you think sports people *win* / *earn* too much money?
5 What is the best way to *know* / *meet* new friends?
6 Is it sometimes OK to *say* / *tell* a lie?

5 LISTENING

a With a partner, think of three things that could go wrong when you are on holiday.

b Match the words to their definitions.

1 [E] a mon<u>soon</u> /mɒnˈsuːn/   5 [ ] a <u>bli</u>zzard /ˈblɪzəd/
2 [ ] an <u>earth</u>quake /ˈɜːθkweɪk/ 6 [ ] a flood /flʌd/
3 [ ] a tsu<u>na</u>mi /tsuːˈnɑːmi/   7 [ ] a <u>fo</u>rest fire
4 [ ] a <u>cy</u>clone /ˈsaɪkləʊn/   /ˈfɒrɪst faɪə/

A a very bad storm with snow and strong winds
B a very strong wind that moves in a circle
C a big fire that can destroy many trees and houses
D a very large wave in the sea
E when it rains very heavily for three months or more
F when there is too much water in a river and it comes onto the streets or fields
G when the ground suddenly shakes very strongly

c ◁4 6))) Listen to what happened to Mr and Mrs Svanström. Mark their route on the map. What natural disaster happened in each place?

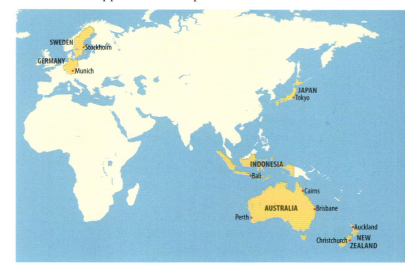

d Listen again and answer the questions.
1 How long did they have to wait at Munich airport?
2 What weather were they expecting in Bali?
3 Where were the streets full of smoke?
4 Where did they sleep in Cairns?
5 Why did they fly to Auckland and not to Christchurch in New Zealand?
6 What were they doing when the Japanese earthquake struck?
7 Where did they go for the last part of their holiday? Did anything happen to them there?

e Do you think they were lucky or unlucky? Why?

G **possessive pronouns**
V adverbs of manner
P sentence rhythm

You must be mine.

Yes. I'll be yours.

8C You must be mine

Girl
BY O. HENRY
PART 1

"I've found where she lives," said the detective quietly. "Here is the address."
   Hartley took the piece of paper. On it were the words "Vivienne Arlington, No. 341 East 49th Street."
5 "She moved there a week ago," said the detective. "I can follow her if you want. It will only cost you $7 a day and expenses…"
   "No, thank you," interrupted Hartley. "I only wanted the address. How much is it?"
10 "One day's work," said the detective. "Ten dollars."
   Hartley paid the man. Then he left the office and took a tram to Broadway. After walking a short distance he arrived at the building that he was looking for. Hartley rang the bell. The door opened.
15 He went in and began to climb the stairs.
   On the fourth floor he saw her standing in an open door. Vivienne was about twenty-one. Her hair was red gold, and her eyes were sea-blue. She was wearing a white top and a dark skirt.
20 "Vivienne," said Hartley, "you didn't answer my last letter. It took me a week to find your new address! Why didn't you answer me? You knew I was waiting to see you and hear from you."

1%

1 READING

a You are going to read and listen to a short story. First look at the picture and answer the questions.
   1 What do the people look like? What are they wearing?
   2 Where are they?
   3 In what century do you think the story takes place?

b 4 7))) Read and listen to Part 1. Then answer the questions with a partner.
   1 What did the detective give Hartley? What did he offer to do?
   2 What did Hartley do when he got the address?
   3 What did Vivienne look like?
   4 Why was Hartley angry with her?
   5 Why do you think she didn't answer his letter?

c Look at the following words and phrases in the story. With a partner, guess what they mean.

   moved (line 5)   expenses (line 7)   tram (line 12)
   rang the bell (line 14)   climb (line 15)

d 4 8))) Read and listen to Part 2. Then answer the questions with a partner.
   1 Why wasn't Vivienne sure about accepting Hartley's offer?
   2 How did Hartley try to persuade her?
   3 Where did Hartley and Vivienne first meet?
   4 What did Hartley think was the reason why Vivienne didn't say yes to his offer?
   5 What do you think Hartley wanted Vivienne to do?
   6 Who do you think Héloïse is?

> 🔍 **Adverbs of manner**
> We often use adverbs of manner in writing to show how the characters are feeling, behaving, or speaking.

e Look at the highlighted adverbs. With a partner, guess what they mean.

64

PART 2

The girl looked out the window *dreamily*. "Mr Hartley," she said *slowly*, "I don't know what to say to you. I understand all the advantages of your offer, and sometimes I feel sure that I could be happy with you. But, then sometimes I am less sure. I was born a city girl, and I am not sure that I would enjoy living a quiet life in the suburbs."

"My dear girl," said Hartley, "You will have everything that you want. You can come to the city for the theatre, for shopping, and to visit your friends as often as you want. You can trust me, can't you?"

"I can trust you *completely*," she said, smiling at him. "I know you are the kindest of men, and that the girl who you get will be very lucky. I heard all about you when I was at the Montgomerys'."

"Ah!" exclaimed Hartley, "I remember so well the evening I first saw you at the Montgomerys'. I will never forget that dinner. Come on, Vivienne, promise me. I want you. Nobody else will ever give you such a happy home."

Vivienne didn't answer. Suddenly Hartley was suspicious. "Tell me, Vivienne," he asked, "is there – is there someone else?"

"You shouldn't ask that, Mr. Hartley," she said. "But I will tell you. There is one other person – but I haven't promised him anything."

"Vivienne," said Hartley, *masterfully*. "You must be mine."

Vivienne looked him in the eye.

"Do you think for one moment," she said *calmly*, "that I could come to your home while Héloise is there?"

Glossary
advantage *n* a positive thing
suburbs *n* an area where people live outside the centre of the city
trust *v* believe that somebody is good, honest, etc.
suspicious *adj* feeling that somebody has done something wrong

2 PRONUNCIATION sentence rhythm

a))) Listen to the last five lines of Part 2. What tells the speakers…?
   a where to pause
   b in what way to say the dialogue

> **Reading aloud**
> Reading stories or poems aloud gives you the opportunity to focus on pronunciation, especially sentence rhythm.

b ▶ **Communication** *Reading dialogue p.104*. Practise reading the dialogue with a partner.

3 LISTENING

a))) Listen to Part 3 of the story. Answer the questions.
   1 What did Hartley say about Héloise?
   2 What did Vivienne promise to do?
   3 Who do you think the lady in the white dress is?

b))) Listen to Part 4 of the story.
   1 Who was the lady?
   2 Who was Vivienne?
   3 Who was Héloise?

c Did the ending surprise you? Why (not)?

4 GRAMMAR possessive pronouns

a Look at some extracts from the story. Complete them with *my, mine, your,* or *yours*.
   1 'Vivienne, you didn't answer ____ last letter.'
   2 'I understand all the advantages of ____ offer.'
   3 'Vivienne … you must be ____.'
   4 'My answer is yes. I will be ____.'

b ▶ **p.140 Grammar Bank 8C.** Learn more about possessive pronouns and practise them.

c))) Listen. Say the sentences with a possessive pronoun.

   ))) It's my book.   It's mine.

5 WRITING using adverbs

a Make adverbs from the following adjectives.

   angry   lazy   quiet   sad   serious   slow

b))) Listen to some lines from stories. Add an adverb from **a** after 'said' to show how the person is speaking.
   1 'I'm sorry, but I don't love you,' he said ____.
   2 'Give me back all my letters,' she said ____.
   3 'I think… I have an idea,' he said ____.
   4 'Don't make a noise. Everyone is asleep,' she said ____.
   5 'I don't feel like doing anything,' he said ____.
   6 'This is a very important matter,' she said ____.

c In pairs, write a short scene between Hartley's wife and Héloise, when she is telling the cook to leave. Include at least two adverbs of manner after *said*.

7 & 8 Revise and Check

GRAMMAR

a Circle a, b, or c.

1 I need _____ some emails.
   a to answer   b answer   c answering
2 The situation is difficult _____.
   a for explain   b explain   c to explain
3 I don't know what _____.
   a do   b to do   c that I do
4 I don't really mind _____ housework.
   a do   b to do   c doing
5 _____ is one of the best forms of exercise.
   a Swiming   b Swimming   c Swim
6 _____ bring our books tomorrow?
   a Do we have to
   b Have we to
   c Do we must
7 It's free. You _____ pay.
   a don't have to   b mustn't   c haven't to
8 You must _____ your grandmother.
   a to call   b calling   c call
9 You _____ drink so much coffee.
   a not should   b don't should   c shouldn't
10 I think you should _____ to her about it.
   a to talk   b talk   c talking
11 If she _____, she won't come back.
   a goes   b went   c 'll go
12 If they don't come soon, we _____ them.
   a don't see   b won't see   c aren't see
13 Call me if you _____ a taxi.
   a won't find   b don't find   c didn't find
14 **A** Whose book is that? **B** It's _____.
   a my   b mine book   c mine
15 She forgot his birthday, but he didn't forget _____.
   a her   b she   c hers

VOCABULARY

a Circle the right verb.

1 When did you *know / meet* your husband?
2 Did you *tell / say* Mark about the party?
3 If we don't run, we'll *miss / lose* the train!
4 I really *wait / hope* she's passed the exam.
5 My mother always *carries / wears* a lot of jewellery.

b Complete with a verb from the list.

| enjoy   finish   forget   hate   learn   mind   promise   try |

1 Don't _____ to turn off the light before you go.
2 I want to _____ to speak Italian.
3 Can you _____ to make less noise, please?
4 I _____ to pay you back next week.
5 I really _____ making cakes.
6 Do you _____ waiting here until I'm ready?
7 My parents are very punctual – they _____ being late.
8 When are you going to _____ using the computer? I need it!

c Complete the modifiers.

1 **A** How are you?   **B** V_____ well, thanks. And you?
2 I was **in**_____ lucky – I won £100.
3 She's a **b**_____ tired – she needs to rest.
4 You're driving **r**_____ fast – slow down!
5 My bag is **q**_____ heavy because I've got my laptop in it.

d Complete the *get* phrases.

1 We didn't have satnav in the car and we **got** _____ on the way home from Edinburgh.
2 I'm always really hungry when I **get** _____ from school.
3 She was very ill, but luckily she's **getting** _____.
4 We **got** two _____ for the theatre to see a show.
5 I **get** _____ very well with my brothers and sisters.
6 They were married for ten years, but six months ago they **got** _____.
7 I **got** a text _____ from Carol. She says she's going to be late.

PRONUNCIATION

a Circle the word with a different sound.

1 m**i**ne   f**i**nd   r**igh**t   g**i**ve
2 w**i**n   f**i**t   ch**i**ld   prom**i**se
3 ch**oo**se   c**ou**ld   w**ou**ld   l**oo**k
4 **sh**ould   impre**ss**ion   di**c**tionary   sandwi**ch**
5 **ear**n   w**ear**   l**ear**n   h**ear**d

b Underline the stressed syllable.

1 pre|tend   3 re|mem|ber   5 qui|et|ly
2 im|por|tant   4 sa|la|ry

CAN YOU UNDERSTAND THIS TEXT?

a Read the article once. What does Michael think is the main reason the British aren't good at speaking languages?

b Read the article again and tick the reasons why, according to the writer, the British are bad at languages.

1 ☐ British people rarely travel abroad.
2 ☐ English is an international language.
3 ☐ British people who live abroad often find the local language too difficult to learn.
4 ☐ British people who live abroad often don't socialize with the local people.
5 ☐ Language teachers in British schools are not very good.
6 ☐ Many British secondary school pupils don't study a foreign language.
7 ☐ British children don't know enough about their own grammar.
8 ☐ British people don't want to waste money learning languages.

c Look at the highlighted words or phrases in the text. Guess their meaning from the context. Check with your teacher or with a dictionary.

Why are the British so bad at learning languages?

Michael Reece has lived and worked in France for fifteen years.

The British are bad at speaking foreign languages. It's a fact. In any city around Europe you can find British tourists asking for the restaurant menu in English. At best they will try to say a couple of phrases they have learnt from a phrase book, but they will stop making an effort the moment they discover the waiter knows a little English.

I read a survey once which found that only 5% of British people could count to 20 in another language. So why is this? I think laziness is possibly the key factor. There is a general feeling among British people that 'everyone speaks English nowadays so it's not worth learning other languages'. In multinational companies English is often the official language of communication within the company. Also, British people who live abroad can always find other British expatriates to talk to, to watch British TV with, even to go to British pubs with – all reasons for never bothering to learn the local language.

The situation in British schools doesn't help. Ten years ago, about 80% of children at secondary school studied a foreign language. Today, that number has gone down to 48%. And even the few pupils who study foreign languages at school don't have as many hours of classes as pupils in other European countries. I think it is also a problem that British children don't study English grammar any more, which makes it more difficult for them to learn the grammar of another language.

CAN YOU UNDERSTAND THESE PEOPLE?

🔊 15 **In the street** Watch or listen to five people and answer the questions.

Stacey   Heba   Ruth   Ben   Nick

1 Stacey thinks that happiness is having _____.
  a somewhere nice to live and a lot of friends
  b a lot of money and a close family
  c a reasonable amount of money and friends and family

2 Heba _____.
  a speaks a little Arabic and a little French
  b speaks Arabic and French very well
  c speaks Arabic well and a little French

3 If Ruth has relationship problems, she talks to _____.
  a her friends
  b her mother
  c her mother and her friends

4 Ben thinks people who have problems sleeping should _____.
  a drink less coffee and do more exercise
  b do physical work before going to bed
  c drink less coffee and try to relax more

5 Nick thinks that Americans are bad at learning languages because _____.
  a they don't want to learn languages
  b they find learning languages too difficult
  c they aren't interested in travelling abroad

CAN YOU SAY THIS IN ENGLISH?

Do the tasks with a partner. Tick (✓) the box if you can do them.

Can you...?

1 ☐ talk about something you would like to learn to do, and someone you think would be interesting to meet
2 ☐ talk about three things you like, love, and hate doing
3 ☐ talk about the rules in your (language) school using *must* and *have to*
4 ☐ give someone advice about learning English using *should* and *shouldn't*
5 ☐ remember three of Murphy's Laws in English
6 ☐ say two true sentences using *mine* and *yours*

Short films Learning a language
Watch and enjoy a film on iTutor.

G if + past, would + infinitive (second conditional)
V animals
P word stress

9A What would you do?

> What would you do if you saw a bear?
>
> I'd run away.

1 READING & SPEAKING

a Read the quiz questions and answers. Complete each question with an animal from the list.

> bee   bull   dog   jellyfish   shark   snake

b Look at the highlighted verbs and verb phrases. With a partner, try to guess their meaning from the context.

c Read the quiz again and circle your answers, a, b, or c.

d ▶ **Communication** *Would you know what to do?* **A** *p.104* **B** *p.108* **C** *p.110*. Read the answers to one section and tell the others. Did you all choose the right answers?

e Have you ever been in any of these situations? What did you do?

2 GRAMMAR
if + past, *would* + infinitive

a Look at questions 1–6 again. Are they about a past situation or an imagined future situation? What tense is the verb after *if*?

b ▶ p.142 **Grammar Bank 9A**. Learn more about the second conditional and practise it.

c Complete the sentences so that they are true for you. Compare with a partner.

1 If I had five extra hours every week,…
2 I would be very happy if…
3 If I could live anywhere in the world,…
4 I would learn English more quickly if…
5 If I won a lot of money in the lottery,…

3 VOCABULARY animals

a ▶ p.161 **Vocabulary Bank** *Animals*.

b 🔊 4 18 Listen. Which animals can you hear?

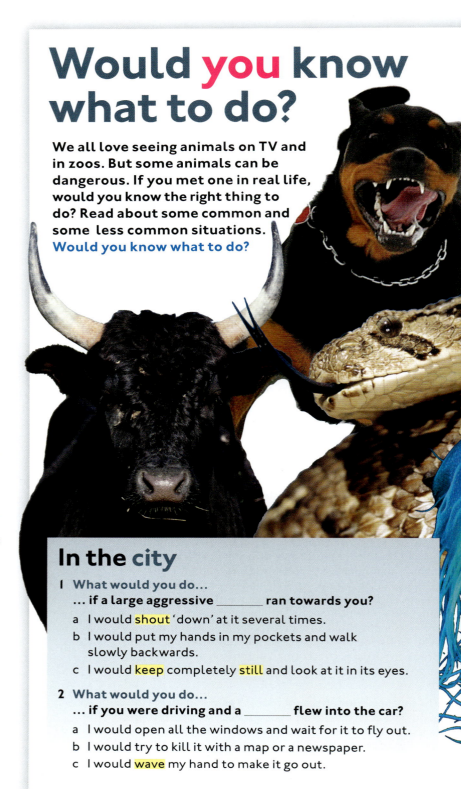

Would you know what to do?

We all love seeing animals on TV and in zoos. But some animals can be dangerous. If you met one in real life, would you know the right thing to do? Read about some common and some less common situations.
Would you know what to do?

In the city

1 What would you do…
   … if a large aggressive _____ ran towards you?
   a I would shout 'down' at it several times.
   b I would put my hands in my pockets and walk slowly backwards.
   c I would keep completely still and look at it in its eyes.

2 What would you do…
   … if you were driving and a _____ flew into the car?
   a I would open all the windows and wait for it to fly out.
   b I would try to kill it with a map or a newspaper.
   c I would wave my hand to make it go out.

In the country

3 What would you do…
… if a poisonous _____ bit you on the leg, and you were more than 30 minutes from the nearest town?
a I would put something very cold on it, like a water bottle.
b I would suck the bite to get the poison out.
c I would tie something, e.g. a scarf on my leg above the bite.

4 What would you do…
… if you were in the middle of a field and a _____ started running towards you?
a I would run to the gate.
b I would throw something (e.g. a hat or a bag) in another direction.
c I would shout and wave my arms.

In the water

5 What would you do…
… if you were in the sea and a _____ stung you?
a I would rub the sting with a towel to clean it.
b I would wash the sting with fresh water.
c I would wash the sting with vinegar or sea water.

6 What would you do…
… if you were in the sea quite near the shore and you saw a _____?
a I would swim to the shore as quickly and quietly as possible.
b I would float and pretend to be dead.
c I would shout for help.

4 PRONUNCIATION word stress

> **Stress in words that are similar in other languages**
> Some words in English, e.g. for animals, are similar to the same words in other languages, but the stress is often in a different place.

a Look at the animal words below. Can you remember which syllable is stressed? Under<u>line</u> it.

| ca|mel cro|co|dile dol|phin e|le|phant |
| gi|raffe kan|ga|roo li|on mo|squi|to |

b 4 19)) Listen and check. Are any of these words similar in your language? Is the stress in the same place?

c In pairs, ask and answer the questions.
1 What's the most dangerous animal in your country?
2 If you went on a safari, what animal would you most like to see?
3 What's your favourite film about an animal?
4 What's your favourite cartoon animal?
5 Are there any animals or insects you are really afraid of?
6 Do you (or did you) have a pet? What?
7 Are you allergic to any animals or insects?
8 If you could be an animal, which animal would you like to be?

5 SPEAKING

Work in groups of three. Take turns to choose a question and ask the others in the group. Then answer it yourself.

> ### What would you do…
> … if you saw a **mouse** in your kitchen?
> … if you saw somebody being attacked by a **dog**?
> … if a **bird** or a **bat** flew into your bedroom?
> … if you saw a large **spider** in the bath?
> … if it was a very hot day and you were on a beach that was famous for **shark** attacks?
> … if someone offered to buy you a fur coat?
> … if your neighbour's **dog** barked all night?
> … if a friend asked you to look after their **cat** or **dog** for the weekend?
> … if you went to somebody's house for dinner and they gave you…?
> a **horse** meat   b **goat**   c **kangaroo**

> **Talking about imaginary situations**
> I think I'd (probably)…
> I (definitely) wouldn't…
> I don't think I'd…

G present perfect + *for* and *since*
V phobias and words related to fear
P sentence stress

9B I've been afraid of it for years

Do you have any phobias?

Yes, I've been afraid of spiders since I was a child.

1 VOCABULARY
phobias and words related to fear

a Look at the picture. How many things can you see that some people have a phobia of?

b Look at the names of five phobias. Match them to explanations A–E.

1 a<u>c</u>rophobia   3 <u>gl</u>ossophobia   5 a<u>rach</u>nophobia
2 <u>ag</u>oraphobia   4 <u>cl</u>austrophobia

| A | | People with this phobia are terrified of spiders. Rupert Grint, the actor who played Ron Weasley in the Harry Potter films, has this phobia, and so does his character Ron. |

| B | | This phobia can have a severe effect on sufferers' lives. These people are frightened of being in open and public spaces like shops and busy streets. They often feel panic when they go out and only feel safe at home. |

| C | | People with this phobia are afraid of being in closed spaces like lifts, or travelling on the underground. This phobia can make life very difficult for people who live and work in cities. |

| D | | People who suffer from this phobia are scared of heights, and they get very nervous if they have to go up high, for example on a ski lift or if they are on a balcony on the 20th floor. |

| E | | People with this phobia suffer from a fear of public speaking. They get very nervous if they have to speak in front of other people, for example at work or in class or at a conference. The actor Harrison Ford has been afraid of public speaking all his life. He even gets nervous when a character in a film he is making has to make a speech. |

c Read the explanations again. Find in the texts…

1 the noun made from the adjective *afraid* _____
2 one adjective which means *very afraid* _____
3 two synonyms for *afraid* _____, _____

2 LISTENING & SPEAKING

a **4 20))** Listen to three people talking about their phobias. Answer question 1 for each person.

	1	2	3
1 What is he / she afraid of?			
2 When did it start?			
3 How does it affect his / her life?			

b Listen again and answer questions 2 and 3 for each person. Which person do you think is most affected by their phobia?

c Ask and answer with a partner.
1 Which of the phobias in this lesson do you think is the most irrational?
2 Which do you think makes the sufferers' lives most complicated?
3 Do you or anyone you know have a phobia? When and how did it start? How does it affect your or their lives?

My brother is really afraid of flying. He gets very nervous before he flies somewhere. It started about ten years ago when…

3 GRAMMAR present perfect + *for* and *since*

a Look at this extract from the first interview in **2**. Answer the questions.

> 'How long have you had this phobia?'
> 'I've had it for about 40 years. Since I was 12 years old.'

1 When did she begin to be afraid of bats?
2 Is she afraid of bats now?
3 What tense do we use to talk about something that started in the past and is still true now?
4 Complete the rule with *for* or *since*.
   Use _____ with a period of time.
   Use _____ with a point in time.

b ▶ **p.142 Grammar Bank 9B.** Learn more about the present perfect + *for* and *since*, and practise it.

c (4 22)) Listen and say the phrase with *for* or *since*.

))) 1984   since 1984

4 PRONUNCIATION sentence stress

a (4 23)) Listen and repeat. Copy the rhythm.

1 for ten years → worked here for ten years
   → I've worked here for ten years.
2 since 2002 → lived here since 2002
   → We've lived here since 2002.
3 known him → have you known him
   → How long have you known him?

b (4 24)) Listen and write five sentences.

5 SPEAKING

a Look at the questions below. What two tenses are they? What are the missing words?

		Name
have	/ a pet? How long / it?	
	/ a bike ? How long / it?	
live	/ in a modern flat ? How long / there?	
	/ near this school ? How long / there?	
know	/ anybody from another country? How long / him (her)?	
be	/ a fan of a football team? How long / a fan?	
	/ a member of a club or organization? How long / a member?	
	/ married? How long / married?	

b Move around the class and ask other students. If they answer *Yes, I do* or *Yes, I am* to the first question, ask the second question. Try to find a different person for each question.

6 READING

a Do you know of any kinds of treatment for people who have phobias?

b Read the text and mark the sentences **T** (true) or **F** (false).

1 30% of people have some kind of phobia.
2 Doctors have created a new drug to cure phobias.
3 In exposure therapy people learn to relax when they are exposed to something they are afraid of.
4 Exposure therapy is always successful.
5 The drug affects the way people learn and remember things.
6 The study showed that the drug helped people to lose their fear.

Scared of spiders? Take this pill.

There are many different kinds of phobias and they affect at least a quarter of the population. But doctors believe that they may soon have a cure. They have discovered that a drug, which is given to patients suffering from tuberculosis, can also help people to overcome their phobias.

The normal treatment for people with strong phobias is some kind of exposure therapy. The most commonly used exposure therapy involves gradually exposing people to the object or situation that produces the fear. For example, if you have a dentist phobia, you might first sit in the waiting room of a dentist, then talk to the dentist, and then sit in the dentist's chair. These exposures are combined with relaxation techniques.

However, exposure therapy does not work for everybody, and doctors think that the new drug, which causes changes to a part of the brain which is used in learning and memory, could be used in the future to make this therapy more effective. Michael Davis at Emory University School of Medicine in Atlanta, Georgia did a study with 30 acrophobics – people who are scared of heights – and put them in a glass lift that appeared to go up and down. The people who were given the pill felt much less afraid then those who took a placebo.

Adapted from a British newspaper

c With a partner, guess the meaning of the highlighted words and phrases.

d What stages of exposure therapy do you think could be used for a someone with
a) arachnophobia b) claustrophobia?

G present perfect or past simple? (2)
V biographies
P word stress, /ɔː/

9C Born to sing

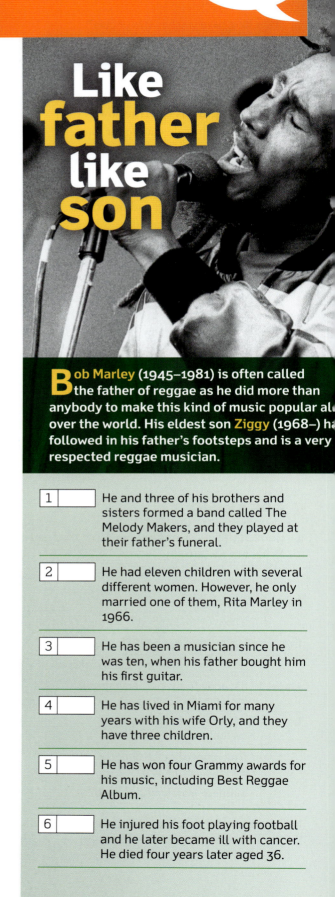

He was born in Jamaica.

How many Grammy's has he won?

1 VOCABULARY & PRONUNCIATION
biographies, word stress, /ɔː/

a ◆4 25⟩⟩ Look at the highlighted words in the list below. Which syllable is stressed? Listen and check.

Events in your life
- ☐ be born
- ☐ marry sb / get married
- ☐ go to primary school
- ☐ have children
- ☐ go to secondary school
- ☐ go to university
- ☐ leave school
- ☐ separate
- ☐ get a job
- ☐ get divorced
- ☐ retire
- ☐ fall in love
- ☐ die

b Number the expressions in what you think is the most logical order. Compare with a partner. Do you agree?

c ◆4 26⟩⟩ Listen and repeat the words and sound.

| 🐴 horse | born | divorced | fall |

d Practise saying these words. Circle the ones with the /ɔː/ sound.

more   work   world   small   walk   worse
talk   ball   form   bought   four   word

e ◆4 27⟩⟩ Listen and check. What rule can you see for words with *wor* + consonant?

2 READING

a Look at the photos of Bob and Ziggy Marley and read the introduction. Have you heard their music? Do you like it?

b Read ten facts about the lives of the two men. In pairs, decide which five are about Bob Marley (**BM**) and which five are about Ziggy Marley (**ZM**).

c Work in pairs. **A** re-read the facts about Bob Marley and **B** about Ziggy Marley. Close your books and tell your partner what you can remember.

3 GRAMMAR present perfect or past simple? (2)

a Answer the questions.
1 Look at the five facts about Bob Marley. What tense are all the verbs? Why?
2 Look at the five facts about Ziggy Marley. What three tenses are there? Why?

b ▶ p.142 Grammar Bank 9C. Learn more about the difference between the present perfect and the past simple, and practise it.

Like father like son

Bob Marley (1945–1981) is often called the father of reggae as he did more than anybody to make this kind of music popular all over the world. His eldest son **Ziggy** (1968–) has followed in his father's footsteps and is a very respected reggae musician.

1 ☐ He and three of his brothers and sisters formed a band called The Melody Makers, and they played at their father's funeral.

2 ☐ He had eleven children with several different women. However, he only married one of them, Rita Marley in 1966.

3 ☐ He has been a musician since he was ten, when his father bought him his first guitar.

4 ☐ He has lived in Miami for many years with his wife Orly, and they have three children.

5 ☐ He has won four Grammy awards for his music, including Best Reggae Album.

6 ☐ He injured his foot playing football and he later became ill with cancer. He died four years later aged 36.

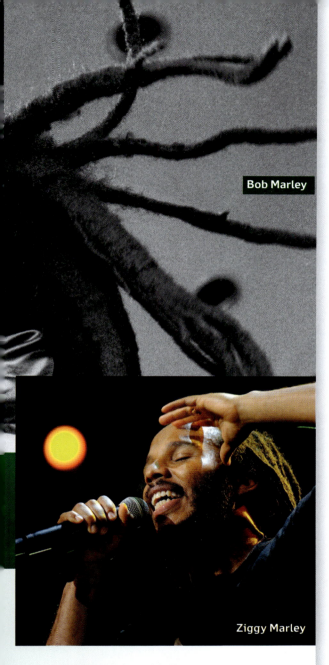

Bob Marley

Ziggy Marley

7	He was born in a small village in Jamaica. His father was a captain in the British army.
8	He was born in Kingston, Jamaica in 1968 and he was 13 years old when his father died. His father's last words to him were 'Money can't buy you life.'
9	His music was very influenced by social problems in his homeland, Jamaica.
10	With his band, The Wailers, he made eleven albums. His most famous songs included *No Woman, No Cry*, *Three Little Birds*, and *I Shot the Sheriff*.

4 LISTENING

a Look at the photos of another famous father and son, Julio and Enrique, who are both singers. What's their surname? Who do you think is more famous?

Julio

1 Madrid 1975
2 Miami
3 Enrique Martinez
4 'Enrique Iglesias' 1995
5 'Escape' 2001
6 Anna Kournikova
7 100 million

Enrique

b You are going to listen to a radio programme about Enrique. Look at the information. Before you listen, guess what the connection is to him.

⟨ I think he was born in Madrid in 1975.

c ▶ 4 29))) Now listen and make notes. Compare with a partner.

d Do you think Ziggy and Enrique have been successful because of their surnames, or because they are genuinely talented? Do you think it's common for children to want to do the same job as their parents?

5 SPEAKING & WRITING

a Think about an older person, a friend or a member of your family, who is alive and who you know well. Prepare to answer the questions below about their life and to tell your partner any other interesting information about them.

The past
- When / born?
- Where / born?
- What / do after (he / she) leave school? (e.g. get a job, go to university, get married, have children, etc.)

The present
- Where / live now?
- How long / live there?
- What / do? (job) How long...?
- What / do in (his / her) free time?

- Do you think (he / she) has had a good life? Why (not)?

b Interview your partner about his / her person. Ask for more information. Do your two people have anything in common?

I'm going to tell you about my grandmother. ⟩ ⟨ When was she born?

c ▶ p.116 **Writing** *A biography.* Write a biography of a person you know, or a famous person.

6 ▶ 4 30))) SONG *You're My #1* ♫

Practical English Getting around

EPISODE 5

1 🎬 HOLLY AND ROB IN BROOKLYN

a (4 31)) Watch or listen to Rob and Holly. Mark the sentences **T** (true) or **F** (false).

1 Rob has just done an interview.
2 He is in a hurry.
3 He has another interview in Manhattan.
4 He has another coffee.
5 Barbara phones Rob.
6 The restaurant is booked for 7 o'clock.

> **British and American English**
> *rest room* = American English; *toilet* = British English
> *the subway* = American English; *the underground* = British English

b Watch or listen again. Say why the **F** sentences are false.

2 VOCABULARY directions

a Look at the pictures and complete the phrases.

1 Turn _____.
2 Go _____ on.
3 Take the _____ turning on the right.
4 Turn right at the _____ lights.
5 Go round the _____ and take the third exit.

b (4 32)) Listen and check.

3 🎬 ASKING HOW TO GET THERE

a (4 33)) Cover the dialogue and watch or listen. Mark Rob's route on the map.

b Watch or listen again. Complete the **You Hear** phrases.

You Say	))) You Hear
How do I get to Greenwich Village on the subway?	Go to the subway station at Prospect Park. _____ the B train to West 4th Street.
How many stops is that?	Six or seven.
OK. And then?	From West 4th Street take the A train, and get _____ at 14th Street.
Could you say that again?	OK. From Prospect Park take the B train to West 4th Street, and then take the A train to 14th Street. That's only one _____.
Where's the restaurant?	Come out of the subway on Eighth Avenue, go _____ on for about 50 yards and take the _____ left. That's Greenwich Avenue. The restaurant's on the _____. It's called The Tea Set.
OK, thanks. See you later.	And don't get _____!

c))) 4 34 Watch or listen and repeat the **You Say** phrases. Copy the rhythm.

d Practise the dialogue with a partner.

e In pairs, roleplay the dialogue.

  A **B** is at Prospect Park. Choose a destination on the subway map. Give **B** directions. You start with *Go to the subway station at…*.
  B Follow **A**'s directions, and tell **A** which subway stop you have arrived at. Were you right?

f Swap roles.

  Take the A train to… Then…

4 ROB IS LATE…AGAIN

a))) 4 35 Watch or listen to Rob and Jenny. Is the date a success?

b Watch or listen again and answer the questions.
  1 What excuse does Rob give for being late?
  2 How long has Jenny waited for him?
  3 What does Rob suggest they do?
  4 What does Jenny say that Rob could do?
  5 Who is Rob interested in: Holly or Jenny?

c Look at the **Social English phrases**. Can you remember any of the missing words?

Social English phrases
Rob I'm so _____.
Rob I _____ I'm sorry.
Jenny I don't want to _____ here any more.
Jenny I don't _____ like a walk.
Jenny It's been a _____ day.
Jenny I didn't _____ to say that.

d))) 4 36 Watch or listen and complete the phrases.

e Watch or listen again and repeat the phrases. How do you say them in your language?

  Can you…?
  ☐ give and understand directions in the street
  ☐ give and understand directions for using public transport
  ☐ apologize

G passive
V verbs: *invent, discover*, etc.
P /ʃ/, -ed, sentence stress

10A The mothers of invention

> I think it was invented by a woman.
>
> Are you sure?

1 LISTENING

a Look at the photos. Five of these things were invented by women. In pairs, decide which five you think they are.

b ◀ 37))) Now listen to a radio programme about inventions. Were you right? Complete the sentences with the invention.

1 The _____ was invented by Josephine Cochrane in 1886.
2 _____ were invented by Mary Anderson in 1903.
3 _____ were invented by Marion Donovan in 1950.
4 _____ was invented by Bette Nesmith Graham in 1956.
5 The _____ was invented by Stephanie Kwolek in 1966.

c Listen again and answer the questions.

1 What happened after Josephine Cochrane's dinner parties?
2 What was the problem with cars in 1903 when it rained or snowed?
3 How many disposable nappies are used every day?
4 What was Bette Nesmith Graham's job?
5 What was special about the material Stephanie Kwolek invented?

d Which of the five inventions do you think was the best?

2 GRAMMAR passive

a Make five true sentences using the words in the chart.

The dishwasher	is called	Tipp-Ex today.
Disposable nappies	was invented	by Marion Donovan.
More than 55 million nappies	are protected	every day.
Mrs Graham's invention	were invented	by the bullet-proof vest.
Policemen all over the world	are used	by an American woman.

The dishwasher was invented by an American woman.

b Look at the two sentences below and answer the questions.

a An American woman invented the dishwasher.
b The dishwasher was invented by an American woman.

1 Do the sentences have the same meaning?
2 In which sentence is the focus more on the dishwasher?
3 In which sentence is the focus more on the woman?

c ▶ **p.144 Grammar Bank 10A.** Learn more about the passive and practise it.

3 READING & VOCABULARY
verbs: *invent*, *discover*, etc.

a Match the verbs to the dictionary definitions.

base	design	discover	invent

1 _____ *verb* to find or learn sth for the first time, e.g. *DNA was ~ in 1953.*
2 _____ *verb* to make sth using sth else as a starting point, e.g. *This film is ~ on a true story.*
3 _____ *verb* to draw a plan which shows how to make sth, e.g. *The building was ~ by a German architect.*
4 _____ *verb* to make or think of sth for the first time, e.g. *Who ~ the bicycle?*

b Complete the 'Did you know...?' text with the past participle of a verb from the list.

base	call	design	discover	give
invent	open	play	show	use

c Read the text again. One of the pieces of information is not true. Which one do you think it is?

4 PRONUNCIATION /ʃ/, -ed, sentence stress

a **4 39** Listen and repeat the words and sounds.

∫ shower	di**sh**wa**sh**er inven**ti**on
	spe**ci**al wa**sh**ing ma**ch**ine

b What four ways can you see for spelling the /ʃ/ sound? Which one do you think is not typical? Go to the **Sound Bank** *p.167* and check.

c How is *-ed* pronounced in these past participles? Put them in the right column.

bas|ed   call|ed   cre|a|ted   de|sign|ed   di|rec|ted
di|sco|vered   in|ven|ted   pain|ted   pro|duced   us|ed

🐕 dog	👕 tie	/ɪd/

d **4 40** Listen and check. Underline the stressed syllable in each multi-syllable verb.

e **4 41** Listen and write six sentences. Then listen again and repeat. Copy the rhythm.

5 SPEAKING

▶ **Communication** *Passives quiz* **A** *p.105* **B** *p.109.* Make sentences for your partner to decide if they are true or false.

Did you know...?

One of the most famous logos in the world is the **Nike** logo. It was ¹_____ by an American student, Carolyn Davidson, in 1971. Ms Davidson was only paid $35 dollars for her design. However, she was later ²_____ a gold ring in the shape of the logo and Nike shares.

Tinned food was ³_____ in 1810 in Britain by Peter Durand. Unfortunately, he did not also invent a tin opener, so tins were ⁴_____ with difficulty using a knife and a hammer. It wasn't until nearly 50 years later that the American Ezra Warner invented the tin opener.

When people at toy company Parker Brothers were first ⁵_____ the board game '**Monopoly**', they were not interested. They said it had 52 fundamental errors, including taking too long to play. However, a few days later the company president saw the game and took it home to try it. He stayed up until 1 a.m. to finish playing it, and the next day he wrote to the inventor, Charles Darrow, and offered to buy it!

The modern game of **golf** was invented in Scotland in the 18th century. It was originally only ⁶_____ by men, and was ⁷_____ 'golf' because of the rule **G**entlemen **O**nly **L**adies **F**orbidden. This is how the word *golf* entered into the English language.

Botox was first ⁸_____ in 1985 to correct strabismus (lazy eye) in children. The possibility of using it to make people's faces look younger was only ⁹_____ 20 years later.

The character Gregory House in the hit TV series **House M.D.** is ¹⁰_____ on Conan Doyle's detective Sherlock Holmes. Like Holmes, House uses his intelligence and knowledge of psychology to solve cases. House's relationship with his friend Dr James Wilson is similar to that between Holmes and his friend, Dr John Watson, and the address on his driving licence is 221B Baker St, a direct reference to Holmes's address.

G used to
V school subjects
P used to / didn't use to

10B Could do better

"Did you use to like primary school?" "Yes, I did. I used to have a great time."

1 VOCABULARY school subjects

a Read the report and match the subjects and pictures.

Subject	Mark
art	65%
foreign languages (English, etc.)	72%
geography	86%
history	44%
IT (= information technology)	50%
literature	57%
maths	42%
PE (= physical education)	78%
science (physics, chemistry, and biology)	61%
Behaviour	
Lazy and untidy. Talks a lot in class.	

b **4 42**)) Listen and check.

c Look at the report again. What do *marks* and *behaviour* mean?

d Did you have any other subjects at primary or secondary school? Which subjects were you…?

  a good at   b OK at   c bad at

  I was very bad at maths.

> 🔍 **good at**
> We use **at** after *good* and *bad* to talk about our abilities, e.g. *I was very bad at maths. I'm very good at cooking.*

2 GRAMMAR used to

a When you were at school did you get a report at the end of every term or year? Were they usually good or bad? Did you always show them to your parents?

b Read some extracts from *Could do better*, a collection of famous British people's school reports. Are the comments positive or negative?

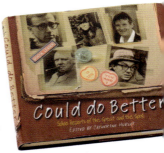

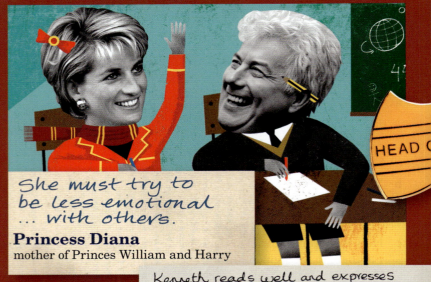

She must try to be less emotional … with others.
Princess Diana
mother of Princes William and Harry

Kenneth reads well and expresses himself well, and is good at arithmetic but everything he does is spoiled by his attitude and his bad behaviour.
Ken Follett
best-selling author of *The Pillars of the Earth*

Constantly late for school and always losing his books and papers.
Winston Churchill
politician, Prime Minister during the Second World War 1940–45

c Read the extracts again and match the people to sentences 1–5. Write **KF, JL, PD, WC,** or **HF**.

1 _____ didn't use to get to school on time.
2 _____ used to make the other children laugh.
3 _____ was clever, but didn't use to behave well.
4 _____ used to use very complicated vocabulary.
5 _____ used to cry a lot at school.

d Look at sentences 1–5 again. Does *used to* refer to…?

1 a the present
  b the past
2 a things that happened once
  b things that happened repeatedly

e ▶ p.144 Grammar Bank 10B. Learn more about *used to* and practise it.

He is… a clown in class and wastes other pupils' time.

John Lennon
musician, member of the Beatles 1960–69

Subject: *English*

Helen must learn not to use such flowery language.

Helen Fielding
author of *Bridget Jones's Diary*

3 PRONUNCIATION used to / didn't use to

🔎 **Pronouncing *used to***
When we say *used to* or *(didn't) use to* we link the two words together. They are both pronounced /ˈjuːstə/.

a ◀4 44))) Listen and underline the stressed words. Then listen and repeat.

1 He used to hate school.
2 I used to be good at French.
3 They didn't use to behave well.
4 She didn't use to wear glasses.
5 Did you use to walk to school?

b ◀4 45))) Now listen and write six more sentences.

4 LISTENING

a ◀4 46))) Listen to six people talking about their memories of school. Write ✓ if they liked it, ✗ if they didn't like it, and ✓✗ if they liked some things but not others.

1 ☐ 2 ☐ 3 ☐ 4 ☐ 5 ☐ 6 ☐

b Listen again and answer the questions.

Who…?
☐ didn't like being at a same-sex school
☐ didn't use to study a lot, but got good marks
☐ had a very good physics teacher
☐ hated doing sport
☐ liked one school, but not another
☐ used to read a lot at school

c Do you identify with any of the speakers? Why?

5 SPEAKING

a Think about when you were at primary or secondary school. Prepare your answers to the questions below. Think of examples you could give.

Did you use to…?
- be disorganized or very organized
- be late for school or on time
- get a lot of homework or a little
- have a teacher you really liked
- be a good or a bad student
- wear a uniform
- have a teacher you hated
- have a nickname

b Work in groups of three. **A** tell **B** and **C** about how you used to be. **B** and **C** listen and ask for more information. Then swap roles. Did you have anything in common?

I used to be very disorganized, for example I often left my books or my sports clothes at home.

6 ◀4 47))) SONG ABC 🎵

G *might*
V word building: noun formation
P diphthongs

> Are you going to the party?
> I might go, but I might not.

10C Mr Indecisive

> Go to the party or stay in?
> Car or taxi?
> Get there early or get there late?
> Come on! Make up your mind!

1 GRAMMAR *might*

a Do you know anybody who is very indecisive? What is he / she indecisive about?

b (4 48)) Cover the dialogue and listen. What does Adrian decide in the end?

c Listen again and complete the dialogue.

Tina Hi, Adrian.
Adrian Oh. Hi, Tina.
T It's Alice's party tonight. You are going, aren't you?
A I don't know. I'm not sure. I might _____, but I might not. I can't decide.
T Oh, come on. It'll be good. Lots of Alice's friends are going to be there. You might _____ _____.
A Yes, that's true… OK. I'll go then.
T Great. Shall we get a taxi there?
A No, I'll take my car… No, wait. It might _____ _____ to park. Let's get a taxi.
T Fine. What time shall I get the taxi for? 9.30?
A Yes… No… Listen. I'll take my car. I'll pick you up at 9.00.
T Are you sure about that?
A Yes, I'm sure… I think.

d (4 49)) Adrian phones Tina later. What happens?

e Underline the verb phrases in the dialogue with *might*. Do we use them for…?
1 an obligation   OR   2 a possibility

f ▶ p.144 **Grammar Bank 10C.** Learn more about *might* and practise it.

g Take turns to ask and answer the questions below. Use *I'm not sure. I might…* and give two possibilities each time.

> What are you going to do after class?
> I'm not sure. I might go home or I might go shopping. What about you?

1 What are you going to do after class?
2 What are you going to have for dinner tonight?
3 What are you going to do on Saturday night?
4 Where are you going to have lunch on Sunday?
5 Where are you going to go for your next holiday?

2 PRONUNCIATION diphthongs

a (4 51)) Listen and repeat the picture words and sounds.

b Look at the other words. Which one has a different sound?

1	aɪ bike	might buy smile since	5	ɪə ear	here idea engineer where
2	eɪ train	may fail key break	6	ʊə tourist	sure bus Europe curious
3	əʊ phone	know although trousers won't	7	aʊ owl	round towel south borrow
4	eə chair	near there wear careful	8	ɔɪ boy	town noisy enjoy annoy

c (4 52)) Listen and check.

80

3 SPEAKING & READING

a Interview your partner with the questionnaire. Ask for more information. Which of you is more indecisive?

ARE YOU INDECISIVE?

Do you have problems deciding…?
- what to buy when you go shopping
- what to wear when you go out
- what to eat in a restaurant
- what to do in your free time
- where to go on holiday

Do you often change your mind about things? What kind of things?
Do you think you are indecisive?
☐ Yes ☐ No ☐ I'm not sure

b Read the article carefully. Complete it with sentences A–E.

> **A** And it isn't just in the coffee bar.
> **B** But if all this choice is bad for us, what can we do about it?
> **C** Buying a cup of coffee isn't as easy as it used to be.
> **D** People often think that being able to choose from a lot of options is a good thing.
> **E** Research shows that we feel happier when we have less choice.

c Do you agree that there is too much choice in the following? Why (not)?

a in supermarkets   d in coffee shops
b on TV   e in restaurants
c in clothes shops

4 VOCABULARY
word building: noun formation

> 🔍 **Noun formation**
> With many verbs you can make a noun by adding *-ion*, *-sion*, or *-ation*, e.g.
> decide → decision   imagine → imagination
> Other verbs change when you form a noun, e.g.
> see (verb) → sight (noun)

a With a partner try to complete the chart.

Verb	Noun (+ -ion, -sion, or -ation)
opt	option
decide	decision
imagine	imagination
inform	
elect	
invite	
organize	
educate	
confuse	
Verb	**Noun (new word)**
choose	
live	
die	
succeed	

b 🔊 4 53)) Listen and check. Underline the stressed syllable in the verbs and nouns.

Is too much choice making us unhappy?

¹_____. Years ago there were only two kinds of coffee – black or white. But nowadays when you go into a coffee shop in the UK you are given about twenty different options. Do you want a Cappuccino, a Latte, a Caramel Macchiato, an Americano, or a White Mocha?

²_____. In big supermarkets we have to choose between thousands of products – my local supermarket has 35 different kinds of milk! When we are buying clothes or electrical gadgets, looking for a hotel on a travel website, or just deciding which TV channel to watch, we are constantly forced to choose from hundreds of possibilities.

³_____. However, university researchers have discovered that too much choice is making us feel unhappy and dissatisfied. The problem is that we have so many options that we get stressed every time we have to make a decision, because we are worried about making the wrong one. Then when we choose one thing we feel bad because we think we are missing other opportunities, and this makes us dissatisfied with what we have chosen.

⁴_____. Professor Mark Lepper at Stanford University in America found that people who tried six kinds of jam felt happier with their choice than those who were offered 24 jams to taste.

⁵_____. Professor Lepper suggests that we should try to relax when we have to choose something to buy. 'Don't take these choices too seriously or it will become stressful,' he says. 'If you pick a sofa from IKEA in 30 seconds, you'll feel better than if you spend hours researching sofas – because you won't know what you're missing.'

Adapted from a British newspaper

9 & 10 Revise and Check

GRAMMAR

Circle a, b, or c.

1. If I _____ a snake, I'd be terrified.
   a see   b saw   c seen
2. What _____ if a large dog attacked you?
   a you would do
   b will you do
   c would you do
3. I _____ that bike if I were you.
   a wouldn't buy   b didn't buy   c won't buy
4. I _____ in this house since I was 12.
   a live   b lived   c have lived
5. We haven't seen my uncle _____ a long time.
   a since   b during   c for
6. _____ have you had this car?
   a How long   b How much   c How long time
7. I _____ married for 15 years. I got divorced in 2010.
   a have been   b am   c was
8. When _____ Queen Victoria die?
   a did   b has   c was
9. The dishwasher _____ in 1886.
   a were invented   b was invented   c is invented
10. The first book in the series was _____ ten years ago.
    a write   b wrote   c written
11. The *Mona Lisa* was painted _____ da Vinci.
    a for   b by   c to
12. When I was a child I _____ have very long hair.
    a use to   b used to   c used
13. Jack _____ like sport when he was at school.
    a don't use to
    b didn't used to
    c didn't use to
14. I might _____ Sophie a ring for her birthday.
    a buy   b to buy   c buying
15. Sue _____ come tonight. She has to work late.
    a might no   b not might   c might not

VOCABULARY

a Make nouns from the verbs.

1. elect _____
2. decide _____
3. choose _____
4. organize _____
5. die _____
6. succeed _____
7. imagine _____

b Circle the word that is different.

1. butterfly   goat   fly   mosquito
2. pig   sheep   cow   lion
3. spider   shark   jellyfish   whale
4. scared   afraid   frightened   fear
5. maths   marks   history   biology

c Complete with a verb from the list in the right form.

base   design   discover   fall   retire

1. In Britain most people _____ when they are 65.
2. I _____ in love for the first time when I was 15.
3. Penicillin was _____ by Alexander Fleming in 1928.
4. The *Lord of the Rings* films were _____ on the books written by Tolkien.
5. The first Apple computer was _____ by Steve Wozniak.

d Write the words for the definitions.

1. k_____ a wild animal that lives in Australia
2. b_____ an insect that makes honey
3. cr_____ a reptile that lives in rivers in Africa and Australia
4. b_____ a male cow
5. t_____ very afraid
6. s_____ a couple usually do this before they get divorced
7. s_____ a school subject that includes physics, chemistry, and biology
8. r_____ information you get from your school at the end of each term which says how you have done

PRONUNCIATION

a Circle the word with a different sound.

1. f**ea**r   n**ea**r   **i**d**ea**   b**ea**r
2. ph**o**bia   c**ow**   sh**ow**   h**o**mework
3. pr**i**mary   ch**i**ldren   sp**i**der   m**igh**t
4. sc**a**red   th**e**re   n**er**vous   w**ea**r
5. /ju/   s**u**bject   st**u**dent   **u**sed   conf**u**sion

b Underline the stressed syllable.

1. gi|raffe   2 e|le|phant   3 se|con|dary   4 re|tire   5 de|sign

CAN YOU UNDERSTAND THIS TEXT?

a Read the article once. How did the dolphins protect the swimmers from the shark?

b Read the article again and mark the sentences **T** (true) or **F** (false).
1 The swimmers were swimming very near the beach.
2 The dolphins were doing strange things.
3 Mr Howes and Helen were separated from the other two swimmers.
4 One of the dolphins jumped out of the water.
5 Mr Howes saw a big fish swimming around the other two girls.
6 Mr Howes understood that the dolphins were trying to help them.
7 The dolphins stopped the shark from attacking them.
8 In the end the swimmers were rescued by lifeguards.
9 An expert said that dolphins very often behave in this way.

c Look at the highlighted words or phrases in the text. Guess their meaning from the context. Check with your teacher or with a dictionary.

DOLPHINS SAVE SWIMMERS FROM A SHARK ATTACK

Lifeguard Rob Howes, his daughter Niccy, 15, Karina Cooper, 15, and Helen Slade, 16, were swimming 100m out to sea at Ocean Beach in New Zealand when suddenly seven dolphins swam towards them.

'They were behaving really weirdly,' Mr Howes said, 'swimming in circles around us, and hitting the water with their tails.' One dolphin swam towards Mr Howes and Helen, who were about 20m away from the other two, and was trying to push them towards the other two girls.

'Then suddenly I saw another huge fish swimming around me and Helen,' said Mr Howes. It was in fact a three metre-long great white shark.

'It was only about two metres away from us,' he said. At that point, he realised that the dolphins 'were trying to herd the four of us together to protect us'.

The shark then went towards the other two girls. Mr Howes was terrified, especially because one of the swimmers was his daughter. But the dolphins pushed the four swimmers back together and circled around them for another 40 minutes. Mr Howes decided not to tell the three girls a shark was sharing the water with them.

Fortunately, the shark finally swam away, and the swimmers all reached the beach safely.

'I swim with dolphins perhaps three or four times a year and I have never seen them behave like that,' said Mr Howes. However, dolphin expert Ingrid Visser said that there have been other reports from around the world about dolphins protecting swimmers. She said that, in this case, the dolphins probably sensed the humans were in danger and took action to protect them.

Adapted from a British newspaper

CAN YOU UNDERSTAND THESE PEOPLE?

4 54)) In the street Watch or listen to five people and answer the questions.

David   Joanna   Polly   Sarah Jane   Justin

1 David has had _____ since he was a child.
  a arachnophobia
  b agoraphobia
  c claustrophobia
2 Joanna would like to see leopards in the wild because _____.
  a they have always been her favourite animals
  b she saw them before on a safari and loved them
  c they are one of the wild animals she hasn't seen yet
3 When Polly was at school _____.
  a she didn't have many friends
  b she liked most subjects
  c she didn't like French or maths
4 Sarah Jane has been a teacher _____.
  a since 2006   b for 6 years   c for 16 years
5 Justin loves the Empire State Building because _____.
  a he thinks it's in exactly the right place
  b he loves its height, and the view from the top
  c it's one of the oldest skyscrapers in New York

CAN YOU SAY THIS IN ENGLISH?

Do the tasks with a partner. Tick (✓) the box if you can do them.

Can you…?
1 ☐ say what you would do if…
  a a dog attacked you
  b you won the lottery
  c you had more free time
2 ☐ talk about how long you have…
  a lived where you are now
  b had your laptop or computer
  c been at this school
3 ☐ describe your life story
4 ☐ talk about when three things were invented or built
5 ☐ talk about three things you used to do when you were a child
6 ☐ say three things you might do next week

Short films Marwell Wildlife
Watch and enjoy a film on iTutor.

G expressing movement
V sports, expressing movement
P sports

11A Bad losers

Where did the ball go?

It went over the bar.

1 PRONUNCIATION & SPEAKING sports

a What sports can you see in the photos?

b 🔊 4 55)) Look at the sports in the list. How do you pronounce them in English? Listen and check, and under<u>line</u> the stressed syllable. Do you know the names of any other sports in English?

> ath|le|tics   base|ball   ba|sket|ball   box|ing   cy|cling
> foot|ball   golf   hand|ball   ho|ckey   mo|tor ra|cing
> rug|by   ski|ing   te|nnis   vo|lley|ball   wind|sur|fing

> 🔍 **Verbs with sports**
> 1 We use **play** for sports with a ball, e.g. *I play hockey at school.*
> 2 With sports ending in *-ing* (cycling, skiing, windsurfing, etc.) we normally use the verb, e.g. *I **cycle** at weekends*, or **go** + **sport**, e.g. *I **go cycling** at weekends.*
> 3 We use **do** for sport and exercise in general, e.g. *I **do sport** at weekends*, and for martial arts, athletics, yoga, Pilates, etc., e.g. *I **do yoga** twice a week.*

c Ask and answer with a partner. Give and ask for as much information as you can.

SPORT — YOU **LOVE** IT OR YOU **HATE** IT.
- Do you do any sport or exercise?
  ☐ Yes. What? Do you enjoy it?   ☐ No. Why not?
- Did you use to do any other sports or exercise? Why did you stop?
- Which sports do you think are the most exciting to watch?
- Which sports do think are the most boring?
- Are you (or is anyone in your family) a fan of a sports team? Which one?
- Do you (or they) watch their matches?
- What is the most exciting sporting event you have ever seen?

2 VOCABULARY
sports, expressing movement

a Put these words in the correct column. Do you know any other words connected to these sports?

> bunker   corner   hole   lap   match point
> penalty   serve   track

athletics	football	golf	tennis

b 🔊 4 56)) Listen to the sports commentaries. What are the four sports?

c Listen again and complete the sentences with one word. Then match sentences 1–4 with pictures a–d.

1 ☐ The ball has gone _____ the lake.
2 ☐ The ball has gone _____ the bar.
3 ☐ Now they have to run _____ the track one more time.
4 ☐ That's a very hard return, but the ball has gone _____!

d ▶ p.162 **Vocabulary Bank** *Expressing movement.*

3 GRAMMAR expressing movement

a Complete the sentences with a verb from the list.

hit kick run throw

1. In basketball you have to _____ the ball **through** a ring with a basket.
2. In football you have to _____ the ball **into** a goal.
3. In tennis you have to _____ the ball **over** a net.
4. In the 800 metres you have to _____ twice **round** the track.

b Look at the sentence below. Try to think of three different verbs you could put in the gap, e.g. *walked*.

The man _____ **along** the street until he got to the corner.

c ▶ p.146 **Grammar Bank 11A.** Learn more about expressing movement and practise it.

d Look at the photos in **1**. Say what the people are doing.

He's hitting the ball over the net.

4 READING & SPEAKING

a When you play a sport or a game with family or friends, how do you react if you lose? Are you a good or bad loser? Are any of your family or friends bad losers?

b Read the text and answer with a name. Which of the bad losers…?

1. insulted the match official
2. did not want to do his job after the match
3. became very emotional when he couldn't take part
4. tried to hit somebody
5. said sorry after the event

c Read the text again and complete the gaps with the prepositions in the list.

down in out out of (x2) past

d Look at the highlighted words in the text which are all related to sport. With a partner guess their meaning.

e In pairs answer the questions.

1. Who do you think was the worst loser?
2. Whose behaviour do you think was understandable?
3. Do you know any famous sportspeople who are bad losers?

5 WRITING

a Talk to a partner. Do you think there is too much football on TV? Why (not)?

b ▶ p.117 **Writing** *An opinion essay*. Read a model essay about football on TV, and then write one.

6 4 59)) SONG *The Final Countdown* ♫

Bad losers?

The hardest lesson to learn in sport is how to lose with dignity, without blaming your defeat on the referees or refusing to shake hands with your opponent. Here are some famous moments when losing was just too hard…

In 1981 at Wimbledon a young John McEnroe was serving. The umpire said that his serve was [1]_____, but McEnroe thought it was [2]_____. He became furious and shouted 'You CANNOT be serious!' at the umpire. He also called the umpire 'an incompetent fool!'

In the 2003 Athletics World Championship the 100 metres runner, Jon Drummond, was disqualified for a false start. Drummond lay [3]_____ on the track and began to cry. Two hours later his coach told journalists: 'He's still crying. We're making him drink water because he's becoming dehydrated.'

In the 1982 German Grand Prix Nelson Piquet was winning the race. He was trying to pass Eliseo Salazar (who was last in the race), but Salazar didn't let him go [4]_____ him and Piquet crashed into Salazar. Piquet jumped [5]_____ his car and started trying to hit and kick Salazar (without much success!).

South Korean footballer Ahn Jung-Hwan scored the goal that sent Italy [6]_____ the 2002 World Cup when they beat them 2–1. But Jung-Hwan also played for the Italian football club Perugia. After the match the president of the club, Luciano Gaucci, announced that the player's contract would not be renewed. 'That gentleman will never set foot in Perugia again,' Gaucci said. 'I have no intention of paying a salary to somebody who has ruined Italian football.' Gaucci later apologized, but Ahn Jung-Hwan left the club and never went back to an Italian club.

When England won the Rugby World Cup in 2003 by beating Australia in the last minute of the match, the Australian Prime minister, John Howard, was so angry that in the medals ceremony he almost threw the medals at the English players. His behaviour was described by a journalist as being 'like an unhappy five-year-old at a birthday party who starts throwing toys around.'

Adapted from a British newspaper

G word order of phrasal verbs
V phrasal verbs
P linking

What's the first thing you do when you wake up?

I turn on the radio.

11B Are you a morning person?

1 SPEAKING & READING

a Answer the questions with a partner.

1 What time do you wake up during the week?
2 Do you use an alarm clock to wake up? If not, what makes you wake up?
3 Do you get up immediately after you wake up?
4 When you first get up do you feel...?
   a awful
   b quite sleepy
   c awake and energetic

b Read an interview with Sara Mohr-Pietsch. Match the questions and answers.

A Do you choose what you wear the night before?
B Do you have anything to eat before you go to work?
C Do you use an alarm clock to wake up?
D How do you feel when you wake up?
E How do you get to work?
F How does this affect your social life?
G ~~What time do you get up when you're doing the Breakfast show?~~
H What time do you go to bed when you're working the next day?
I Would you like to change your working hours?

c Cover the answers and look at the questions. With a partner remember her answers.

d Answer the questions with a partner.

1 Would you like to work the same hours as the radio presenter?
2 In general are you a morning or evening person?

Early bird!

Sara Mohr-Pietsch tells us what it's like to be an early morning presenter on the Breakfast programme on BBC Radio 3.

1 *What time do you get up when you're doing the Breakfast show?*
I get up at 4.45 a.m. and leave the house at 5.20.

2 _____
Yes. I usually set my radio alarm to come on at 4.30 so that I can wake up slowly as I listen to the world news. I set my phone alarm for 4.45 and leave it on the other side of the room so I have to get up to turn it off!

3 _____
It depends – some mornings I feel rested and awake, but other mornings it's quite hard to get out of bed. It depends on the season. I find I need much more sleep in the winter.

4 _____
If I'm slow to get up, then I wait until I'm in the studio before having breakfast, but most mornings I have a bowl of cereal before I leave the house.

5 _____
That depends on the season too. In the summer I usually wait until the morning to decide. But in the winter I often leave clothes out the night before so that I can stay in bed until the last minute!

6 _____
A car picks me up at 5.20.

7 _____
In the winter, any time between 8.30 and 9.30 p.m. In the summer, usually more like 9.00 to 10.00 p.m.

8 _____
What social life? I certainly can't go out for a wild night during the week, but I'm lucky because a lot of my closest friends live near me, so I can see them in the evenings and still go to bed quite early.

9 _____
Sometimes I think I would like to have more normal working hours, but I love my job so much that I'd never want to give it up. The buzz of being 'live' on the radio early in the morning as people start their days is really wonderful.

2 VOCABULARY phrasal verbs

a Look at some sentences from the interview. With a partner say what the highlighted phrases mean.

> 'I leave it on the other side of the room so I have to **get up** to **turn it off**!'
>
> 'A car **picks me up** at 5.20.'
>
> 'I love my job so much that I'd never want to **give it up**.'

> **Phrasal verbs**
> *Wake up, get up, turn on / off, give up*, etc. are common phrasal verbs (verbs with a preposition or adverb).
> Sometimes the meaning of the two separate words can help you guess the meaning of the phrasal verb, e.g. *turn off*. Sometimes the meaning of the two words does not help you, e.g. *give up*.

b Read the information box. Can you think of a phrasal verb which means…?
  1 to try to find something you have lost
  2 to put on clothes in a shop to see if they are the right size
  3 to have a friendly relationship (with somebody)

c ▶ p.163 Vocabulary Bank *Phrasal verbs.*

3 GRAMMAR word order of phrasal verbs

a Look at the picture and underline the **object** of the phrasal verb in each sentence.

1 Turn off the alarm clock!
2 Turn the alarm clock off!
3 Turn it off!

b Complete the rules about separable phrasal verbs with *noun* or *pronoun*.
  1 If the object of a phrasal verb is a _____, you can put it **after** the verb + *up, on*, etc. **OR between** the verb and *up, on*, etc.
  2 If the object of a phrasal verb is a _____, you <u>must</u> put it **between** the verb and *up, on*, etc.

c ▶ p.146 Grammar Bank 11B. Learn more about the word order of phrasal verbs and practise it.

4 PRONUNCIATION linking

a 5 4))) Listen and write the missing words.
  1 There's a wet towel on the floor. Please ____ ____ ____.
  2 I can't concentrate with that music on. Please ____ ____ ____.
  3 If you don't know what the word means, ____ ____ ____.
  4 Why have you taken your coat off? ____ ____ ____!
  5 This book was very expensive. Please ____ ____ ____.
  6 Why are you wearing your coat in here? ____ ____ ____!

b Practise saying the sentences. Try to link the phrasal verbs and pronouns, e.g. pick‿it‿up.

5 SPEAKING

a Read the questions in the questionnaire and think about your answers.

b Work in pairs. Interview your partner with the questions.

PHRASAL VERB QUESTIONNAIRE

- Have you ever forgotten to **turn** your mobile phone **off** in a concert or the cinema?
- Do you **throw away** old clothes or do you give them to other people?
- Do you enjoy **trying on** clothes when you go shopping?
- Do you often **go away** at the weekend? Where to?
- Before you go shopping do you usually **write down** what you have to buy? Do you only buy what's on the list?
- Do you enjoy **looking after** small children? Why (not)?
- Have you ever asked your neighbours to **turn** the TV or the music **down**? What happened?
- What's the first thing you **turn on** after you **wake up** in the morning?

G *so, neither* + auxiliaries
V similarities
P sentence stress, /ð/ and /θ/

11C What a coincidence!

> I have a son called James.
>
> So do I.

'I'm Jim.'

'So am I.'

In the USA, identical twin brothers were adopted soon after they were born. One brother was adopted by a couple named Lewis in Lima, Ohio, and his brother was adopted by a couple named Springer in Dayton, Ohio. By coincidence, both boys were called 'Jim' by their new parents. When Jim Lewis was six years old, he discovered that he had an identical twin brother. When he was thirty-nine, he decided to find and contact his brother. Six weeks later, he met Jim Springer in a café in Dayton, and they probably had a conversation something like this...

1 GRAMMAR *so, neither* + auxiliaries

a Look at the photos and describe the two men.

b Read about the two men and answer the questions.
  1 Who are Jim Springer and Jim Lewis?
  2 Why didn't they know each other?
  3 What did Jim Lewis decide to do when he was 39?
  4 How long did it take him?

c 5 5)) Cover the dialogue. Listen once. Try to remember three things they have in common.

d Listen again and complete the gaps.

> A Hi! I'm Jim.
> B So ¹_____ I. Great to meet you. Sit down. Are you married, Jim?
> A Yes... well, I've been married twice.
> B Yeah? So ²_____ I. Do you have any children?
> A I have one son.
> B So ³_____ I. What's his name?
> A James Allen.
> B That's amazing! My son's name is James Allen too!
> A Did you go to college, Jim?
> B No, I didn't.
> A Neither ⁴_____ I. I was a terrible student.
> B So ⁵_____ I. Hey, this is my dog Toy.
> A I don't believe it! My dog's called Toy too!
> B He wants to go outside. My wife usually takes him. I don't do any exercise at all.
> A Don't worry. Neither ⁶_____ I. I drive everywhere.
> B What car do you have?
> A A Chevrolet.
> B So ⁷_____ I!
> A+B Let's have a beer, Jim.
> A What beer do you drink?
> B Miller Lite.
> A So ⁸_____ I!

e Which coincidence do you think is the most surprising?

f Look at the dialogue again. Answer the questions with a partner.
  1 Find two phrases that the twins use…
     when they have something ➕ in common.
     when they have something ➖ in common.
  2 Why do you think the auxiliary verb changes?

g ▶ p.146 **Grammar Bank 11C.** Learn more about *so, neither,* etc. and practise them.

2 PRONUNCIATION sentence stress, /ð/ and /θ/

a 5 7))) Listen and repeat the words and sounds.

/ð/	mo**th**er	bro**th**er	nei**th**er	**th**ey
/θ/	**th**umb	bo**th**	**th**irty	**th**row

b 5 8))) Add four words to each row. Listen and check.

al**th**ough ma**th**s o**th**er **th**ere **th**ing **th**irsty **th**rough wi**th**out

c 5 9))) Listen and repeat the dialogues. <u>Underline</u> the stressed words.

1 **A** I like tea. **B** So do I. 3 **A** I don't smoke. **B** Neither do I.
2 **A** I'm tired. **B** So am I. 4 **A** I'm not hungry. **B** Neither am I.

d 5 10))) Listen and respond. Say you're the same.

))) I catch the bus to work.   So do I.

3 SPEAKING

a Complete the sentences so they are true for you.

Me	Who else in the class?
I love _____. (a kind of music)	
I don't like _____. (a drink)	
I'm very _____. (adjective of personality)	
I'm not very good at _____. (sport or activity)	
I'm going to _____ after class. (an activity)	
I have to _____ every day. (an obligation)	
I don't eat _____. (a kind of food)	

b Move around the class saying your sentences. For each sentence try to find someone like you, and write down their name. Respond to other people's sentences. Say *So do / am I*, or *Neither do / am I* if you have something in common.

A I love heavy metal. **B** Really? I hate it! **C** So do I.

4 VOCABULARY similarities

a Read about some more similarities between the two Jims. Complete the text with a word from the list.

as both i<u>den</u>tical like <u>nei</u>ther <u>sim</u>ilar so

b Complete the sentences about you and your family. Tell your partner.
1 I have the same colour eyes as my _____.
2 I look like my _____.
3 My personality is quite similar to my _____'s.
4 My _____ and I both like _____.
5 I like _____ and so does my _____.
6 I don't like _____ and neither does my _____.

5 LISTENING

Facebook coincidence brings couple together

a 5 11))) Look at the photo of a couple and listen to a news story about them. What is the coincidence?

b Listen again and answer the questions.
1 Why did Kelly Hildebrandt put her name into Facebook?
2 What did she discover?
3 What did she do next?
4 What other things do they have in common?
5 Why were they worried?
6 What do they call each other?
7 What problem did they once have?
8 What are they definitely *not* going to do?

c Have you ever put your name into Google or Facebook? Did you discover anything interesting?

As schoolboys, the two Jims looked exactly ¹_____ each other. They ²_____ liked maths and carpentry – but hated spelling. After school they had ³_____ jobs: Lewis was a security guard and Springer was a deputy sheriff. Jim Lewis first married a woman called Linda, and then a woman called Betty, exactly the same names ⁴_____ Jim Springer's first and second wives. Even their tastes in sport are ⁵_____ – Jim Springer likes baseball and ⁶_____ does Jim Lewis. Jim Lewis doesn't like basketball and ⁷_____ does Jim Springer.

Practical English Time to go home

EPISODE 6

1 ROB AND JENNY TALK ABOUT THE FUTURE

a **5 12))** Watch or listen to Rob and Jenny. Mark the sentences **T** (true) or **F** (false).

1 Rob is going home today.
2 He says it will be difficult to stay in touch.
3 Jenny suggests that she could go to London.
4 Rob thinks it's a good idea.
5 They're going to a restaurant tonight.
6 Barbara wants to talk to Jenny.

> **British and American English**
> *You just missed him* = American English;
> *You've just missed him* = British English
> *cell (phone)* = American English;
> *mobile (phone)* = British English

b Watch or listen again. Say why the **F** sentences are false.

2 ON THE PHONE

a **5 13))** Cover the dialogue and watch or listen. Answer the questions.

1 Who does Rob want to speak to?
2 How many times does he have to call?

b Watch or listen again. Complete the **You Hear** phrases.

))) You Hear	You Say
Hello. *Broadway Grill*.	Oh, sorry. I have the wrong number.
NewYork24seven. _____ can I help you?	Hello. Can I speak to Barbara Keaton, please?
Just a second. I'll put you _____. ... Hello.	Hi, is that Barbara?
No, I'm sorry. She's not at her _____ right now.	Can I leave a message, please?
Sure.	Can you tell her Rob Walker called? I'll call back later.
I'll give her the _____. You could try her cell phone.	Yes, I'll do that. Thank you.
I'm sorry, I can't take your _____ at the moment. Please _____ a message after the beep.	Hello, Barbara. This is Rob returning your call.
NewYork24seven. How can I help you?	Hello. It's Rob again. Can I speak to Barbara, please?
Just a second. I'm sorry, the line's _____. Do you want to hold?	OK, I'll hold.
Hello.	Hi, Barbara. It's me, Rob.
Rob, hi! I tried to call you earlier.	What did you want to talk about?

c (5 14))) Watch or listen and repeat the **You Say** phrases. Copy the rhythm.

d Practise the dialogues with a partner.

e In pairs, roleplay the dialogue.

A (book open) You are the Broadway Grill, the receptionist, etc. You start *Hello. Broadway Grill.*
B (book closed) You want to speak to Barbara.

f Swap roles.

3 IN CENTRAL PARK AGAIN

a (5 15))) Watch or listen to Rob and Jenny. Is it a happy ending or a sad ending?

b Watch or listen again and answer the questions.
1 Who has some news?
2 What did Barbara offer Rob?
3 What did Jenny do this morning?
4 What does Jenny ask Barbara to do?

c Look at the **Social English** phrases. Can you remember any of the missing words?

Social English phrases
Rob You _____ first.
Jenny That's great _____.
Jenny I'll _____ her.
Jenny I'll explain _____.
Barbara Is everything _____ _____?
Jenny _____ better.

d (5 16))) Watch or listen and complete the phrases.

e Watch or listen again and repeat the phrases. How do you say them in your language?

Can you...?
☐ phone somebody and say who you are / who you want to talk to
☐ leave a message for somebody
☐ respond to news

G past perfect
V verb phrases
P contractions: had / hadn't

12A Strange but true!

Why did the people shout? Because a shark had come into the pool.

NEWS ROUND THE WORLD

Here is our selection of last week's true stories

AUSTRALIA

In Sydney, early in the morning, some swimmers were having a swim in an outdoor swimming pool which was very close to the sea. The swimmers were very surprised when suddenly the pool assistants started shouting 'Get out of the water! Quickly!' The swimmers immediately got out. Then they realized that there was a shark at the other end! _____ Fortunately none of the swimmers were hurt and the shark was caught in a net and put back into the sea.

ENGLAND

Security guards at Stansted airport were amazed when they saw a dog getting off a train and walking on its own towards the airport terminal. They caught the dog and took it to the police. Thanks to a microchip in its neck, they discovered that its name was Diesel and that it belonged to a woman called Sarah Chapman, who lived in London, 50 kilometres away. Sarah had gone on holiday for a few days and had left Diesel with some friends. _____ It had then got on a train and had travelled 50 kilometres to Stansted airport, changing trains on the way. Sarah said: 'I'm sure Diesel went to the airport to look for me!'

1 READING & SPEAKING

a Read the stories and look at the pictures. Complete the gaps with one of the sentences below.

AUSTRALIA
1 The shark had already attacked three people.
2 A large wave had carried the shark into the pool during the night.

ENGLAND
3 Unfortunately, the dog had bitten one of her friends.
4 The dog had run away and had gone to the local railway station.

ITALY
5 He had decided that he couldn't live with his mother and father for another day.
6 He had robbed a bank the night before.

SWEDEN
7 The woman had got confused at the check-in desk.
8 The woman had left her passport at home.

b Match verbs 1–10 with phrases A–J.

1 [H] get into / out of   A on the belt
2 [ ] get on / off   B a swim
3 [ ] free somebody   C holiday
4 [ ] realize   D in prison
5 [ ] put the luggage   E from prison
6 [ ] go on   F a train
7 [ ] have   G a woman
8 [ ] leave the dog   H the swimming pool
9 [ ] be   I with friends
10 [ ] belong to   J that there was a shark in the pool

ITALY

An Italian man who was in prison for stealing was freed early from prison on the condition that he promised to live with his parents at their house. But after a week he arrived at his local police station and said 'Please arrest me again!'

Guido Beneventi, 30, told the police: 'My parents spent all their time telling me to do housework. It was like being a child again!'

SWEDEN

Airport workers in the luggage area at Arlanda airport in Sweden were surprised to see an old lady sitting on the luggage belt next to her suitcase. She had put her luggage on the belt and then had sat down on the belt herself. A spokesman at Stockholm's Arlanda airport said 'Unfortunately, she did not understand when she was given check-in instructions. She got on the belt together with her bag. Luckily, it wasn't a long ride – only a few metres.'

2 GRAMMAR past perfect

a Look at these highlighted verbs from the Australia story. Answer the questions.

A Then they realized that there was a shark at the other end!

B A large wave had carried the shark into the pool during the night.

1 Which action happened first, **A** or **B**?
2 What are the two parts of the verb in sentence **B**?

b Look at the other three stories again (including the missing sentences) and underline examples of *had* + past participle. Did these actions happen before or after the main part of the story?

c ▶ **p.148 Grammar Bank 12A.** Learn more about the past perfect and practise it.

d Complete the following sentences in your own words. Use the past perfect.

1 When I got to the check-in desk I suddenly realized that…
2 When we arrived back from our holiday we found that…
3 When the film started I realized immediately that…
4 I couldn't answer any of the exam questions because I…
5 We spent 20 minutes in the car park looking for the car because we couldn't remember…

e Compare with a partner. Are your sentences the same or different?

f Work with a partner. **A** re-read the story about Australia, **B** re-read the story about Italy. Underline the key words and events. Then **A** (books closed) re-tell the story in your own words. **B** (books open) help **A** when necessary. Then swap.

3 PRONUNCIATION
contractions: *had / hadn't*

> 🔍 **Contractions: past perfect**
> In conversation we often contract *had* in the past perfect after a subject pronoun (*I, you*, etc.), e.g.
> When I got to the airport I realized that **I'd** forgotten my passport.
> I suddenly remembered that we **hadn't** told Sue about the party.

a 🔊 5 18 Listen and write six past perfect sentences. Then practise saying the sentences.

b ▶ **Communication** *What had happened?* **A** p.104 **B** p.109. Try to guess your partner's sentences.

4 LISTENING

a 🔊 5 19 Listen to another news story. Then number the events in order.

☐ Joey attacked her.
☐ Joey sat on her plate.
☐ Joey went to sleep.
☐ Katie came home from work.
☐ Katie met her neighbour.

b With a partner, try to guess what you think had happened.

c 🔊 5 20 Now listen and find out what had happened. Had anybody guessed right?

G reported speech
V say or tell?
P double consonants

12B Gossip is good for you

She told him she was leaving.
He said that he would write.

1 SPEAKING & LISTENING

a Read the dictionary definition and then answer the questions with a partner.

> **gossip** /ˈgɒsɪp/ *(v and n)* to talk about other people, especially their private life

1 What kind of people gossip more?
   a people in cities or people in small towns
   b young people or old people
   c men or women
2 Who do people most often gossip about?
   a their neighbours
   b people at work or school
   c celebrities
3 Do you have any friends who gossip a lot?
4 How do you feel when people gossip about *you*?

b 5 21))) Listen to a conversation between Rosemary and Iris. What has happened to Jack and Emma? Listen again and answer the questions.

1 Jack and Emma are the woman's…
   a neighbours. b friends. c children.
2 Rosemary thinks she heard them having…
   a a conversation.
   b a party.
   c an argument.
3 According to Rosemary, Emma said she was…
   a seeing another man.
   b looking for a new job.
   c going to stay with her mother.
4 She said she had…
   a left the dog with a neighbour.
   b left the children with her sister.
   c left the dinner in the microwave.
5 Iris is going to…
   a tell her husband.
   b tell her family.
   c tell another neighbour.

c 5 22))) Now listen to what Jack and Emma *really* said last night. Was Rosemary right about everything?

2 GRAMMAR reported speech

a Look at some extracts from the conversations. Compare what Emma said (direct speech) with what Rosemary says that she said (reported speech). Underline the words which are different in the highlighted reported speech.

1 **What Emma said**
   I'm going to stay with my mum.
   I won't come back…
   I've taken the children to my sister…

2 **What Rosemary and Iris said**
   She said that she was going to stay with her mum! She told him that she wouldn't come back.
   Ooh, how awful. What about the children?
   She said she'd taken them to her sister.

b ▶ p.148 **Grammar Bank 12B.** Learn more about reported speech and practise it.

c 5 24))) Listen to some sentences in direct speech. Say them in reported speech. Begin *He said…* or *She said…*

))) I'm in a hurry.   She said that she was in a hurry.

))) I'll write.   He said that he would write.

3 VOCABULARY say or tell?

Complete the sentences with the right form of *say* or *tell*.
1 'I have a problem,' Annie _____ .
2 Annie _____ us that she had a problem.
3 Lisa _____ that she was leaving her husband.
4 He _____ the teacher that he had left his homework at home.
5 His teacher _____ that he didn't believe him.
6 Can you _____ Mark that I can't meet him tonight?
7 What did you _____ to her?
8 When I was a child my mother used to _____ us not to _____ hello to people we didn't know.

4 SPEAKING

a Work in pairs. **A** tell your partner the following. **B** Listen and take notes. Then swap roles.

- something about your parents or grandparents
- a place you have been to
- something that you're planning to do in the summer
- something that you did last weekend

The information can be true or invented, but it must be interesting!

b Change partners. Tell partner 2 what partner 1 said. Decide together whether you think your previous partners were telling the truth or had invented the information.

He told me (that)...   He said (that)...

5 PRONUNCIATION double consonants

a Look at five groups of words. Match each group to a vowel sound.

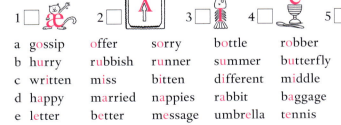

	1	2	3	4	5
a	gossip	offer	sorry	bottle	robber
b	hurry	rubbish	runner	summer	butterfly
c	written	miss	bitten	different	middle
d	happy	married	nappies	rabbit	baggage
e	letter	better	message	umbrella	tennis

b 🔊 5 25 Listen and check.

> 🔍 **Double consonants**
> The vowel sound before a double consonant is normally short when it is the stressed syllable, e.g. gossip /ɒ/, hurry /ʌ/, written /ɪ/, happy /æ/, and letter /e/.
> Double consonants are pronounced the same as single consonants.

c How do you think you pronounce the words below? Check the pronunciation and meaning with your dictionary.

kettle   nanny   pottery   slippers   supper

6 READING

HERE'S A SECRET:
Gossip might be good for you

We all enjoy gossiping about people we know, although sometimes we might **feel guilty** about it afterwards. However, new research shows that gossiping might be good for us.

Professor McAndrew, a professor of psychology, believes that gossiping is in our genes and we feel pleasure when we **share** interesting information. McAndrew says that gossiping is a **social skill**, and we need to learn to do it well. According to the professor, gossip can be a positive thing when people use it to build connections with other people in their social group. But it can be a negative thing when somebody gossips about another person only to make themselves feel more important in the group.

Professor McAndrew's research also showed that people were happy to **pass on** good news but only if it was about a friend. They also enjoyed passing on negative information about other people when it was about somebody they disliked.

Another thing that the new study showed was that men and women gossip differently. **In general**, the men in the study shared gossip with their wives or girlfriends, but not with their male friends. Women however, gossiped with both partners and friends.

Adapted from a British newspaper

a Read the article and mark the sentences **T** (true) or **F** (false).
1 We sometimes feel bad after we gossip.
2 Professor McAndrew says that we are programmed to gossip.
3 Gossiping can be good or bad – it depends on why we do it.
4 People enjoy sharing bad news about people they like.
5 Men gossip with their friends more than with their family.

b Look at the **highlighted** words and phrases. With a partner, guess their meaning.

c Do you agree with what the article says about the way men and women gossip?

7 🔊 5 26 SONG
I Heard It Through the Grapevine 🎵

G questions without auxiliaries
V revision
P revision

12C The *English File* quiz

"Who painted that picture?"
"I can't remember."

1 GRAMMAR questions without auxiliaries

a With a partner, see how many of the quiz questions you can answer from memory.

b Now try to find the answers you couldn't remember in Files 1–11.

c Look at 1 and 2 in the quiz. Answer these questions.
1 How is question 1 different from question 2?
2 What is the subject of the verb in question 1?
3 What is the subject of the verb in question 2?
4 Which other questions in the quiz are similar grammatically to question 1?

d ▶ p.148 **Grammar Bank 12C.** Learn more about questions without auxiliaries and practise them.

The **ENGLISH FILE** QUIZ

1 Who painted *Mr and Mrs Clark and Percy*?
2 How did Caroline de Bendern lose a fortune?
3 Which airport in Asia has a pet hotel?
4 What does *toy boy* mean?
5 Whose wedding dress did Lindka Cierach design?
6 What vitamin does sunlight produce?
7 Who plays Dr House in the series *House M.D.*?
8 What did Captain Edward Murphy give his name to?
9 How many natural disasters did Mr and Mrs Svanström experience on their round-the-world trip?
10 Who wrote the short story *Girl*?
11 Which singer made reggae popular all over the world?
12 Who invented the dishwasher, a man or a woman?
13 Who never arrived at school on time when he was a child?
14 Who shouted 'You CANNOT be serious!' at a tennis umpire at Wimbledon?
15 What is Kelly Hildebrandt's husband called?

2 WRITING & SPEAKING

a ▶ **Communication** *General knowledge quiz* **A** *p.105* **B** *p.110*. First write the questions. Then ask them to your partner.

b With a partner, make your own quiz. Write two questions with or without auxiliaries for each category. Make sure you know the answers!

c Ask your questions to another pair.

HISTORY

MUSIC

SCIENCE

ART

CINEMA

11 & 12 Revise and Check

GRAMMAR

Circle a, b, or c.

1 The golf ball _____ the hole, and everybody cheered.
   a went on   b went   c went into
2 The door opened and two men _____.
   a came out   b came out of   c out
3 Your towel's on the floor. _____!
   a Pick up it   b Pick up   c Pick it up
4 I've lost my keys. Can you help me _____?
   a look them for
   b look for them
   c look after them
5 A I love travelling.   B _____.
   a So do I   b Neither do I   c So am I
6 A I can't do this exercise.   B _____.
   a So can I
   b Neither can't I
   c Neither can I
7 A I went to the cinema last night.
   B _____. What did you see?
   a So went I   b So I did   c So did I
8 I was too late and when I got to the station _____.
   a the train has left
   b the train had left
   c the train left
9 When we got to the airport we remembered that we _____ all the windows in our house.
   a hadn't closed
   b didn't close
   c haven't closed
10 Lisa told me that she _____ to marry Nigel.
   a wants   b want   c wanted
11 Kevin said he _____ back in ten minutes.
   a would be   b was   c will be
12 My grandfather _____ that he had worked in a factory when he was young.
   a said us   b told   c told us
13 Who _____ in the house next door?
   a lives   b live   c does live
14 Where _____ that dress?
   a you bought   b bought you   c did you buy
15 How many people _____ to go on the excursion?
   a do want   b does want   c want

VOCABULARY

a Complete with a word from the list.

along   down   into   off   out   back   past   towards   through   up

1 We drove _____ a lot of tunnels on our way to St Moritz.
2 When it started to rain we went _____ a café to wait until it stopped.
3 She walked _____ the street, looking in all the shop windows.
4 When the dog started running _____ me I was terrified.
5 Go _____ the petrol station, and it's the next turning on the right.
6 You have to take _____ your shoes before going into the temple.
7 If you don't know the meaning of a word, look it _____ in the online dictionary.
8 Can you turn _____ the heating? It's very hot in here.
9 If you don't like the jacket, take it _____ to the shop.
10 Can you find _____ what time the film finishes?

b Complete the missing words.

1 Julia and Jane are **i**_____ twins.
2 I live in the same street **a**_____ my sister.
3 Her new novel is quite **s**_____ to her last one.
4 Dave isn't very tall and **n**_____ is his son.
5 My parents **b**_____ love classical music.

c Complete the phrases with a verb from the list.

do   get   give   go   have   leave   look   put   tell   turn

1 _____ skiing   6 _____ up the music
2 _____ on your coat   7 _____ a swim
3 _____ me a story   8 _____ off the train
4 _____ forward to sth   9 _____ up smoking
5 _____ your dog with friends   10 _____ karate

PRONUNCIATION

a Circle the word with a different sound.

1 ʌ   hurry   rugby   summer   put
2 ɪ   find   written middle   fill
3 aʊ   around   down   through   out
4 θ   neither throw   nothing   both
5 dʒ   gossip   together message   negative

b Underline the stressed syllable.

1 ath|le|tics   2 to|wards   3 for|ward   4 si|mi|lar   5 di|fferent

CAN YOU UNDERSTAND THIS TEXT?

a Read the article once. What was the amazing coincidence?

b Read the article again and number the events in the order they happened

- [ ] Their daughter was born.
- [ ] They both had a heart operation in the same hospital.
- [ ] Alistair had another heart operation.
- [ ] They got married.
- [ ] They discovered that they had been in the same hospital twenty years earlier.
- [ ] They discovered they had the same heart problem.
- [ ] They met at a swimming pool.
- [ ] Alistair asked Alison to marry him.

c Look at the highlighted words or phrases in the text. Guess their meaning from the context. Check with your teacher or with a dictionary.

Heart couple's amazing coincidence

When Suzanne met Alistair Cotton at a swimming pool in the UK in 1995, they were amazed to discover that they both suffered from the same extremely rare heart condition. They started going out together and fell in love, but several months later they discovered an **even** bigger coincidence.

Almost twenty years earlier when they were children (Suzanne was seven and Alistair was fourteen) they had both had a life-saving heart operation in the same hospital, on the same day performed by the same **heart surgeon**. After their operations, they had spent several days **recovering** in the same hospital ward (although they have no memories of seeing or speaking to each other.) They certainly had no idea that twenty years later they would meet and fall in love with the child in the next bed. Suzanne, now 43, said, 'We were very shocked by the coincidence. We were obviously **destined** to be together.'

After Alistair and Suzanne moved in together Alistair continued to have difficulties with his heart and he had to have another **major** heart operation. As soon as he woke up after the operation, he **proposed** to Suzanne and the couple got married in 2002.

The following year, Suzanne **became pregnant** and baby Hannah was born in 2004 and is now a happy, healthy child who shows no signs of having **inherited** any heart problems from her parents. Suzanne said, 'Many heart patients can't have children or their children are born with heart problems themselves, so for our amazing story to have such a happy ending is just wonderful.'

Adapted from a British newspaper

CAN YOU UNDERSTAND THESE PEOPLE?

5 28)) **In the street** Watch or listen to five people and answer the questions.

Nick　　Ruth　　Hew　　Andy　　Alison

1 The twins that Nick knows _____.
  a have very similar personalities
  b are very similar in appearance
  c have the same appearance and personality
2 Ruth doesn't mind losing when _____.
  a the person who wins is better than she is
  b she has really enjoyed the game
  c she thinks she hasn't played very well
3 The sport Hew doesn't mention is _____.
  a cycling b hockey c rugby
4 Andy _____.
  a was an evening person in the past
  b was a morning person in the past
  c has never been good in the morning
5 Alison thinks that _____.
  a women gossip more than men
  b men gossip more than women
  c men and women both gossip

CAN YOU SAY THIS IN ENGLISH?

Do the tasks with a partner. Tick (✓) the box if you can do them.

Can you…?

1 [ ] describe three things that you have to do in certain sports using a verb and a preposition of movement
2 [ ] make true sentences with *take off*, *turn down*, and *look after*
3 [ ] say true things about you – your partner responds with *so (am I, etc.)* and *neither (do I, etc.)*
4 [ ] continue these sentences with the past perfect:
   a I got to the station, but…
   b When I saw him I was surprised because…
5 [ ] report two things that somebody said to you yesterday using *said* or *told me*
6 [ ] ask your partner three questions without an auxiliary verb beginning with *Who*, *How many*, and *Which*

Short films Sports in New Zealand
Watch and enjoy a film on iTutor.

Communication

1A WHAT'S HIS NAME? HOW DO YOU SPELL IT? Student A

1 Jessica _____   2 _____ Hughes   3 Bethany _____
4 _____ Dixon   5 Abigail _____   6 _____ Kelly

a Ask **B** questions to complete the missing information.

   Photo 1 – What's her surname? How do you spell it?

b Answer **B**'s questions.

> 🔍 **Asking for repetition**
> If you don't hear or understand somebody, you can say:
> Sorry?   Can you say that again?   Can you repeat that?

1B ALEXANDER AND OLIVER Student A

a Ask **B** questions and complete the chart for Oliver.

Name	Alexander	Oliver
How old / ?	32	
Where / from?	London	
Where / live?	Brighton	
What / do?	journalist	
What / like?	modern art, classical music	
What / not like?	sport	

b Answer **B**'s questions about Alexander.

1C DESCRIBE AND DRAW Student A

a Look at your painting for a minute.
b Describe your painting for **B** to draw.
c Listen to **B** describing his / her painting. Try to draw it. Don't look at it. Ask **B** questions to help you.
d Now compare your drawings with the original paintings. Are they similar?

2B AT, IN, ON Student A

a Ask **B** your questions.
   1 When were you born?
   2 Where do you usually have breakfast?
   3 What time do you usually have lunch?
   4 What days of the week do you usually go out in the evening?
   5 What time of day do you usually do your English homework?
   6 When do you usually have a holiday?
   7 Where do you normally listen to music?
   8 When's your birthday?

b Answer **B**'s questions using *at*, *in*, or *on*. Ask *What about you?* for each question.

2C HAPPY ENDING

1 Why didn't Hannah see the man who was crossing the road?
2 Who was the man?
3 Why did he cross without looking?
4 Where did they go after that?
5 What did they order?
6 Why was Jamie in the High Street?
7 What and when was the concert?
8 What was special about the day?

3A WHAT ARE YOUR PLANS?
Student A

a Ask **B** your questions using *going to*. Ask for more information.

- What / you / do after class?
- What time / you / get up tomorrow?
- Where / you / have lunch tomorrow?
- What / you / do on Saturday night?
- Where / you / go for your next holiday?
- / you / study English next year?

b Answer **B**'s questions. Give more information.

3C WHAT'S THE WORD? Student A

a Look at the six words or phrases on your card. Think for a minute how you are going to define them.

photo   lazy   trainers

go sightseeing (*verb*)   Arrivals   passenger

b You have two minutes to communicate your words to **B**. Remember you <u>can't</u> use any part or form of the words on the card.

c Now listen to **B**'s definitions. Try to guess the words.

4A HAS HE DONE IT YET? Students A+B

Look at the picture for one minute and try to remember what's in it. Then go to p.102.

5A HOW FAST IS YOUR LIFE?
Students A+B

Check your partner's score and tell him or her. Then read to see what it means.

How to score:
1 point for never
2 points for sometimes
3 points for often

Is your score between 6 and 9? You are living life in the slow lane. Compared to most people you take things easy and don't get stressed by modern-day living. You are patient, relaxed, and easy-going. Most of the time this is good news, but sometimes it can be a problem. For example, are you sometimes late for appointments?

Is your score between 10 and 14? You have a medium pace of life. You are probably somebody who can change the speed at which you live depending on the situation.

Is your score between 15 and 18? You are living life in the fast lane, rushing around and trying to do many different activities and projects at the same time. You are impatient and you find it difficult to relax. You are probably very productive, but your relationships and health could suffer as a result.

Adapted from Richard Wiseman's Quirkology website

Communication

4A HAS HE DONE IT YET?
Students A+B

a Work individually. Look at the list of things Max always does every morning. Has he already done them? Try to remember what was in the picture. Write sentences.

He's already made the bed.
OR *He hasn't made the bed yet.*
- make the bed
- wash up his coffee cups
- tidy his desk
- pick up his towel
- take the dog for a walk
- turn off his computer
- put his clothes in the cupboard
- have a shower
- have breakfast

b Work in pairs. Compare your sentences with your partner. Are they the same? Then go back to p.101 and compare your sentences with the picture. Were you right?

5B THE FRIENDLIEST CITY   Student A

a Read about what happened when Tim did the three tests in New York. Try to remember the information.

New York

The photo test
I asked an office worker who was eating his sandwiches to take a photo of me. He was really friendly and said 'Of course I'll take your picture.' When I asked him to take more photos he said 'Sure! No problem.' When he gave me back my camera he said 'Have a nice day!'

The shopping test
I went shopping near Times Square and I bought an 'I love New York' T-shirt and some drinks from two different people. I gave them too much money, but they both gave me the exact change back.

The accident test
I went to Central Park and I fell over. I only had to wait about thirty seconds before a man came to help me. 'Is this your camera?' he said, 'I think it's broken.'

b In your own words tell **B** and **C** what happened in New York.

First he did the photo test...

c Listen to **B** and **C** tell you what happened in Paris and Rome.

d Together decide which of the cities is the friendliest so far.

6B I'LL / SHALL I? GAME   Students A+B

Play the game.

6C DREAMS Student A

a Last night you dreamt about these things. Prepare to tell **B** about your dream.

b **B** is a psychoanalyst. Tell him / her about your dream. He / she will tell you what it means.

> Last night I dreamt about a river...

c Swap roles. Now you are a psychoanalyst. Listen to **B**'s dream. Number the things below in the order he / she talks about them.

- ☐ **Ice cream** – you will get some money (from the lottery or from a relative).
- ☐ **Long hair** – you want to be free. Perhaps you have problems with your family or a partner.
- ☐ **A key** – you have a problem and you are looking for a solution.
- ☐ **People speaking other languages** – you think your life is boring and you would like to have a more exciting life.
- ☐ **Travelling by bus** – you are worried about a person who is controlling your life.

d Now use the information in **c** to interpret **B**'s dream.

> 🔍 **Useful language**
> First you dreamt about...
> This tells me that...
> This means you are going to...
> This represents...

7A HOW TO... Student A

a Read the article **How to survive at a party**. Then without looking at the text tell **B** the five tips. When you finish decide with **B** which is the most important tip.

> ### How to... Survive at a Party (when you don't know anybody)
>
> 1 **Don't stand in the corner.** You need to be positive. Find somebody you think you would like to talk to and introduce yourself.
> 2 **Try to ask impersonal questions** like 'I love your bag. Where did you get it?' This will help to start a conversation.
> 3 **Don't dominate the conversation.** When you are nervous it's very easy to talk about yourself all the time. Nobody wants to listen to your life story when they have just met you for the first time.
> 4 **Smile!** Use your body language to give a positive, friendly impression.
> 5 **If you need to escape** from a really boring person, say that you are going to the bar to get a drink or that you need to go to the bathroom. Don't come back!

b **B** will tell you five tips for **How to survive a first date**. Listen and when he or she finishes decide together which is the most important tip.

8A WHAT SHOULD I DO? Student A

a Read problem 1 to **B**. He / she will give you some advice.

> **Problems**
> 1 I don't know what to get my boyfriend / girlfriend for his / her birthday. It's tomorrow!
> 2 I have problems going to sleep at night.
> 3 My children want a dog, but my husband / wife is allergic to animals.
> 4 My neighbour's dog barks all the time and it's driving me crazy!
> 5 My laptop isn't working well – it's very slow.

b Thank **B** and say:

That's a good idea.
OR Thanks, but that's not a very good idea because...

c Now listen to **B**'s problem 1. Give him / her advice. Begin with one of the phrases below.

I think you should...   You shouldn't...   I don't think you should...

d Continue with problems 2–5.

Communication

8C READING DIALOGUE Students A+B

a   Work with a partner. First practise saying the names.

Hartley /ˈhɑːtli/   the Montgomerys /mɒnˈɡʌməriːz/
Vivienne /ˈvɪvien/   Héloise /eluːˈiːz/

b   Act out the dialogue. Use the adverbs in brackets to help you, and remember to pause at the commas.

H   (anxiously) Vivienne, you didn't answer my last letter. It took me a week to find your new address! Why didn't you answer me? You knew I was waiting to see you and hear from you.

V   (slowly) Mr. Hartley, I don't know what to say to you. I understand all the advantages of your offer, and sometimes I feel sure that I could be happy with you. But then sometimes I am less sure. I was born a city girl, and I am not sure that I would enjoy living a quiet life in the suburbs.

H   My dear girl, you will have everything that you want. You can come to the city for the theatre, for shopping, and to visit your friends as often as you want. You can trust me, can't you?

V   (seriously) I trust you completely. I know you are the kindest of men, and that the girl who you get will be very lucky. I heard all about you when I was at the Montgomerys'.

H   Ah! I remember so well the evening I first saw you at the Montgomerys'. I will never forget that dinner. Come on, Vivienne, promise me. I want you. Nobody else will ever give you such a happy home.
(suspiciously) Tell me, Vivienne, is there – is there someone else?

V   (defensively) You shouldn't ask that, Mr. Hartley. But I will tell you. There is one other person – but I haven't promised him anything.

H   (masterfully) Vivienne, you must be mine.

V   (calmly) Do you think for one moment that I could come to your home while Héloise is there?

c   Change roles.

12A WHAT HAD HAPPENED? Student A

a   Look at the odd numbered sentences (1, 3, 5, 7, 9, and 11) and think of the missing verb (+ = positive verb, − = negative verb). Don't write anything yet!

1 Diana was very angry because her husband _____ the dinner. −
2 We went back to see the house where we **had lived** when we were children.
3 He couldn't catch the plane because he _____ his passport. +
4 The flat was very dirty because nobody **had cleaned** it for a long time.
5 We went back to the hotel where we _____ on our honeymoon. +
6 The crocodile was hungry because it **hadn't eaten** anything for two days.
7 After I left the shop I suddenly remembered that I _____ for the jacket. −
8 I ran to the station, but the last train **had gone**.
9 Miriam was surprised to hear that she _____ the exam. +
10 I didn't want to lend Jane the book because I **hadn't read** it.
11 Jack was angry because I _____ him to my party. −
12 They got to the cinema late and the film **had started**.

b   Read sentence 1 to **B**. If it's not right, try again until **B** tells you 'That's right'. Then write in the verb.

c   Listen to **B** say sentence 2. If it's the same as 2 above, say 'That's right'. If not, say 'Try again' until **B** gets it right.

d   Take it in turns with sentences 3–12.

9A WOULD YOU KNOW WHAT TO DO? Student A

a   Read the answers to **In the city**.

b   Tell **B** and **C** the right answers, and why the other ones are wrong.

c   Listen to **B** and **C** tell you about the other sections (**In the country** and **In the water**). Check your answers.

> **In the city**
>
> 1 **The answer is b.** Dogs like to attack any part of you that is moving, usually hands or arms. It is also dangerous to turn your back on the dog. You shouldn't look the dog in its eyes because this will make him angry. Shouting 'down' or 'go away' at the dog will not work because dogs usually only react to their master's voice.
>
> 2 **The answer is a.** Bees will usually fly out of an open window, but don't wave your hands around as bees follow movement and might try to sting you. And you mustn't hit the bee as this will make the bee very angry. Of course, as soon as you can you should stop the car and open the doors.

10A PASSIVES QUIZ Student A

a Complete your sentences with the verb in the passive and the right answer.

1 Until 1664 New York _____ (call)…
   a New Amsterdam
   b New Hampshire
   c New Liberty
2 The *Star Wars* films _____ (direct) by…
   a George Lucas
   b Steven Spielberg
   c Stanley Kubrick
3 The noun which _____ (use) most frequently in conversation is…
   a money   b time   c work
4 Penguins _____ (find)…
   a at the South Pole
   b at the North Pole
   c in Alaska
5 The Italian flag _____ (design) by…
   a Garibaldi   b Mussolini   c Napoleon
6 The first mobile phones _____ (sell) in…
   a 1963   b 1973   c 1983
7 The politician Winston Churchill _____ (born)…
   a on a train   b in a toilet   c under a bridge
8 The electric chair _____ (invent) by…
   a a teacher   b a dentist   c a politician

b Read your sentences to **B**. **B** will tell you if you are right.

c Now listen to **B**'s sentences. Say if he / she is right.

B's answers
1 The Smartphone was invented by IBM.
2 The *Lord of the Rings* films were directed by Peter Jackson.
3 The book which is stolen most often from libraries is *The Guinness Book of Records*.
4 In the world, 16,000 babies are born every hour.
5 Chess was invented by the Chinese.
6 The first Levi jeans were worn by miners.
7 Football was first played by the British.
8 In 1962 the original London Bridge was bought by a rich American.

12C GENERAL KNOWLEDGE QUIZ Student A

a Complete your questions with the verb in brackets in the past simple.

1 Who _____ the battle of Waterloo in 1815? (lose)
   a Duke of Wellington
   b Bismarck
   c **Napoleon**
2 Which Spanish actress _____ an Oscar in 2006? (win)
   a **Penelope Cruz**
   b Salma Hayek
   c Cameron Diaz
3 Who _____ the film *Avatar*? (direct)
   a Steven Spielberg
   b **James Cameron**
   c Ridley Scott
4 Which Formula 1 driver _____ in 2007, but returned to racing in 2010? (retire)
   a Fernando Alonso
   b **Michael Schumacher**
   c Sebastian Vettel
5 Which Roman Emperor _____ 'I came I saw I conquered'? (say)
   a Augustus   b Nero   c **Julius Caesar**
6 Who _____ the world record for the 100 and 200 metres race at the Beijing Olympics? (break)
   a **Usain Bolt**
   b Carl Lewis
   c Michael Johnson
7 Which painter _____ off part of his ear? (cut)
   a Picasso   b **Van Gogh**   c Matisse
8 Who _____ penicillin? (discover)
   a **Alexander Fleming**
   b James Watson
   c Thomas Edison

b Ask **B** your questions. Give your partner one mark for each correct answer.

c Answer **B**'s questions. Who got the most right answers?

Communication

1A WHAT'S HIS NAME? HOW DO YOU SPELL IT? Student B

1 _____ Dylan 2 Kieran _____ 3 _____ Webb
4 Cally _____ 5 _____ Scott 6 Michael _____

a Answer **A**'s questions.

b Ask **A** questions to complete the missing information.

   Photo 1 – What's her first name? How do you spell it?

> **Asking for repetition**
> If you don't hear or understand somebody, you can say:
> Sorry?   Can you say that again?   Can you repeat that?

1B ALEXANDER AND OLIVER Student B

a Answer **A**'s questions about Oliver.

Name	Alexander	Oliver
How old / ?		25
Where / from?		Scotland
Where / live?		London
What / do?		doctor
What / like?		sport, music, good books and films
What / not like?		clubs and discos

b Ask **A** questions and complete the chart for Alexander.

1C DESCRIBE AND DRAW Student B

a Look at your painting for a minute.

b Listen to **A** describing his / her painting. Try to draw it. Don't look at it. Ask **A** questions to help you.

c Now describe your painting for **A** to draw.

d Compare your drawings with the original paintings. Are they similar?

2B AT, IN, ON Student B

a Answer **A**'s questions using *at*, *in*, or *on*. Ask *What about you?* for each question.

b Ask **A** your questions.
  1 Where were you born?
  2 What time do you usually get up during the week?
  3 Where do you usually have lunch?
  4 What time of day do you usually meet friends?
  5 When do you usually go shopping?
  6 Where do you usually do your English homework?
  7 When do you do housework?
  8 Where can you have a nice walk near where you live?

3A WHAT ARE YOUR PLANS? Student B

a Answer **A**'s questions. Give more information.

b Ask **A** your questions using *going to*. Ask for more information.
- / you / go out this evening?
- What / you / have for dinner tonight?
- What / you / wear tomorrow?
- / you / go anywhere next weekend?
- What / you / do next summer?
- When / you / do your English homework?

3C WHAT'S THE WORD? Student B

a Look at the six words or phrases on your card. Think for a minute how you are going to define them.

a painting   generous   shorts

book a flight (*verb*)   Check-in   a nurse

b Listen to **A**'s definitions. Try to guess the words.

c You have two minutes to communicate your words to **A**. Remember you <u>can't</u> use any part or form of the words on the card.

5B THE FRIENDLIEST CITY Student B

a Read about what happened when Tim did the three tests in Paris. Try to remember the information.

> ### Paris
>
> **The photo test**
> I was standing in front of the Eiffel Tower and I asked some gardeners to take some photos of me. They couldn't stop laughing when they saw my hat, but they took the photos.
>
> **The shopping test**
> I went to a greengrocer's and I bought some fruit. I gave the man a lot of euro coins and he carefully took the exact amount.
>
> **The accident test**
> I fell over in the Champs Elysées. The street was very busy, but after a minute someone stopped and said to me, 'Are you OK?' He was Scottish!

b Listen to **A** tell you what happened in New York.

c In your own words tell **A** and **C** what happened in Paris.

> *First he did the photo test...*

d Listen to **C** tell you what happened in Rome.

e Together decide which of the cities is the friendliest so far.

7A HOW TO... Student B

a Read the article **How to survive a first date**.

b **A** will tell you five tips for **How to survive at a party**. Listen and when he or she finishes decide together which is the most important tip.

c Look again quickly at **How to survive a first date**. Then without looking at the text tell **A** the five tips. When you finish decide with **A** which is the most important tip.

How to ... Survive a First Date (and make a success of it)

1. **Think carefully about what to wear** for the date. If you are a man, try to dress smartly but casually (no suits!). If you are a woman, it's important not to dress too sexily. Don't wear too much perfume or aftershave!
2. **Choose a place that isn't too expensive** (you don't know who is going to pay). Try to go somewhere that isn't very noisy.
3. **Don't be too romantic** on a first date. For example, arriving with a red rose on a first date isn't a good idea!
4. **Remember to listen more than you talk** but don't let the conversation die. Silence is a killer on a first date! Be natural. Don't pretend to be somebody you aren't.
5. **If you are a man,** be a gentleman and pay the bill at the end of the evening. **If you are a woman,** offer to pay your half of the bill (but don't insist!).

Communication

6C DREAMS Student B

a   Last night you dreamt about these things. Prepare to tell **A** about your dream.

b   You are a psychoanalyst. Listen to **A**'s dream. Number the things below in the order he / she talks about them.

- ☐ **Having a bath** – you have a secret which nobody knows about.
- ☐ **Dogs** – you are looking for friends.
- ☐ **Losing hair** – you are going to lose some money.
- ☐ **Lost luggage** – a problem you have will soon get better.
- ☐ **A river** – you are going to be very lucky.

c   Now use the information in **b** to interpret **A**'s dream.

> **Useful language**
> First you dreamt about…
> This tells me that…
> This means you are going to…
> This represents…

d   Swap roles. Now **A** is a psychoanalyst. Tell him / her about your dream. **A** will tell you what it means.

Last night I dreamt about ice-cream…

8A WHAT SHOULD I DO? Student B

a   Listen to **A**'s problem 1. Give him / her advice. Begin with one of the phrases below.

I think you should…   You shouldn't…   I don't think you should…

b   Read your problem 1 to **A**. He / she will give you some advice.

> **Problems**
> 1   I share a flat with a friend but he / she never does the washing-up!
> 2   I want to take my boyfriend / girlfriend somewhere really special on Saturday night.
> 3   I need some new clothes for a wedding, but I don't know what to buy.
> 4   I think I'm getting a cold – I have a headache and a cough.
> 5   My sister always borrows my clothes, and when I want to wear them they're dirty.

c   Thank **A** and say:

That's a good idea.
OR Thanks, but that's not a very good idea because…

d   Continue with problems 2–5.

9A WOULD YOU KNOW WHAT TO DO? Student B

a   Read the answers to **In the country**.

> **In the country**
> 3   **The answer is c.** If you tie a bandage or a piece of material above the bite, this will stop the poison from getting to your heart too quickly. However, be careful not to tie it too tightly. You shouldn't put ice or anything cold on the bite, as this will make it more difficult to get the poison out later, and never try to suck out the poison. If it gets into your mouth, it might go into your blood.
> 4   **The answer is b.** If you are lucky, the bull will change direction to follow the hat or bag and give you time to escape. It doesn't matter what colour the shirt is, bulls don't see colour, they only see movement. Don't try to run away, as bulls can run incredibly fast, and you mustn't shout or wave your arms because this will attract the bull's attention even more.

b   Listen to **A** tell you about **In the city**. Check your answers.

c   Tell **A** and **C** the right answers for **In the country**, and why the other ones are wrong.

d   Listen to **C** tell you about **In the water**. Check your answers.

10A PASSIVES QUIZ Student B

a Complete your sentences with the verb in the passive and the right answer.

1 The Smartphone _____ (invent) by…
   a Apple   b Nokia   c IBM
2 The *Lord of the Rings* films _____ (direct) by…
   a Steven Spielberg
   b James Cameron
   c Peter Jackson
3 The book which _____ (steal) most often from libraries is…
   a The Bible
   b *The Guinness Book of Records*
   c *The Lord of the Rings*
4 In the world, 16,000 babies _____ (born)…
   a every second   b every hour   c every day
5 Chess _____ (invent) by…
   a the Egyptians   b the Indians   c the Chinese
6 The first Levi jeans _____ (wear) by…
   a miners   b farmers   c cowboys
7 Football _____ first _____ (play) by…
   a the British   b the Romans   c the Greeks
8 In 1962 the original London Bridge _____ (buy) by…
   a a rich American
   b a museum
   c the Royal family

b Listen to **A**'s sentences. Say if he / she is right.

A's answers
1 Until 1664 New York was called New Amsterdam.
2 The *Star Wars* films were directed by George Lucas.
3 The noun which is used most frequently in conversation is *time*.
4 Penguins are found at the South Pole.
5 The Italian flag was designed by Napoleon.
6 The first mobile phones were sold in 1983.
7 The politician Winston Churchill was born in a toilet.
8 The electric chair was invented by a dentist.

c Read your sentences to **A**. **A** will tell you if you are right.

12A WHAT HAD HAPPENED? Student B

a Look at the even numbered sentences (2, 4, 6, 8, 10, and 12) and think of the missing verb (+ = positive verb, - = negative verb). Don't write anything yet!

1 Diana was very angry because her husband **hadn't cooked** the dinner.
2 We went back to see the house where we _____ when we were children. +
3 He couldn't catch the plane because he **had forgotten** his passport.
4 The flat was very dirty because nobody _____ it for a long time. +
5 We went back to the hotel where we **had stayed** on our honeymoon.
6 The crocodile was hungry because it _____ anything for two days. -
7 After I left the shop I suddenly remembered that I **hadn't paid** for the jacket.
8 I ran to the station, but the last train _____. +
9 Miriam was surprised to hear that she **had passed** the exam.
10 I didn't want to lend Jane the book because I _____ it. -
11 Jack was angry because I **hadn't invited** him to my party.
12 They got to the cinema late and the film _____. +

b Listen to **A** say sentence 1. If it's the same as 1 above, say 'That's right'. If not, say 'Try again' until **A** gets it right.

c Read sentence 2 to **A**. If it's not right, try again until **A** tells you 'That's right'. Then write in the verb.

d Take it in turns with sentences 3–12.

2C SAD ENDING

1 Why didn't Hannah see the man who was crossing the road?
2 What happened?
3 Where did she go then and what did she do?
4 Who arrived at her house two hours later?
5 What news did she have for Hannah?
6 How was Jamie?
7 What did she tell Hannah about the car and the driver?
8 What happened in the end?

Communication

12C GENERAL KNOWLEDGE QUIZ Student B

a Complete your questions with the verb in brackets in the past simple.

1 Who _____ President of the USA eight years after his father had been the US president? (become)
  a Bill Clinton
  b John F Kennedy
  c **George Bush**
2 Who _____ the part of the mother in the film *Mamma Mia*? (play)
  a **Meryl Streep**
  b Julia Roberts
  c Sandra Bullock
3 Which tennis player _____ Wimbledon five years in a row between 2003 and 2007? (win)
  a **Roger Federer**
  b Rafael Nadal
  c Novak Djokovic
4 Who _____ the Sistine Chapel? (paint)
  a Leonardo da Vinci
  b **Michelangelo**
  c Raphael
5 Which film _____ eleven Oscars in 2003? (win)
  a *The King's Speech*
  b *The Queen*
  c ***The Return of the King***
6 Who _____ a wooden horse to enter the city of Troy? (use)
  a **the Greeks**
  b The Romans
  c The Persians
7 Which famous boxer _____ to fight in the Vietnam war in 1967? (refuse)
  a **Muhammad Ali**
  b Joe Frazier
  c Sugar Ray Robinson
8 Who _____ the telephone? (invent)
  a Marconi   b **Bell**   c Stephens

b Answer A's questions.

c Ask A your questions. Give your partner one mark for each correct answer. Who got the most right answers?

5B THE FRIENDLIEST CITY Student C

a Read about what happened when Tim did the three tests in Rome. Try to remember the information.

Rome

The photo test
I asked a very chic woman who was wearing sunglasses to take some photos. She took a photo of me with my hat on, then without my hat. Then another photo with my sunglasses. Then she asked me to take a photo of her!

The shopping test
I bought a copy of *The Times* newspaper from a newspaper seller near the railway station. It was three euros. I gave the man four euros and he didn't give me any change.

The accident test
I went to a busy street near the station. When I fell over about eight people immediately hurried to help me.

b Listen to **A** and **B** tell you what happened in New York and Paris.

c In your own words tell **A** and **B** what happened in Rome.

First he did the photo test...

d Together decide which of the cities is the friendliest so far.

9A WOULD YOU KNOW WHAT TO DO? Student C

a Read the answers to **In the water**.

In the water

5 **The answer is c.** If a jellyfish stings you, you should clean the sting with vinegar as this stops the poison. If you don't have any vinegar, then use sea water. But don't use fresh water, for example water from a tap or mineral water, as this will make the sting hurt more. And you shouldn't rub the sting as this will make it worse too. After you have washed the sting, you should clean off any bits of tentacles that are on your skin. And take a pain killer!

6 **The answer is a.** If you are near the shore and the shark is not too close, you can probably swim to the shore without attracting its attention. For this reason it is important to swim smoothly and not splash or make sudden movements. Keeping still is dangerous because if the shark swims in your direction it will see you and it will attack you. Don't shout because shouting will provoke the shark and it will attack you.

b Listen to **A** and **B** tell you the answers in the other sections (**In the city** and **In the country**). Check your answers.

c Tell **A** and **B** the right answers for **In the water**, and why the other ones are wrong.

Writing

1 DESCRIBING A PERSON

a Read Charlie's email. The computer has found ten mistakes. They are grammar, punctuation, or spelling mistakes. Can you correct them?

From: Charlie [barcacarlos@hotmail.com]
To: Lucy [lucyathome1989@yahoo.com]
Subject: Hi from Spain

Hi Lucy

My name's Charlie. Well, it's really Carlos but everyone calls me Charlie. I'm from Barcelona and I live at home with my parents and my dog. I have 21 years old, and I'm at university. I'm studing physics. I'm in my last year and I really like it.

I'm going to tell you about myself. As you can see from the foto, I have black hair and browns eyes. My father always says I have a big nose, but I don't think so, I think it's a Roman nose!

I think I'm a positive person. My freinds say I'm funny and it's true, I like making people laugh. But I can to be serious too when I need to be!

I dont have many free time becuase when I'm not in class I have to do projects or write reports. But when I can, I like watching TV series, especially science fiction series and comedies. I watch them in english with subtitles. I also like playing computer games like *World of Warcraft* and *Starcraft*.

Please write soon and tell me about you and your life.

Best wishes

Charlie

b Read the email again from the beginning. Then cover it and answer the questions from memory.

1. Where's Charlie from?
2. What's his real name?
3. Who does he live with?
4. What does he do?
5. What does he look like?
6. What's he like?
7. What are his favourite free time activities?

c Write a similar email about you or a person you know. Write four paragraphs.

Paragraph 1	name, nationality, age, family, work / study
Paragraph 2	physical appearance
Paragraph 3	personality
Paragraph 4	hobbies and interests

d Check your email for mistakes (grammar, punctuation, and spelling).

◀ p.7

Writing

2 MY FAVOURITE PHOTO

📷 MY FAVOURITE PHOTO BLOG

POST YOUR FAVOURITE PHOTO ON THE WEBSITE, TOGETHER WITH A SHORT DESCRIPTION OF WHY THE PHOTO IS IMPORTANT TO YOU.

This week's winner is Ellie, a student from Cardiff.

1. One of my favourite photos is this one of my friend Anna.
2. I took the photo _____ the summer of 2011 when I was _____ holiday with some friends _____ Ireland.
3. We were at a place called Tara. It's a hill which is famous because there's a big stone _____ top of it, and people say that the old kings of Ireland were crowned there. Anna was telling us all about the history of the stone, and she put her arms _____ it. When I took the photo we thought she was meditating, but in fact we later realised she was sleeping! She woke up after a few minutes and she said the magic of the place made her sleepy!
4. I love this photo because it's mysterious, like the place, and it reminds me of a lovely holiday.
5. I have the photo _____ my phone and _____ my computer with other photos _____ Ireland.

a Match the questions with paragraphs 1–5.
- [ ] What was happening when you took the photo?
- [ ] Where do you keep it?
- [ ] Why do you like it?
- [ ] What's your favourite photo?
- [ ] Who took it? When? Where?

b Complete the text with *in*, *of*, *on*, or *round*.

🔍 **You can keep a photo...**

in	an album.	on	the wall.	by	your bed.
	your wallet.		a table.		
	your bedroom.		your phone.		
	a frame.		your computer.		

c Write about your favourite photo. Answer the questions in **a** in the right order.

d Check your description for mistakes (grammar, punctuation, and spelling). Attach a copy of the photo if you can. Show your description to another student. Is the photo similar in any way to yours?

◀ *p.15*

3 AN INFORMAL EMAIL

a Goran is a student from Croatia who's going to study English in the UK. He's going to stay with a family. Read the email from Mrs Barnes and complete it with expressions from the list.

> Best wishes   Dear Goran
> PS   Looking forward to hearing from you

b Read the email again and answer the questions.

1. When is Goran coming to the UK?
2. How is he travelling?
3. Who is going to meet him at the airport?
4. Does Goran have to share a room?
5. Does *Looking forward to hearing from you* mean…?
   a I hope you write again soon.
   b I'm going to write to you again soon.
6. Does *PS* mean…?
   a This isn't very important information.
   b I forgot to say this before.
7. Why does Mrs Barnes send Goran a photo?

c Imagine you are going to stay with Mrs Barnes. Answer her email using your own information. Write three paragraphs. End the email with *Best wishes* and your name.

Paragraph 1	Thank her for her email.
Paragraph 2	Say when you are arriving, etc.
Paragraph 3	Answer her other questions.

d Check your email for mistakes (grammar, punctuation, and spelling).

◀ *p.23*

From: Sally Barnes [Barnes@hotmail.com]
To: Goran [gorangrec@yahoo.com]
Subject: Your trip

1 _____

Thank you for your email. We're very happy that you're coming to stay with us this summer, and we're sure you're going to enjoy your stay with us.

What time are you arriving at Stansted airport? If you send us your flight number and arrival time, we can all meet you in Arrivals. Can you send us your mobile number too?

Could you also give us some other information? What day are you going back to Croatia? Is there anything you can't eat or drink? Do you want your own room, or do you prefer to share a room with another student? Is there anything special you would like to do or see in the UK?

2 _____ .

3 _____

Sally Barnes

4 _____ I'm attaching a photo of the family, so you can recognize us at the airport!

Writing

4 DESCRIBING WHERE YOU LIVE

a Read the text and complete it with these words.

area   city   food   historic   modern
nature   population   rivers   weather

b Match the questions with paragraphs 1–5.

- [ ] What's it famous for?
- [ ] What's the weather like?
- [ ] What's the best thing about it? Do you like living there?
- [ ] What's your home town like? What is there to see there?
- [ ] Where do you live? Where is it? How big is it?

c Write a description of the place where you live. Write five paragraphs. Answer the questions in **b** in the right order. First, make notes on the questions in **b**.

d Check your email for mistakes (grammar, punctuation, and spelling). Show your description to other students in your class. Which place that you read about would you most like to visit?

◀ p.39

THE PLACE WHERE I LIVE

1. I live in Kayseri, which is an important ¹_city_ in Central Anatolia in Turkey. It has a ²_____ of over 1,000,000 people. It's near the famous Cappadocia ³_____, so there are a lot of tourists in the summer.

2. Kayseri is one of the richest cities in Turkey because it has a lot of industry. It is a university town, and there are also many ⁴_____ buildings, for example Kayseri Castle, Hunat Hatun Mosque, and the Grand Bazaar around Cumhuriyet Square, with its famous statue of Ataturk. But Kayseri also has ⁵_____ residential areas full of luxury blocks of flats, shopping centres, and stylish restaurants.

3. The ⁶_____ in Kayseri is typical of the Middle Anatolia Region. Winters are cold and snowy – great for skiing – and summers are hot and dry. It sometimes rains in the spring and autumn.

4. Kayseri is famous for its mountains. Mount Erciyes is the symbol of the city and it has a well-known ski resort, and on Mount Ali there are national and international paragliding championships. It's also famous for its ⁷_____ and has many local specialities like *pastirma*, which is dried beef with spices, and *manti*, which is a kind of Turkish ravioli. They're delicious!

5. What I like best about Kayseri is that we are so close to ⁸_____. When I'm tired of city life, I can easily get out and enjoy the mountains, ⁹_____, waterfalls, and thermal spas, which are only a short distance away.

5 A FORMAL EMAIL

From: Antonio Ricci [antonior@tiscali.net]
To: The Priory Language School [enquiries@prioryedinburgh]
Subject: Information about courses

Dear Sir / Madam,

I am writing to ask for information about your language courses. I am especially interested in an intensive course of two or three weeks. I am 31 and I work in the library at Milan University. I can read English quite well, but I need to improve my listening and speaking. The book I am currently studying is 'pre-intermediate' (Common European Framework level A2).

I have looked at your website, but there is no information about intensive courses next summer. Could you please send me information about dates and prices? I would also like some information about accommodation. If possible I would like to stay with a family. My wife is going to visit me for a weekend when I am at the school. Could she stay with me in the same family?

I look forward to hearing from you.

Yours faithfully,

Antonio Ricci

a Read the email to a language school. Tick (✓) the questions that Antonio wants the school to answer.
- [ ] How much do the courses cost?
- [ ] When do the courses start and finish?
- [ ] How many students are there in a class?
- [ ] Are there Business English classes?
- [ ] Where can I stay?
- [ ] Where are the teachers from?

b Look at the highlighted expressions. How would they be different in an informal email (or letter)?

Formal	Informal
Dear Sir / Madam,	
I am writing	
I would like	
I look forward to hearing from you.	
Yours faithfully,	

Painting courses in Tuscany

Learn to paint in Tuscany, Italy.
- One-week courses, from April to October
- Your accommodation in Tuscany is included
- Beginners welcome

Email us for more information at **painttuscany@blueelephant.com**

Golf lessons in Florida

- One- or two-week courses in different parts of the state
- Professional golf coaches
- All levels, beginners to advanced
- Small groups or private lessons

For more information email us at **info@golfinflorida.com**

c Read the advertisements and choose a course. Think of two or three questions you would like to ask.

d Write a formal email asking for information. Write two paragraphs.

Paragraph 1	Explain why you are writing and give some personal information.
Paragraph 2	Ask your questions, and ask them to send you information.

e Check your email for mistakes (grammar, punctuation, and spelling).

◀ p.57

Writing

6 A BIOGRAPHY

a Read the biography of Norah Jones. Then cover the text and try to remember three things about her.

b Put the verbs in brackets in the past simple or present perfect.

> 🔍 **Writing a biography – use of tenses**
>
> If you write a biography of a person who is dead, the verbs will all be in the **past simple**.
>
> If the person is alive, all finished actions will be in the **past simple** (such as the person's early life, e.g. *was born, went to university*, etc. or specific actions in their life, e.g. *got married, moved to another town*, etc.).
>
> However, you must use the **present perfect** for unfinished actions which started in the past and are still true now (and which might change), e.g. *She has won nine Grammy awards. She has appeared in several films.*
>
> Use the **present simple** (or **present continuous**) to talk about the present day, e.g. *She lives in New York. She's working on a new album.*

c Write a biography of someone you know, or of a famous person, who is still alive. Write three paragraphs. Make notes before you begin.

Paragraph 1	where and when they were born, their early life (past simple)
Paragraph 2	their life as a young adult (mostly past simple)
Paragraph 3	their later life and their life now (past simple, present perfect, present simple / present continuous)

d Check your biography for mistakes (grammar, punctuation, and spelling). Show your biography to other students in the class. Which of your classmates' biographies is the most interesting?

◂ p.73

Norah Jones

Norah Jones is an American singer-songwriter and actress. She ¹*was born* (**be born**) in 1979 in New York. Her father is Ravi Shankar, a famous Indian sitar player, and her mother is the concert producer Sue Jones. In 1986 her parents ²_____ (**separate**) and later got divorced, and Norah went to live in Texas with her mother.

Norah ³_____ (**be**) interested in music all her life. When she was young she played the saxophone and she was in two different choirs. She ⁴_____ (**go**) to the University of North Texas to study jazz piano, and while she was there she ⁵_____ (**meet**) Jesse Harris. She started a band with him a year later, and since then they ⁶_____ (**work**) together on many different projects.

In 1999 she ⁷_____ (**move**) to New York, and in 2001 she signed a contract with Blue Note records. Since then she ⁸_____ (**make**) five albums, and they have all been very successful. She ⁹_____ (**win**) nine Grammy awards and has sold over 37 million albums worldwide. She has also appeared in several films, including *My Blueberry Nights*.

She has been in only one relationship, with Lee Alexander, but they ¹⁰_____ (**break up**) in 2007. She still lives in New York. At the moment she is working on a new album.

7 AN OPINION ESSAY

a Read the article once. Do you agree with what it says?

'THERE IS TOO MUCH FOOTBALL ON TV.' DO YOU AGREE?

Every time I turn on the television, I'm sure to find a football match on one of the channels. If I change channels, there will probably be football on other channels too, especially at the weekend. ¹*In my opinion* there is definitely too much football on TV for the following reasons.

² _____, if you compare football with other sports, football completely dominates. The only place where you can watch other sports is on special sports channels, which you usually have to pay for. This is not fair for people who like other sports, ³_____ tennis, basketball, or athletics.

Secondly, the football matches on TV are not only the important matches. Every week they show boring matches from the second or third divisions.

⁴_____, I also believe that, at weekends, most people want to relax in front of the television. Many people, including me, don't like football and prefer to see good films or funny series.

⁵_____, I think that even on news programmes there is too much football. It is very annoying when they talk about football for hours every day, especially when there are more important things happening in the world.

⁶_____, I think TV should show fewer football matches and programmes about football, especially at the weekend. ⁷_____ it should show other sports too, and more films. On news programmes they should talk about important things that are happening in the world, not about football.

b Read the article again and complete the gaps with a word or phrase from the list. Use capital letters where necessary.

finally   firstly   for example   thirdly
~~in my opinion~~   instead   to conclude

c You are going to write an article called **'There are too many reality shows on TV'. Do you agree?** With a partner decide if you agree or not, and think of three of four reasons.

d Write the article. Write four or five paragraphs.

Paragraph 1	Write an introduction. You can adapt the introduction in the model article. Say if you agree or not.
Middle paragraphs	Give your reasons. Begin the paragraphs with *Firstly*, *Secondly*, (*Thirdly*,) and *Finally*.
Last paragraph	Write a conclusion (this should be a summary of what you write in the middle paragraphs).

e Check your article for mistakes (grammar, punctuation, and spelling). Show your article to other students in the class. How many of your classmates agree with you? How many disagree?

◀ p.85

Listening

1 14))
My first impression of Alexander was that he was much older than me. In fact he was 32, but I thought he was older. But when we started talking I really liked him. He was extrovert and funny and he had a very good sense of humour. He works for a TV company and he told me a lot of good stories about his work. He was also interested in the same things as me – art and music, and we talked a lot about that. Physically he wasn't really my type. It's difficult to say why. He was tall and dark and quite good-looking and he had a nice smile but there just wasn't any chemistry between us. I could imagine going to a concert or theatre with him, but as a friend. Sorry Mum, but no.

1 15))
When I first saw Oliver I thought he looked warm and friendly, and more attractive than Alexander. He was quite tall with short blond hair and he had lovely blue eyes, a bit like the actor Jude Law. He was a bit shy and quiet at first but when we started chatting he relaxed and we found we had a lot of things in common – we both like books, and the cinema. He was generous too – he wanted to pay for everything. I really enjoyed the evening. When it was time to go he asked for my phone number and said he wanted to meet again. We walked out of the restaurant and went to look for a taxi. And then something happened, and I knew that it was impossible for me to go out with him. He said 'At last!' and took out a packet of cigarettes. That was it, I'm afraid. I could never have a boyfriend who was a smoker. I think perhaps for my next date I'm going to choose the man myself. I don't think another person can really choose a partner for you.

1 24))
Mr and Mrs Clark and Percy is by the British artist David Hockney, and it's considered to be one of the greatest British paintings of the 20th century. It was painted in 1971 and it's a portrait of two of his friends, Ossie Clark and his wife Celia, and their cat Percy. Ossie Clark and Celia were fashion designers and they had a very successful clothes shop in London. In the 1960s they dressed a lot of the famous pop stars of the time, including The Rolling Stones and Eric Clapton. Hockney painted Ossie and Celia a few months after they got married in their flat at Notting Hill in London. He painted them in their bedroom, because he liked the light there, and on the wall on the left of the window you can see one of his own paintings.

Mr and Mrs Clark and Percy is a very big painting, approximately 3 metres wide and 2 metres high. The couple are wearing typical clothes of the late 1960s. Celia is wearing a long dress, and in fact she was expecting a baby at that time. Her husband isn't wearing any shoes, and he's putting his feet into the carpet. This was because Hockney had a lot of problems painting his feet. He just couldn't get them right.

Hockney said that his aim with this painting was to paint the relationship between the two people. Traditionally, when a painter paints a married couple the woman is sitting down and the man is standing up. In this painting the man is sitting and the woman is standing. Usually in a painting the married couple are close together, but in this painting they are separated by a big open window which symbolizes the distance between them. The white cat, sitting on Mr Clark, is a symbol of infidelity. It seems that Hockney didn't think that their marriage was going to be very happy, and in fact the couple got divorced four years later.

Celia often posed as a model for Hockney, but she says that this painting, his most famous picture of her, is not her favourite. She said "It's a wonderful painting, but it makes me look too heavy." In 1996, twenty five years after this picture was painted, Ossie Clark died. He was murdered by his lover in his Kensington flat.

1 26))
My name's Jenny Zielinski. I live and work in New York. I'm the assistant editor of a magazine called *NewYork24seven*. A few months ago, I visited our office in London to learn more about the company. I met the manager, Daniel O'Connor. I had lots of meetings with him, of course. And a working dinner on my birthday… But I spent more time with Rob Walker. He's one of the writers on the London magazine. We had coffees together. We went sightseeing. I even helped Rob buy a shirt! He was fun to be with. I liked him a lot. I think he liked me too. Rob isn't the most punctual person in the world, but he is a great writer. We invited him to work for the New York magazine for a month… and he agreed! So now Rob's coming to New York. I know he's really excited about it. It's going to be great to see him again.

1 29))
Jenny So, here you are in New York at last.
Rob Yeah, it's great to be here. It's really exciting.
Jenny And how's your hotel?
Rob It's fine. My room is really…nice.
Jenny Do you have a good view from your room?
Rob I can see lots of other buildings.
Jenny Tomorrow I'm going to show you around the office and introduce you to the team. Barbara's looking forward to meeting you. You remember, Barbara, my boss?
Rob Oh…yeah, sorry.
Jenny And then you can start thinking about your blog and the column. Have you got any ideas yet, Rob? … Rob?
Rob What? Sorry, Jenny.
Jenny You must be really tired.
Rob Yes, I am a bit. What time is it now?
Jenny It's nine o'clock.
Rob Nine o'clock? That's two o'clock in the morning for me.
Jenny Let's finish our drinks. You need to go to bed.
Rob I guess you're right.
Jenny So, I'll see you in the office at eleven in the morning.
Rob At eleven?
Jenny Is that OK?
Rob It's perfect. Thanks, Jenny.
Jenny There's just one thing.
Rob What's that?
Jenny Don't be late.
Rob By the way. It's great to see you again.
Jenny Yeah. It's great to see you, too.

1 34))
Mia It was a really terrible holiday. It was my fault, I mean I wanted to go to Thailand, but I knew before I went that I didn't really want to have a serious relationship with Joe. And the holiday just showed how different we are. He irritated me all the time. He wanted to stay in some really cheap hostels, because he thought the hotels were too expensive. I didn't want 5-star luxury, but when I go on holiday I want to be comfortable. The places where Joe wanted to stay were very basic and had very small rooms. There's nothing worse than being in a very small room with someone when you're not getting on very well. Another thing I didn't like was that Joe got very jealous. When you're travelling, part of the fun is talking to other travellers, but he hated it if I talked to other people, especially other men. And then he kept taking photos! Hundreds of them. Every time we saw a monument he said 'Go and stand over there so I can take a photo.' I hate being in photos. I just wanted to enjoy the sights. The holiday was all a big mistake. Never go on holiday with a boyfriend if you're not sure about the relationship. It's sure to be a disaster!

1 35))
Linda Oh, it was a wonderful holiday. I loved every moment! Venice is just a paradise. We did everything – we went on a gondola, we saw all the museums, and we had some fantastic meals. And you know, everyone says that Venice is expensive, but I didn't think it was – it wasn't an expensive holiday at all. I thought it was quite reasonable. We all got on very well. I think I'm going to suggest to Isabelle and Laura that we go on holiday together again next year…

1 44))
In May 1968, I came back to Paris. It was a very exciting time. There were a lot of demonstrations, and fighting between students and the police. I wasn't really interested in politics – I wasn't a communist or an anarchist. But I loved the atmosphere. All the students were fighting for freedom, for revolution, and the French police were everywhere. On May the 15th I was with thousands of other young people. We were walking towards the Place de la Bastille. I was tired, so a friend picked me up and I sat on his shoulders. Another boy who was walking next to us was carrying a Vietnamese flag (it was the time of the Vietnam war) and he said to me 'Hey, could you carry the flag for me?' and I said OK. There was so much happening that I didn't notice all the photographers. The next day the photo was on the cover of magazines all over the world. When my grandfather saw it, he immediately ordered me to come to his house. He was furious – really really angry. He said 'That's it! You're a communist! I'm not going to leave you anything. Not a penny!' I walked out of the room and I never saw him again. Six months later he died, and I didn't get any money from him. Nothing.

1 50))
Happy ending
Narrator Suddenly, a man ran across the road. He was wearing a dark coat so Hannah didn't see him at first. Quickly she put her foot on the brake. She stopped just in time. She got out of her car and shouted at the man.
Hannah Don't you usually look before you cross the road? I nearly hit you. I didn't see you until the last moment.
Jamie Sorry! Hey, Hannah it's me. It's Jamie.
Hannah Jamie! What are you doing here? I nearly killed you!
Jamie I was buying something. I was in a hurry and I crossed the road without looking.
Hannah Come on. Get in!
Narrator Hannah and Jamie drove to the coffee bar. They sat down in their usual seats and ordered two cups of coffee.

Waiter Here you are. Two cappuccinos.
Hannah / Jamie Thanks.
Hannah What an evening! I nearly killed you.
Jamie Well, you didn't kill me, so what's the problem?
Hannah But what were you doing in the high street? I thought you were here, in the café, waiting for me.
Jamie I went to the theatre to buy these tickets for the Scouting For Girls concert. I know you wanted to go. And it's on the 15th of October – next Saturday. Our anniversary.
Hannah Our anniversary?
Jamie Yes. Three months since we first met. We met on Saturday the 15th of July. Remember?
Hannah Gosh, Jamie. I can't believe you remember the exact day! What a romantic! It's lucky I didn't hit you in the street…

1 51)))
Sad ending
Narrator Suddenly, a man ran across the road. He was wearing a dark coat so Hannah didn't see him at first. Quickly she put her foot on the brake. Although Hannah tried to stop she couldn't. She hit the man. Hannah panicked. She drove away as fast as she could. When she arrived at the coffee bar Jamie wasn't there. She called him but his mobile phone was turned off. She waited for ten minutes and then she went home. Two hours later a car arrived at Hannah's house. A policewoman knocked at the door.
Policewoman Good evening, Madam. Are you Hannah Davis?
Hannah Yes, I am.
Policewoman I'd like to speak to you. Can I come in?
Narrator The policewoman came in and sat down on the sofa.
Policewoman Are you a friend of Jamie Dixon?
Hannah Yes,
Narrator said Hannah.
Policewoman Well, I'm afraid I have some bad news for you.
Hannah What? What's happened?
Policewoman Jamie had an accident this evening.
Hannah Oh no! What kind of accident?
Policewoman He was crossing the road and a car hit him.
Hannah When…When did this happen? And where?
Policewoman This evening at 5.25. He was crossing the road in the high street by the theatre.
Hannah Oh no! How is he?
Policewoman He's in hospital. He's got a bad injury to his head and two broken legs.
Hannah But is he going to be OK?
Policewoman We don't know. He's in intensive care.
Hannah Oh no. And the driver of the car?
Policewoman She didn't stop.
Hannah She?
Policewoman Yes, it was a woman in a white car. Somebody saw the number of the car. You have a white car outside don't you, Madam? Is your number plate XYZ 348S?
Hannah Yes…yes, it is.
Policewoman Can you tell me where you were at 5.25 this evening?

1 55)))
Olivia
Interviewer Excuse me, do you have a moment?
Olivia Yes, sure.
Interviewer Where are you going?
Olivia To Nicaragua.
Interviewer For a holiday?
Olivia No, I'm going to do voluntary work. I'm going to teach English to young children.
Interviewer Where exactly in Nicaragua are you going?
Olivia To a town called Esteli. It's about 150 kilometres from Managua.
Interviewer How long are you going to be there for?
Olivia I'm going to be in Esteli for six weeks and after that I'm going to travel round Nicaragua for a month.
Interviewer That sounds amazing.
Olivia Yes, I'm really looking forward to it.
Interviewer Are you feeling nervous at all?
Olivia A bit, because I don't speak much Spanish. But they're going to give us a 40-hour language course when we arrive, so I hope that's enough to start with.
Interviewer Well, good luck and have a great time.
Olivia Thanks. I'm sure it's going to be a fantastic experience.

Matthew
Interviewer Excuse me, do you have a moment?
Matthew Yeah, OK.
Interviewer Where are you going?
Matthew To Australia.
Interviewer That's a long flight. Are you going to stop on the way?
Matthew No, I'm going direct to Melbourne.
Interviewer Why Melbourne?
Matthew I'm going to work there. I'm a model and we're going to do a photo shoot for a magazine.
Interviewer That sounds exciting. What kind of clothes are you going to model?
Matthew Winter clothes, for next season. It's winter in Australia now so it's going to be quite cold. That's why we're going there.
Interviewer Of course, it's their winter. How cold do you think it's going to be?
Matthew I'm not quite sure. About eight or nine degrees during the day and colder at night, I suppose.
Interviewer Well, have a good trip, and I hope the photos are fabulous!
Matthew Thanks.

Lily
Interviewer Excuse me, do you have a moment?
Lily OK, sure.
Interviewer Where are you going?
Lily To Budapest.
Interviewer Why are you going there?
Lily I'm going to a conference.
Interviewer So it's a work trip.
Lily Yes. But I'm also going to see an old friend there. Actually, an old boyfriend. Someone I went out with a long time ago.
Interviewer When did you decide to meet up again?
Lily Well, I knew he was working at Budapest University, so when the conference came up about a month ago I got in touch with him on Facebook.
Interviewer Is he going to meet you at the airport?
Lily I don't think so! But who knows?
Interviewer How do you feel about it?
Lily Quite excited. It's going to be strange meeting again after all these years.
Interviewer Well, good luck. I'm sure you're going to have a great time. And enjoy the conference, too.
Lily Thanks very much.

1 62)))
Ben Hi. This is Ben West. Sorry I can't take your call. Please leave a message.
Lily Hi Ben. It's me, Lily. Hope you're OK. I've booked my flight and hotel. I'm coming on Sunday the 2nd of May – I couldn't get a flight on the first. I'm flying from Gatwick with Easyjet and I'm arriving at Budapest airport at 14.40. I'm going back on Saturday the 8th leaving at 16.35. I'm staying at a lovely old hotel, quite a famous one I think. It's called the Hotel Gellert or Jellert – I'm not sure how you pronounce it, but it's G-E-double L-E-R-T. I'm sure you know it. I'll call you on Sunday night when I get there. See you soon – I'm really looking forward to seeing you again.

2 2)))
Presenter Good evening, ladies and gentlemen and welcome to *What's the word?* And our first contestants tonight are Martin and Lola. Hello to you both. Are you nervous?
Lola Just a bit.
Presenter Well, just try and relax and play *What's the word?* with us. If you're watching the show for the first time, here's how we play the game. As you can see Martin has a TV screen in front of him and six words are going to appear on the screen. Martin has two minutes to describe the words to Lola so that she can guess what they are. But he can't use any part of the words on the screen. So, for example, if the word is taxi driver, he can't use the word taxi or driver or drive.
Presenter Martin, Lola, are you ready?

2 3)))
Presenter Martin, Lola, are you ready?
Martin/Lola Yes.
Presenter OK, Martin you have two minutes to describe your six words starting now!
Martin OK, word number 1. It's a person. It's somebody who works in a hospital.
Lola A doctor.
Martin No, no, no it's the person who helps the doctor and looks after the patients.
Lola Oh, a [bleep].
Martin That's right. Word number 2. It's a place. It's somewhere where people go when they want to buy things.
Lola A shop.
Martin Not exactly. It's bigger and you can buy all kinds of different things there, especially food.
Lola A [bleep].
Martin Yes, well done. OK, word number 3. It's a thing. It's something which we use for everything nowadays. For the internet, for talking to people, for taking photos…It's a kind of gadget. Everyone has one.
Lola A [bleep]?
Martin That's it! Word number 4. It's an adjective. It's the opposite of dark.
Lola Light?
Martin It's like light, but you only use it to describe hair.
Lola [bleep]?
Martin Yes! Word number 5. It's an adjective again. Er…You use it to describe a person who's … er, who's quick at learning things.
Lola Intelligent?
Martin No, but it's similar to intelligent. It's the opposite of stupid.
Lola [bleep]!
Martin Yes, brilliant. And word number six, the last one. OK. It's a verb. For example, you do this to the TV.
Lola Watch?
Martin No… It's what you do when you finish watching TV at night.
Lola Er…go to bed?
Martin No! Come on! You do it to the TV before you go to bed.
Lola Oh, [bleep]?
Martin Yes!

2 8)))
Jenny Well, I think that's everything. What do you think of the office?
Rob It's brilliant. And much bigger than our place in London.
Jenny Oh, here's Barbara. Rob, this is Barbara, the editor of the magazine.
Barbara It's good to finally meet you, Rob.
Rob It's great to be here.
Barbara Is this your first time in New York?
Rob No, I came here when I was eighteen. But only for a few days.
Barbara Well, I hope you get to know New York much better this time!
Jenny Barbara, I'm going to take Rob out for lunch. Would you like to come with us?
Barbara I'd love to, but unfortunately I have a meeting at one. So, I'll see you later. We're meeting at three, I think.
Jenny That's right.
Barbara Have a nice lunch.
Holly Hey, are you Rob Walker?
Rob Yes.

Holly Hi, I'm Holly. Holly Tyler.
Rob Hello, Holly.
Holly We're going to be working together.
Jenny Really?
Holly Didn't Barbara tell you? I'm going to be Rob's photographer!
Jenny Oh, well…We're just going for lunch.
Holly Cool! I can come with you. I mean, I had a sandwich earlier, so I don't need to eat. But Rob and I can talk. Is that OK?
Jenny Sure.
Holly So let's go.

2 11))
Holly So tell me, Rob. What are you going to write about?
Rob Well, to start with, my first impressions of New York. You know, the nightlife, the music, things like that.
Holly Are you planning to do any interviews?
Rob I'd like to. Do you have any suggestions?
Holly Well, I know some great musicians.
Rob Musicians?
Holly You know, guys in bands. And I also have some contacts in the theatre and dance.
Rob That would be great.
Holly Maybe we could go to a show, and after you could talk to the actors.
Rob I really like that idea.
Waitress Can I bring you anything else?
Jenny Could we have the check, please?
Waitress Yes, ma'am. Here's your check.
Jenny Thanks. Excuse me. I think there's a mistake. We had two bottles of water, not three.
Waitress You're right. I'm really sorry. It's not my day today! I'll get you a new check.
Jenny Thank you.
Holly We're going to have a fun month, Rob.
Rob Yeah, I think it's going to be fantastic.
Jenny OK, time to go. You have your meeting with Barbara at three.
Rob Oh yeah, right.

2 22))
Presenter Teenagers today have a bad reputation. People say that they are lazy and untidy and that they do very little to help their parents in the house. But there are some teenagers for whom this description is just not true at all.
It is estimated that there are more than 200,000 teenagers in the UK who have to look after a member of their family, their mother or father or brother or sister. In many cases these young helpers, or 'carers' as they are called, have to do between 25 and 50 hours work helping in their house, as well as doing their school work.

2 23))
Presenter I'd like to welcome to the programme two of these teenagers, Alice and Daniel, who are 17 years old, and who both look after members of their family. Hello, Alice, hello Daniel.
Alice / Daniel Hi.
Presenter Who do you look after?
Alice I look after my mum. She has ME – it's an illness which means that she feels tired all the time and she can't walk very well. And I also look after my younger brother and sister. He's six and she's four.
Daniel I look after my mum too. She had a bad car accident seven years ago and she can't walk. I also look after my little sister.
Presenter You both do a lot of housework. What exactly do you do?
Alice On a normal day I get up early and I clean the house and I do the ironing. After school I sometimes take my mum to the shops in her wheelchair. In the evening my dad makes the dinner – I'm not very good at cooking! But I make sure my brother and sister eat their dinner and then I put them to bed.
Daniel My day's quite similar. I clean the house and iron but I also do the cooking and the shopping. My dad left home four years ago so we're on our own. I take my sister to school and make sure that my mum is OK. I need to give her massages every evening.
Presenter How do you feel about the way you live?
Alice I don't really mind looking after my mum. She's ill and she needs my help. But sometimes I feel a bit sad when I can't go out because there are things to do in the house. And I sometimes get angry with my school friends. They don't really understand the problems I have at home. All they think about are clothes, boys, and going out.
Daniel I enjoy what I do because I'm helping my mum and I'm helping my sister at the same time. Of course it's true that I can't go out much, because I need to spend most of my time at home. I sometimes go out with my friends but I don't like leaving my mum on her own. I always make sure that I have my mobile. If my mum needs anything, she calls me and I go back home. It's not a problem for me. It's just part of my life.
Presenter You're both doing a great job, thanks very much for coming on the programme.

2 26))
1 **Interviewer** Have you ever bought something that you've never worn?
 A Yes – hasn't everyone? I remember some trousers I bought that I never wore.
 Interviewer What was the problem with them?
 A They were very tight, black leather trousers that I bought from a second-hand shop near Portobello Road, when I was about 20 years old. I remember when I was in the changing room I thought they looked fantastic. I thought I looked like Jim Morrison from the Doors. But when I got home, in the cold light of day, I realised that I looked more like one of the women from Abba! That's why I never wore them.
2 **Interviewer** Have you ever bought something that you've never worn?
 A Yes, a karate suit. I decided that I wanted to do karate, and I signed up for a course and bought the suit and the orange belt but then I changed my mind and decided not to do the course.
 Interviewer Why not?
 A I was worried that someone would knock my teeth out.
 Interviewer Do you still have the suit?
 A No, I sold it on eBay.
3 **Interviewer** Have you ever bought something that you've never worn?
 A Sadly it happens to me quite often, because I hate clothes shopping, and I never try things on. For example, I have a shirt in my wardrobe now that I've never worn.
 Interviewer Why not?
 A Well, I bought it in a hurry a few months ago and then I put it away in my wardrobe. A few weeks later I took it out and looked at it and I thought 'Why did I buy this?' It's horrible – pink and purple stripes. And of course I didn't have the receipt, so I couldn't take it back.
4 **Interviewer** Have you ever bought something that you've never worn?
 A Lots of things, I'm afraid. The last one was a brown leather coat.
 Interviewer What was wrong with it?
 A Well, I bought it online, from a website that has cheap offers, but when it arrived it looked completely different from what it looked like on screen and I decided I didn't like it. So it's in my wardrobe. I'm sure I'm never going to wear it, but perhaps I'll give it to someone as a present.

2 32))
Presenter Last Friday Sven, a lawyer from Stockholm, was looking forward to a relaxing two days in the mountains. He and his wife had a reservation in a luxury hotel at a skiing resort, so they could spend the weekend skiing. But the weekend didn't work out exactly as they were expecting. Sven worked until late on Friday evening. His office was on the 12th floor. When he finished, at 8 o'clock, he locked his office and got into the lift … and he didn't get out again until Monday morning!
Sven I pressed the button for the ground floor and the lift started going down but then it stopped. I pressed the button again but nothing happened. I pressed the alarm and shouted but nobody heard me. Most people had already gone home. I tried to phone my wife but my mobile didn't work in the lift. I couldn't do anything. I just sat on the floor and hoped maybe somebody would realize what had happened. But on Saturday and Sunday I knew nobody would be there. I slept most of the time to forget how hungry I was.
Presenter Meanwhile Sven's wife, Silvia, was waiting for her husband to come home.
Silvia I was very worried when he didn't come home on Friday evening and I couldn't understand why his mobile wasn't working. I phoned the police and they looked for him but they couldn't find him anywhere. I thought maybe he was with another woman.
Presenter So Sven was in the lift the whole weekend from Friday evening until Monday morning. At eight o'clock, when the office workers arrived, they phoned the emergency number and somebody came and repaired the lift.
Sven I was very happy to get out. I hadn't eaten since Friday afternoon and I was very hungry. It's lucky that I am not claustrophobic because the lift was very small. The first thing I did was to phone my wife to say that I was OK.
Presenter Sven will soon be the fittest man in his office – from now on he's going to take the stairs every day – even though it's 12 floors.

2 42))
Interviewer Today we talk to Laurel Reece, who's writing a book about how to live more slowly. She's going to give us five useful tips.
Laurel My first tip is something which is very simple to say, but more difficult to do in practice. Whatever you're doing, just try to slow down and enjoy it. If you're walking somewhere, try to walk more slowly; if you are driving, make yourself drive more slowly. It doesn't matter what you are doing, cooking, having a shower, exercising in the gym, just slow down and really enjoy the moment. We all try to do too many things that we just don't have time for. So my second tip is make a list of the three things which are most important for you, your priorities in life. Then when you've made your list make sure that you spend time doing those things. Imagine for example that your three things are your family, reading, and playing sports. Then make sure that you spend enough time with your family, that you have space in your life for reading, and that you have time to do sports. And forget about trying to do other things that you haven't got time for.
Tip number three is don't try to do two things at the same time. The worst thing you can do is to multitask. So for example, don't read your emails while you are talking to a friend on the phone. If you do that, you aren't really focusing on your emails or your friend and you aren't going to feel very relaxed either.
Tip number four is very simple: once a day, every day, sit down and do nothing for half an hour. For example, go to a café and sit outside, or go to a park and sit on a bench. Turn off your phone so that nobody can contact you, and then just sit and watch the world go by. This will really help you to slow down.
OK. My fifth and final tip. One of the most relaxing things you can do is to be near water or even better, to be on water. So if you live near a lake or river, go and sit by the river, or go boating.

If you live near the sea, go and sit on the beach. Relax and listen to the sound of the wind and the water. You will feel your body and mind slowing down as the minutes go past.

2 45))

First I did the photo test. I was near Charing Cross station. I stopped a man who was walking quite slowly down the road and I said, 'Excuse me, could you take my photo?' The man said, 'No, no, no time for that,' and just continued walking. Then I asked a businessman in a grey suit who was walking towards the station. He took one photo, but when I asked him to take another one he walked away quickly.

Next, it was the shopping test. I went to a tourist shop in Oxford Street and I bought a key ring and a red bus. The red bus was very expensive. The total price was forty pounds. I gave the man a hundred pounds. He gave me sixty pounds back.

Finally, it was time for the accident test. For this test I went down into the Tube – the London Underground. As I went down the stairs I fell over and sat on the floor. A man immediately stopped and looked down at me. I thought he was going to help me but he didn't – he just said 'Why don't you look where you're going?'

2 51))

Presenter Next in our list of things which you thought were bad for you is chocolate. Jane, our food expert, is going to tell us why actually it can be good for us.
Jane Well, there have been a lot of studies recently about chocolate. Remember, chocolate is something that we've been eating for hundreds of years, it's not a modern invention. And the studies show that chocolate, like red wine, contains antioxidants. In fact chocolate has more antioxidants than wine. These antioxidants can protect us against illnesses like heart disease.
Presenter Really?
Jane Yes, but, and this is very important, all the good antioxidants are only in dark chocolate. So don't eat milk chocolate or white chocolate – they aren't healthy at all. And of course you also need to remember that although dark chocolate is good for you, it contains quite a lot of calories, so if you're worried about your weight, don't eat too much. One or two pieces a day is enough.
Presenter Great news for me because I love chocolate! And now to Tony, our TV journalist. Tony, newspaper articles are always telling us about studies which say that we watch too much TV, that we spend too much time sitting in front of the TV and that as a result we don't do enough exercise. They also say that watching TV makes us stupid. Is this all true Tony?
Tony Well, it's almost certainly true that we watch too much television, but it probably isn't true that watching TV makes us stupid. I've just finished reading a book by a science writer, Steven Johnson, called *Everything bad is good for you*. One thing he says in his book is that modern TV series like *The Sopranos* or *House* or *Mad Men* are more intellectually stimulating than TV series were 20 years ago. He says that these shows are complicated and very clever and that they help to make us more intelligent.
Presenter Well, I can believe that, but what about reality shows that are so popular on TV. I can't believe that these are good for us.
Tony Well, Steven Johnson says that we can even learn something from reality shows – he says this kind of programme can teach us about group psychology, about how people behave when they're in a group.
Presenter Well, thank you, Tony and Jane. So now you know what to do this evening. You can sit down in front of the TV with a box of dark chocolates…

2 55))

Holly Hey, Rob, come on. Keep up.
Rob Sorry. I'm a bit tired this morning.
Holly You aren't exactly in good shape, are you?
Rob I know, I know. I think I'm eating too much.
Holly Then eat less!
Rob It isn't easy. I eat out all the time. And the portions in American restaurants are enormous.
Holly You don't do enough exercise.
Rob I walk a lot.
Holly Walking isn't enough, Rob. Do you do anything to keep fit?
Rob I cycle when I'm in London…
Holly So why don't you get a bike here?
Rob I'm only here for another three weeks. Anyway, my hotel's near the office. I don't need a bike.
Holly You know, Jennifer goes running all the time. Before and after work. But I just think that running is just so boring. I mean, where's the fun?
Rob Yeah, I'm not very keen on running.
Holly So why don't you play basketball with me and my friends?
Rob OK. That's a great idea! But I don't have any trainers.
Holly Trainers? Sneakers! You can buy some.
Rob Is there a sports shop near here?
Holly Sure, there's one across the street.

2 59))

Rob Hi Jenny.
Jenny Oh, hi.
Rob Have you had a good day?
Jenny Oh, you know. Meetings! What about you?
Rob It was great. I went to Brooklyn and met some really interesting people.
Jenny And you had time to go shopping, too.
Rob What? Oh yeah. I've just bought these.
Jenny What are they?
Rob A pair of trainers – er, sneakers.
Jenny Nice. Why did you buy sneakers?
Rob I think I need to get a bit fitter.
Jenny Oh, I'm impressed. You know, I go running every morning in Central Park.
Rob Do you?
Jenny It's so beautiful early in the morning. Why don't you come with me?
Rob Er… sure. Why not?
Jenny Great! I'll come by your hotel tomorrow morning.
Rob OK. What time?
Jenny Six forty-five?
Rob Six…?
Jenny Forty-five.
Rob Can we make it a bit later? Say, seven forty-five?
Jenny That's too late, Rob. Let's make it seven fifteen.
Rob OK.
Jenny Excellent. See you later.
Rob Great.
Holly Basketball and running, Rob. You must have a lot of energy.
Rob Er… yeah.

3 8))

Presenter Today's topic is 'positive thinking'. We all know that people who are positive enjoy life more than people who are negative and pessimistic. But scientific studies show that positive people are also healthier. They get better more quickly when they are ill, and they live longer. A recent study has shown that people who are optimistic and think positively live, on average, nine years longer than pessimistic people. So, let's hear what you the listeners think. Do you have any ideas to help us be more positive in our lives?

3 9))

Presenter Our first caller this evening is Andy. Hi Andy. What's your tip for being positive?
Andy Hello. Well, I think it's very important to live in the present and not in the past. Don't think about mistakes you made in the past. You can't change the past. The important thing is to think about how you can do things better now and in the future.
Presenter Thank you, Andy. And now we have another caller. What's your name, please?
Julie Hi, My name's Julie. My tip is think positive thoughts, not negative ones. We all have negative thoughts sometimes, but when we start having them we need to stop and try to change them into positive ones. Like, if you have an exam tomorrow and you start thinking 'I'm sure I'll fail', then you'll fail the exam. So you need to change that negative thought to a positive thought. Just think to yourself 'I'll pass'. I do this and it usually works.
Presenter Thank you, Julie. And our next caller is Martin. Hi Martin.
Martin Hi. My tip is don't spend a lot of time reading the papers or watching the news on TV. It's always bad news and it just makes you feel depressed. Read a book or listen to your favourite music instead.
Presenter Thanks, Martin. And our next caller is Miriam. Miriam?
Miriam Hi.
Presenter Hi Miriam. What's your tip?
Miriam My tip is every week make a list of all the good things that happened to you. Then keep the list with you, in your bag or in a pocket, and if you're feeling a bit sad or depressed, just take it out and read it. It'll make you feel better.
Presenter Thanks, Miriam. And our last call is from Michael. Hi Michael. We're listening.
Michael Hi. My tip is to try to use positive language when you speak to other people. You know, if your friend has a problem, don't say 'I'm sorry' or 'Oh, poor you', say something positive like 'Don't worry! Everything will be OK'. That way you'll make the other person think more positively about their problem.
Presenter Thank you, Michael. Well, that's all we've got time for. A big thank you to all our callers. Until next week then, goodbye.

3 13))

Presenter Earlier this year, ten years after Steve sent the letter, some builders were renovating the living room in Carmen's mother's house. When they took out the fireplace they found Steve's letter, and gave it to Carmen's sister, and she sent the letter to Carmen in Paris. Carmen was now 42, and she was still single.
Carmen When I got the letter I didn't call Steve straight away because I was so nervous. I kept picking up the phone and putting it down again. I nearly didn't phone him at all. But I knew that I had to make the call.
Presenter Carmen finally made the call and Steve answered the phone. He was also now 42 and also single.
Steve I couldn't believe it when she phoned. I've just moved house, but luckily I kept my old phone number.
Presenter Steve and Carmen arranged to meet in Paris a few days later.
Steve When we met it was like a film. We ran across the airport and into each other's arms. Within 30 seconds of seeing each other again we were kissing. We fell in love all over again.
Presenter Last week the couple got married, 17 years after they first met.
Carmen I never got married in all those years, but now I have married the man I always loved.
Presenter So Steve and Carmen are together at last. But will they keep their promises?

3 17))

Patient So what does it mean, doctor?
Dr Well, first the party. A party is a group of people. This means that you're going to meet a lot of people. I think you're going to be very busy.
Patient At work?
Dr Yes, at work… you work in an office, I think?

Patient Yes, that's right.
Dr I think the party means you are going to have a lot of meetings.
Patient What about the champagne?
Dr Let me look at my notes again. Ah yes, you were drinking champagne. Champagne means a celebration. It's a symbol of success. So we have a meeting or meetings and then a celebration. Maybe in the future you'll have a meeting with your boss, about a possible promotion?
Patient Well, it's possible. I hope so. What about the garden and the flowers? Do they mean anything?
Dr Yes, yes. Flowers are a positive symbol. So the flowers mean that you are feeling positive about the future. So perhaps you already knew about this possible promotion?
Patient No, I didn't. But it's true, I am very happy at work and I feel very positive about my future. That's not where my problems are. My problems are with my love life. Does my dream tell you anything about that?
Dr Mm, yes it does. You're single, aren't you?
Patient Yes, well, divorced.
Dr Because the violin music tells me you want some romance in your life – you're looking for a partner perhaps?
Patient Yes, yes, I am. In fact I met a woman last month – I really like her… I think I'm in love with her. I'm meeting her tonight.
Dr In your dream you saw an owl in a tree.
Patient Yes, an owl… a big owl.
Dr The owl represents an older person. I think you'll need to ask this older person for help. Maybe this 'older person' is me? Maybe you need my help?
Patient Well, yes, what I really want to know is does this person, this woman… love me?

3 18))
Patient Well, yes, what I really want to know is does this person, this woman… love me?
Dr You remember the end of your dream? You were feeling cold?
Patient Yes, my feet were very cold.
Dr Well, I think perhaps you already know the answer to your question.
Patient You mean she doesn't love me.
Dr No, I don't think so. I think you will need to find another woman. I'm sorry. Perhaps you can find someone on the internet? I have heard of a very good website…

3 23))
Nigel Hi Suze. Sorry I'm a bit late. I was watching the match.
Suzy Come on in then. Mum, this is Nigel. Nigel this is my mum.
Nigel Oh… hello.
Mum Nice to meet you, Nigel.
Suzy And this is my Dad.
Dad Hello, Nigel.
Nigel Hello.
Dad Come on into the living room.

Dad Would you like a drink, Nigel? Orange juice, beer?
Nigel Oh thanks, John. I'll have a beer, please.

Mum You're a vegetarian, aren't you, Nigel?
Nigel Yes, I am. Personally I think eating animals is totally wrong.
Mum Ahem, well, this is vegetable lasagne. I hope you like it. Suzy's Dad made it.

Dad Any more lasagne, Nigel?
Nigel Oh, er, no thanks. I'm not very hungry.
Girl The lasagne is delicious, Dad.
Mum Yes, it is.
Dad Thank you.

Suzy I'll do the washing up, Mum.
Dad No, I'll do it.

Nigel Er, where's the bathroom?

Nigel Did you watch the match this evening, John? Chelsea and Arsenal. It was fantastic!
Dad No, I didn't watch it. I don't like football at all. In fact I hate it.
Nigel Oh.

Mum So…what are you going to do when you finish university, Nigel?
Nigel Er, I don't know.
Dad What are you studying at university?
Nigel Sociology.
Dad Why did you choose sociology?
Nigel Because I thought it was easy.
Mum Is it interesting?
Nigel It's OK. Er … What was Suzy like as a little girl, Marion? Do you have any photos of her?
Mum Photos of Suzy? Yes, we have thousands of photos. She was a lovely little girl, wasn't she John?
Dad Yes, she was. A beautiful little girl.
Nigel Can I see some?
Suzy Oh no, please.
Mum John, can you bring the photo albums?

Mum Look, and this is one when she was three years old.
Dad And this is when we went to Disneyland. That's Suzy with Mickey and Minnie Mouse.
Nigel Ah! She was so sweet.
Dad Would you like another beer, Nigel?
Nigel Yes, please, John.

3 32))
Interviewer Good morning and welcome. In today's programme we're going to talk about singing. In the studio we have Martin, the director of a singing school in London, and Gemma, a student at Martin's school. Good morning to both of you.
Martin / Gemma Good morning.
Interviewer First, Martin, can you tell us, why is it a good idea for people to learn to sing?
Martin First, because singing makes you feel good. And secondly, because singing is very good for your health.
Interviewer Really? In what way?
Martin Well, when you learn to sing you need to learn to breathe correctly. That's very important. And you also learn to stand and sit correctly. As a result, people who sing are often fitter and healthier than people who don't.
Interviewer Are your courses only for professional singers?
Martin No, not at all. They're for everybody. You don't need to have any experience of singing. And you don't need to be able to read music.
Interviewer So how do your students learn to sing?
Martin They learn by listening and repeating. Singing well is really 95% listening.
Interviewer OK. Gemma, tell us about the course. How long did it last?
Gemma Only one day. From ten in the morning to six in the evening.
Martin Could you already sing well before you started?
Gemma No, not well. I've always liked singing. But I can't read music and I never thought I sang very well.
Interviewer So what happened on the course?
Gemma Well, first we did a lot of listening and breathing exercises, and we learnt some other interesting techniques.
Interviewer What sort of things?
Gemma Well, for example we learnt that it's easier to sing high notes if you sing with a surprised look on your face!
Interviewer Oh really? Could you show us?
Gemma Well, I'll try.
Interviewer For those of you at home, I can promise you that Gemma looked very surprised. Were you happy with your progress?

Gemma Absolutely. At the end of the day we were singing in almost perfect harmony. It was amazing. In just one day we really were much better.
Interviewer Could you two give us a little demonstration.
Martin / Gemma Oh, OK…

3 38))
Journalist I arrived at Madrid airport where I met Paula. *Hola Soy Max.*
Paula *Encantada. Soy Paula.*
Journalist Paula took me to my hotel and that evening we went to the centre of Madrid and it was time for my first test. I had to order a sandwich and a drink in a bar then ask for the bill. I sat down at the bar and I tried to order a beer and a ham sandwich. *Por favor, una cerveza y un bocadillo de jamón.*
Waiter *En seguida.*
Journalist Fantastic! The waiter understood me first time. My pronunciation wasn't perfect but I got my beer and my sandwich. I really enjoyed it. But then the more difficult bit. Asking for the bill… *¿Cuánto es?*
Waiter *Seis noventa.*
Journalist *¿Cómo?*
Waiter *Seis noventa.*
Journalist Six ninety. I understood! Paula gave me eight points for the test. I was very happy with that. Next we went out into the street. Test number two was asking for directions and (very important!) understanding them. We were in a narrow street and I had to stop someone and ask them for the nearest chemist, *Una farmacia.* I stopped a woman. At first I didn't understand anything she said!
Passer-by *Siga todo recto y tome la segunda por la derecha. Hay una farmacia en esa calle.*
Journalist I asked the woman to speak more slowly.
Passer-by *Todo recto y tome la segunda calle por la derecha DERECHA.*
Journalist I got it this time, I think. The second street on the right. I followed the directions and guess what? There was a chemist there! Seven points from Paula.
Test number three. I wasn't looking forward to this one. I had to get a taxi to a famous place in Madrid. Paula wrote down the name of the place on a piece of paper. It was the name of the football stadium where Real Madrid play. We stopped a taxi.
Journalist *El Bernabéu, por favor.*
Taxi driver *¿Qué? ¿Adónde?*
Journalist He didn't understand me. I tried again but he still didn't understand. I was desperate so I said *Real Madrid, Stadium, football.*
Taxi driver *¡Ah! El Santiago Bernabéu.*
Journalist Finally! Paula only gave me five because I ended up using English. Still, at least I made the taxi driver understand where I wanted to go. And so to the final test. I had to leave a message in Spanish on somebody's voicemail. I had to give my name, spell it, and ask the person to call me back. Paula gave me the number (it was one of her friends called Lola) and I dialled. I was feeling a bit nervous at this point, because speaking on the phone in a foreign language is never easy.
Lola *Deje su mensaje después de la señal.*
Journalist *Eh. Buenas noches. Soy Max. Max. M-A-X. Eh… Por favour… llamarme esta noche… Oh yes… a las 8.30, eh Gracias.* Well, my grammar wasn't right, but I left the message. Half an hour later, at half past eight Lola phoned me. Success! Paula gave me eight points. That was the end of my four tests. Paula was pleased with me. My final score was seven. I was quite happy with that. So how much can you learn in a month? Well, of course you can't learn Spanish in a month, but you can learn enough to survive if you are on holiday or on a trip. Now I want to go back to England and try and learn some more. *¡Adiós!*

Listening

3 39))

Jenny Are you okay?
Rob Me? Never better.
Jenny It's beautiful here, isn't it? I think this is my favourite place in New York.
Rob Yeah, it's great.
Jenny So how's it all going? Are you happy you came?
Rob To Central Park? At seven fifteen in the morning?
Jenny To New York, Rob.
Rob Yeah. Of course I'm happy. It's fantastic.
Jenny Really? You aren't just saying that.
Rob No, I mean it.
Jenny You need to get in shape, Rob.
Rob I know. I am a bit tired of eating out all the time. It isn't good for my figure.
Jenny It's the restaurants you go to! Why don't you come over to my place after work? I could make you something a little healthier.
Rob I'd really like that. Thanks.
Jenny So, how do you feel now? Are you ready to go again?
Rob Oh yes! I'm ready for anything.
Jenny Are you sure you're okay?
Rob Absolutely.
Jenny Okay. We'll only go around two more times.
Rob Two? Excellent!

3 43))

Rob That was a lovely meal. Thanks, Jenny.
Jenny That's OK.
Rob It's been great being in New York. You know, your offer to work here came at a very good time for me.
Jenny Really?
Rob Yeah, I was looking for something new. Something different. You see, I broke up with my girlfriend a few months before I met you.
Jenny Oh… right.
Rob What about you?
Jenny What about me?
Rob You know… relationships?
Jenny Oh, I've been too busy recently to think about relationships. Getting this job at the magazine was a really big thing for me. I guess that's taken up all my time and energy.
Rob But that isn't very good for you. Only thinking about work, I mean.
Jenny Why didn't you tell me you weren't feeling well this morning? We didn't have to go for a run.
Rob I wanted to go. It was nice.
Jenny Well, I'm glad you're feeling better. Would you like another coffee?
Rob No, thanks. I think I should get back to the hotel now, I've got a really busy day tomorrow. Do you have a telephone number for a taxi?
Jenny Yeah…but it's much easier to get a cab on the street.
Rob Oh, OK, then.
Jenny I'll see you in the morning, if you're feeling OK.
Rob Oh, I'm sure I'll be fine. Thanks again for a great evening.
Jenny Any time.
Rob Goodnight.
Jenny Night, Rob.

3 51))

Presenter Welcome to this morning's edition of *What's the problem?* Today we're talking about friends, so if you have a problem with one of your friends, and you'd like our psychologist Catherine to give you some advice, just phone us on 800 700 550. Our first caller today is Kevin from Birmingham. Hello, Kevin.
Kevin Hi.
Presenter What's the problem?
Kevin Yes. My problem is with my best friend, Alan. Well, the thing is, he's always flirting with my girlfriend.
Presenter Your best friend flirts with your girlfriend?
Kevin Yes, when the three of us are together he always says things to my girlfriend like, 'Wow! You look fantastic today' or 'I love your dress, Suzanna', things like that. And when we're at a party he often asks her to dance.
Presenter Do you think he's in love with your girlfriend?
Kevin I don't know, but I'm getting really stressed about it. What can I do?

3 52))

Presenter Well, let's see if our expert can help. Catherine?
Catherine Hello, Kevin. Have you talked to your girlfriend about this?
Kevin No, I haven't. I don't want Suzanna to think I'm jealous.
Catherine Well, first I think you should talk to her, ask her how she feels and what she thinks of Alan's behaviour. Perhaps she thinks it's fine, and they are just good friends. That it's just his personality. If that's what she thinks, then I think you should accept it and relax.
Kevin What should I do if she also finds it er, difficult, er, uncomfortable?
Catherine Then I think you should talk to Alan. Tell him that he's a good friend, but that you and Suzanna have problems with the way he behaves. I'm sure he'll stop doing it. He's probably never thought it was a problem.
Kevin Thanks very much for that. I'll talk to Suzanna tonight.

3 53))

Presenter And our next caller is Miranda from Brighton. Hi Miranda.
Miranda Hi.
Presenter And what's your problem?
Miranda My problem is with my husband's ex-wife. They divorced five years ago, before I met him. But she still phones him at least once a week to chat, and if she has a problem in her flat or with her car, she always calls him and asks him to come and help her.
Presenter Does your husband have children with his ex-wife?
Miranda No, they don't have any children. That's why I think she should stay out of our lives.
Presenter Catherine, over to you. What do you think Miranda should do?

3 54))

Catherine Hi Miranda. Well, the first thing is have you spoken to your husband about this?
Miranda Yes, I have. He thinks I'm being difficult. He feels sorry for his ex – she's on her own, she doesn't have a partner.
Catherine OK. Miranda, do you have any male friends, men who are just good friends?
Miranda Yes, I have a friend called Bill. We've been friends since I was a teenager.
Catherine That's perfect. My advice is this: when your husband's ex-wife phones and asks him to go and see her, phone Bill and arrange to meet and have a drink or go to the cinema. Every time your husband meets his ex or has a long phone call, then you meet Bill or have a long phone call. He'll soon see what's happening, and he'll stop seeing his ex.
Miranda I think that's a great idea. Thank you, Catherine.
Presenter And the next caller is…

4 6))

Presenter And to finish our programme today, the incredible story of a Swedish couple who went on holiday and survived no fewer than seven natural disasters! Stefan and Erika Svanström started their four-month trip last December. They were travelling with their young baby daughter. First they flew from Stockholm to Munich. But when they arrived in Munich they couldn't get their connecting flight to Thailand because there was a terrible blizzard in South Germany – the worst snowstorm for a hundred years! They had to wait at the airport for 24 hours. Mrs Svanström said:
Mrs Svanström 'We just thought things will get better.'
Presenter When they finally got to Thailand, they had a relaxing few weeks. But that was the last time they could really relax. From Thailand they flew to the island of Bali in Indonesia, a popular holiday destination. When they arrived in Bali they were expecting blue skies and sun, but what they got were terrible monsoon rains – the worst monsoons for many years. Mrs Svanström said:
Mrs Svanström 'Now we were thinking, what will happen next?'
Presenter They decided not to stay in Bali, but to go to Australia. They flew to Perth in Western Australia, but hours after they arrived Perth suffered terrible forest fires, and the streets were full of smoke. They travelled north to Cairns, and arrived just in time for Cyclone Yasi – one of the worst cyclones ever to hit the city. They had to leave their hotel and spend 24 hours in a shopping centre with 2,500 other people.
Could things get any worse? Yes, they could. The Svanström family left Cairns and travelled south to Brisbane to visit friends, but the city was suffering from the worst floods in its history. So they left Brisbane and booked to fly to Christchurch in New Zealand. But just before their plane left Brisbane some friends phoned them to say that Christchurch had been hit by an earthquake and a large part of the city was destroyed. Their plane landed in another city, Auckland. They travelled around New Zealand for a while, and then they flew to Japan. On March 11th they were having lunch in a restaurant in Tokyo when suddenly everything began to shake. It was an earthquake: nine on the Richter scale and one of the worst that ever hit Japan. And after the earthquake came a devastating tsunami. Fortunately, Mr and Mrs Svanström and their child were not hurt. They travelled from Japan to China for the last part of their holiday. Luckily, they didn't have any more natural disasters, and they arrived safely home in Stockholm on 29th March. Mr Svanström said:
Mr Svanström 'We have learnt that in life you should always expect the worst, but hope for the best. Also, you need to be prepared for anything.'

4 10))

Part 3
Hartley "Héloïse will go,"
Reader said Hartley angrily.
Hartley "I haven't had one day without problems since I met her. You are right, Vivienne. Héloïse must go before I can take you home. But she will go. I have decided…"
Vivienne "Then,"
Reader said Vivienne,
Vivienne "my answer is yes. I will be yours."
Reader She looked into his eyes and Hartley could hardly believe his luck.
Hartley "Promise me,"
Reader he said.
Vivienne "I promise,"
Reader repeated Vivienne, softly. At the door he turned and looked at her happily.
Hartley "I will come for you tomorrow,"
Reader he said.
Vivienne "Tomorrow,"
Reader she repeated with a smile. An hour and forty minutes later Hartley stepped off the train when it stopped in the suburbs, and walked to his house. As he walked towards the door a woman ran to him. She had black hair and was wearing a long white dress. They kissed, and walked into the house.

4 11))
Part 4
Hartley's wife "My mother is here,"
Reader the woman said.
Hartley's wife "But she's leaving in half an hour. She came to have dinner, but there's nothing to eat."
Hartley "I have something to tell you,"
Reader said Hartley. He whispered something in her ear. His wife screamed. Her mother came running into the hall. The woman screamed again, but it was a happy scream – the sound of a woman whose husband loved her.
Hartley's wife "Oh, mother!"
Reader she cried,
Hartley's wife "What do you think? Vivienne is coming to be our cook! She is the cook that was with the Montgomery's. She's going to be ours! And now, dear,"
Reader she told her husband,
Hartley's wife "you must go to the kitchen and tell Héloïse to leave. She has been drunk again all day."

4 20))
1 **Interviewer** Do you have any phobias?
   A Yes, I'm terrified of bats.
   Interviewer Really? How long have you had the phobia?
   A I've had it for about forty years! Since I was 12 years old. At my school we had a swimming pool, and the changing rooms were in an old building near the pool. On the first day at school our teacher told us that there were bats in there and that we shouldn't move around too much as they might start flying around and get into our hair. She also said we mustn't turn the lights on because this would wake up the bats. We had to change as quickly and quietly as possible.
   Interviewer Did a bat every fly into your hair?
   A No, nothing ever happened, but I was terrified just at the thought of it.
   Interviewer Does it affect your life at all?
   A Yes, I often feel very nervous or start to panic if I'm outside when it's beginning to get dark, which is when bats appear. If I'm sitting in my garden in the evening, I always have a tennis racket, so if a bat flies near me, I can protect myself. And I can't watch a TV documentary about bats, or even look at them in photos.
2 **Interviewer** Do you have any phobias?
   B Yes, I get very bad claustrophobia.
   Interviewer How long have you had the phobia?
   B It just started one morning about ten years ago. I was going to work on the train and it was very crowded. I started thinking that if there were an accident, I'd never get out. I had a panic attack and I sort of felt my heart beating very quickly. I had to get off the train.
   Interviewer How does your phobia affect your life?
   B Well, I can't travel on crowded trains. I never ever travel on the underground because my worst nightmare would be if the train stopped in the tunnel. I also try to avoid lifts. What else? Oh yes, if I'm flying, I must have an aisle seat. I can't sit by the window.
3 **Interviewer** Do you have any phobias?
   C Yes, I have a pretty unusual phobia. I'm scared of clowns.
   Interviewer Clowns, really? How long have you had it?
   C I've had it for a long time. Since I was a child.
   Interviewer How did it start?
   C Well, I remember I went on a school trip to the circus when I was six or seven years old and there were clowns. I thought they were sort of stupid but I wasn't really afraid of them. Then I went to a birthday party and there were clowns and they were showing us how to paint our faces, and I found I didn't like being near them. At first I just didn't like them, but over the years my feelings have changed to fear.
   Interviewer Does your phobia affect your life at all?
   C Not really because luckily I don't see clowns very often!

4 29))
Good evening and welcome to *Top Sounds*, our weekly music programme, and tonight the focus is on the Latin music star Enrique Iglesias. As I'm sure you all know, Enrique Iglesias is the son of the Spanish singer Julio Iglesias, who is one of the most successful singing artists of all time.
   Enrique was born in Madrid, Spain in 1975. His mother is Isabel Preysler, a journalist and TV host from the Philippines. When he was three years old his parents got divorced and later he moved to Miami to live with his father. He started studying Business at Miami University, but he left after a year because he wanted to become a musician. He didn't want his father to know about his music career and he didn't want to use his famous surname to be successful. So when he sent some of his songs to several record companies he used the name Enrique Martinez and he eventually got a contract with a Mexican record company.
   He made his first album, called *Enrique Iglesias* in 1995, which won him a Grammy. He then made two more albums and he had many hits in the Latin music charts. At first Enrique sang mainly in Spanish but later he began to sing more and more in English too.
   His fourth album, *Escape* in 2001, was his biggest commercial success and included the singles *Escape* and *Hero*, sung in English, which became hits all over the world and made Enrique an international star. Since then he has made five other albums and has also had a few acting parts in films and TV programmes. Also in 2001, he began dating the Russian tennis player, Ana Kournikova, but they kept their relationship very private. Today Enrique Iglesias is recognized as one of the most popular artists in Latin America. He has sold 100 million albums, which makes him one of the best selling artists of all time.

4 31))
Holly That was a good day's work, Rob. You did a great interview.
Rob You took some great photos, too. They're really nice.
Holly Thanks. Hey, let's have another coffee.
Rob I don't know. I have to get to Manhattan.
Holly You don't have to go right now.
Rob I'm not sure. I don't want to be late.
Holly Why do you have to go to Manhattan?
Rob I've got a... erm...
Holly A date? You have a date?
Rob Mm hm.
Holly Is it with anybody I know?
Rob No, it isn't. Anyway, excuse me a minute. I need to go to 'the rest room'.
Holly That's very American. I'll order more coffees.
Rob OK.
Jenny Rob?
Holly Is that you, Jennifer?
Jenny Oh, hi Holly. Erm... is Rob there?
Holly Yeah, one second. Rob! Not anybody I know, huh?
Rob Hi, Jenny.
Jenny Rob? Are you still in Brooklyn?
Rob Yeah.
Jenny You know the reservation at the restaurant's for eight, right?
Rob Don't worry. I'll be there! Oh, how do I get to Greenwich Village on the subway?

4 35))
Rob Jenny! I'm here.
Jenny Hi.
Rob I'm so sorry. There was a problem on the underground.
Jenny We call it the subway here.
Rob Right. Anyway, the train stopped for about twenty minutes. I tried to call but there was no signal.
Jenny I've been here since seven forty-five.
Rob I know. I ran from the underground... subway station... I'm so sorry.
Jenny You're always late. It's funny, isn't it?
Rob I said I'm sorry. Look, why don't we go back inside the restaurant?
Jenny I waited for an hour for you. I don't want to stay here anymore.
Rob Maybe we could... we could go for a walk. We could find another restaurant.
Jenny I don't feel like a walk. It's been a long day.
Rob OK.
Jenny But the night is still young. Maybe you have time to meet up with Holly again.
Rob Holly?
Jenny I'm sorry. I didn't mean to say that.
Rob I don't care about Holly.
Jenny Forget it, Rob. Now if you don't mind, I'd like to go home.
Rob Listen to me, Jenny. Holly is just a colleague.
Jenny I said forget it. It's OK.
Rob No, it isn't OK. Look. I know I'm always late. And I know the underground is the subway. But that's not the point! I'm not interested in Holly. I came to New York because of you. The only person I'm interested in is you!

4 37))
Presenter Good afternoon, and welcome to another edition of *Science Today*. In today's programme we are going to hear about women inventors. When we think of famous inventors we usually think of men, people like Alexander Graham Bell, Guglielmo Marconi, Thomas Edison. But, as Sally will tell us, many of the things which make our lives easier today were invented by women.
Sally That's absolutely right. Let's take the dishwasher for example. This was invented by a woman called Josephine Cochrane in 1886. She was a rich American who gave a lot of dinner parties. But she was annoyed that her servants used to break plates and glasses when they were washing up after a party. So, Josephine decided to try and invent a machine which could wash a lot of plates and glasses safely. Apparently she said: 'If nobody else is going to invent a dishwasher, then I will!' She designed the machine and then she found a company to make it. At first only hotels and restaurants bought Josephine's new machine but today the dishwasher is used by millions of people all over the world.
   The car was invented by a man, but it was a woman, Mary Anderson, who in 1903 solved one of the biggest problems of driving. Until her invention it was impossible for drivers to see where they were going when it was raining or snowing. They had to open their window. The name of Mary's invention? Windscreen wipers.
   An invention that definitely improved the lives of millions of people was disposable nappies. They were invented by a woman called Marion Donovan. Her father and uncle were inventors, and when she had young children she sat down and invented a nappy that you could use and then throw away. Anybody who has a small baby will know what a big difference disposable nappies make to our lives. But although she invented it in 1950, it wasn't until 1961 that an American company bought Marion's idea. Today millions of disposable nappies are used every day and Marion's invention has been made more eco-friendly. Now you can buy biodegradable nappies!
   And now to our next inventor. In 1956, Bette Nesmith Graham was working as a secretary. Like all secretaries at that time she used to get very frustrated and angry when she made typing mistakes. In those days if you made a mistake, you had to get a new sheet of paper and start again from the beginning. Then she had a brilliant

idea, which was to use a white liquid to paint over mistakes. Her invention is called Tipp-Ex today. Mrs Graham was a divorced mother and her invention made her a very rich woman. Her son, Mike Nesmith, became a famous pop star – he was a member of the American group, The Monkees.

And finally… policemen, soldiers, and politicians all over the world are protected by something which was invented by a woman. In 1966 Stephanie Kwolek invented kevlar, a special material which was very light but incredibly strong, much stronger than metal. This material is used to make bullet-proof vests. Stephanie's invention has probably saved thousands of lives.

Presenter Thanks very much, Sally. So, if you thought that everything was invented by men, think again.

4 46)))

1 **Presenter** Did you like school?
   A No, definitely not.
   Presenter Why?
   A I didn't like most of the lessons – I was always bored, and I hated exams. And the worst thing of all was PE. Where I went to school we used to play rugby. Ugh – it was torture.
2 **Presenter** Did you like school?
   B I loved primary school, but I didn't really like secondary school.
   Presenter Why not?
   B Well the school was very big and it was sort of cold and impersonal. It took me a very long time before I felt at home there. And I'm not really very academic, but the school was. We used to get loads of homework which I hated.
3 **Presenter** Did you like school?
   C Er, yes, I did.
   Presenter Why?
   C I was very curious about everything when I was little, so I liked school because I learned about new things. The other thing I used to see my friends every day. The other thing I loved was the library – my school had a fantastic library – I even used to stay on there after class just to read. Oh dear, I sound very goody-goody, but it's true!
4 **Presenter** Did you like school?
   D Not especially
   Presenter Why?
   D It was a boys' school and I got a bit fed up with just being with boys all the time.
5 **Presenter** Did you like school?
   E It was all right – some bits were better than others, of course. The lessons I liked depended very much on the teacher – so for example physics and English were great, but chemistry and history were terrible. I generally liked sport, except in the winter. I made some good friends at school, and I'm still in touch with a few of them 30 years later, so I suppose that's positive!
6 **Presenter** Did you like school?
   F Actually, I used to really love school. Lessons were fine, and I always did well without having to work too hard. But the real reason I loved school was because I had a very good social life. I had lots of friends and we used to play football in the playground at lunchtime. I was one of the gang. I felt that I belonged there. I've never really felt like that since then.

5 11)))

And our last story on today's *News Hour* is about an incredible coincidence. Have you ever put your name into Google or Facebook to see what comes up? One evening last April, an American woman, Kelly Hildebrandt, did just that. She was feeling bored, so she put her name into Facebook. She has quite an unusual name, so she was amazed to discover that there was another person on Facebook with exactly the same name and surname as her – but with one big difference. The other Kelly Hildebrandt was a man, and he lived in Texas. Kelly sent him a message and they began to email each other. Later they started to phone each other every day, and finally they met in person. They discovered that they had more in common than just their name – they both love the beach, and they both really enjoy cooking. Soon they realised that they were in love. At first they were worried that they might be related, but they found out that there was no family connection at all, and in October Kelly asked Kelly to marry him. The two Kelly's call each other 'Kelly girl' and 'Kelly boy', and they say that having the same name often causes confusion – once when Kelly boy booked travel tickets for them the travel agent almost cancelled one ticket because he thought that booking two tickets with the same name was a mistake. But there is one thing that the two Kellys are very clear about – if they have children they definitely won't call them Kelly!

5 12)))

Jenny I can't believe it. Your month here is nearly over. It's gone so fast.
Rob I know. I've had a great time, Jenny.
Jenny Me too. It's been really special. But…
Rob But what?
Jenny It won't be the same when you're in London and I'm here.
Rob But we'll still be in touch. You can visit me in London and I can come back here to see you.
Jenny It still won't be the same.
Rob No. No, it won't.
Jenny Maybe… I could come back to London with you?
Rob You can't do that Jenny. You've just got this job.
Jenny That's true.
Rob Well, we still have some time together. We're going out for dinner tonight!
Jenny Yes, and I'm going to take you somewhere really nice.
Rob Look at the time. I have to go now; it's my last interview in New York. I don't want to be late.
Jenny OK. See you later then.
Rob Bye.
Barbara Jenny, is Rob here?
Jenny Oh, you just missed him, Barbara.
Barbara I really need to talk to him. I'll try him on his cell phone. Hello, Rob? It's Barbara. Can you give me a call? There's something I'd like to talk about.

5 15)))

Rob Jenny!
Jenny Rob! I have something to tell you.
Rob I have something to tell you too. You go first.
Jenny Well. I thought again about moving to London…
Rob But you don't need to move to London.
Jenny What?
Rob Barbara called me earlier.
Jenny What about?
Rob She offered me a job. Here, in New York!
Jenny What?! Oh, that's great news.
Rob You don't seem very pleased.
Jenny I am, I mean, it's great! It's just that…
Rob What?
Jenny I sent Barbara an email this morning.
Rob And?
Jenny I told her I was quitting, and moving to London.
Rob Don't worry. Maybe she hasn't read your email yet.
Jenny I'll call her.
Barbara Hello, Barbara Keaton.
Jenny Barbara? It's Jenny.
Barbara Oh, hi Jenny.
Jenny Um, have you read your emails recently? There's one from me.
Barbara Oh yes. I can see it. I haven't opened it yet.
Jenny Don't open it! Delete it! Please just delete it. I'll explain later.
Barbara OK. It's gone. Is everything alright, Jenny?
Jenny Yes, thanks. Never better.

5 19)))

And finally on *News Today* here's a funny story to cheer you up on a Monday morning.

On Saturday night Katie Parfitt, a nurse from Manchester, came home from work. As soon as she opened the door, she realised that her cat, Joey, was behaving rather strangely. Instead of being pleased to see her, he started attacking her, and then, when she sat down to have something to eat, Joey jumped onto the table and sat on her plate. Then he jumped down onto the floor and immediately went to sleep. He slept all night, snoring very loudly. Katie couldn't understand what the matter was with Joey – he had never behaved like this before. However, when she met her neighbour the next morning, the mystery was solved.

5 20)))

My neighbour told me that he was having a drink in our local pub on Saturday. Suddenly he saw my cat Joey walk in though the door – it was open because it was a hot day. And then one of the people spilled his glass of beer on the floor and Joey starting drinking it – he was probably thirsty. So of course when Joey got home he was completely drunk! I took him to the vet the next day, but luckily he's fine now.

5 21)))

Iris Hello Rosemary. How are you this morning?
Rosemary Hello Iris. I'm fine thanks, but you'll never guess what's happened. Jack and Emma have broken up!
Iris No! Jack and Emma from number 36? That can't be true. I saw them last week and they looked really happy.
Rosemary No, it's definitely true. I heard them shouting. They were having a terrible argument.
Iris No! When?
Rosemary Last night. After he came home from work.
Iris What did they say?
Rosemary Well, I wasn't really listening…
Iris Of course not.
Rosemary But I couldn't help hearing. She was talking so loudly and of course the walls are very thin.
Iris So what did they say?
Rosemary Well, she said she that was going to stay with her mum! She told him that she wouldn't come back.
Iris Ooh, how awful. What about the children?
Rosemary She said she'd taken them to her sister. I suppose she'll take them with her in the end. And anyway, then five minutes later I saw her leaving the house with a suitcase!
Iris No! Why do you think she's leaving him? Is he seeing another woman?
Rosemary I don't know. Ooh, here's my bus.
Iris I must go and tell Mrs Jones at number 14. She always thought there was something… something strange about him…

5 22)))

Jack Hi Emma. I'm back. Where are you?
Emma I'm upstairs in the bedroom. I'm packing.
Jack Why? Where are you going?
Emma I'm going to stay with my mum.
Jack What happened to her?
Emma She's had an accident. She fell over in the street yesterday and she's broken her leg.
Jack How awful. Poor thing. Shall I go and make you a cup of tea?
Emma That'd be lovely. Thanks darling.
Jack How long do you think you'll have to stay?
Emma I won't come back until the weekend I don't think. I'll have to make sure she's OK. I've taken the children to my sister's for the night and she'll take them school tomorrow morning. Can you pick them up after school?
Jack Of course I can darling. Now don't worry about anything. We'll be absolutely fine. Drink your tea and I'll go and get your suitcase.
Emma Thanks, darling. The taxi'll be here in five minutes.

1

1A word order in questions

questions with do / does / did in present simple and past simple

question word	auxiliary	subject	infinitive (= verb)
	Do	you	live with your parents?
	Did	you	have a holiday last year?
Where	does	your sister	work?
When	did	you	start studying English?
What	did	they	talk about?

- Use **ASI** (**A**uxiliary, **S**ubject, **I**nfinitive) and **QUASI** (**Qu**estion word, **A**uxiliary, **S**ubject, **I**nfinitive) to remember word order in questions.

questions with be

question word	be	subject	adjective, noun, etc.
What	Are	you	hungry?
	Is	there	a bank near here?
	was	that	noise?
Where	are	you	from?
	were	you	born?

- Make questions with the verb *be* by inverting the verb and the subject.
  She is a teacher. **Is she** a teacher?

1B present simple

	I / you / we / they	he / she / it
+	I usually **work** at home.	Holly **knows** me very well.
−	They **don't live** near here.	It **doesn't** often **rain** here.
?	**Do** you **speak** French?	**Does** Alice **like** jazz?
✓ ✗	Yes, I **do**. / No, I **don't**.	Yes, she **does**. / No, she **doesn't**.

- Use the present simple for things you do every day / week / year, or for things which are generally true or always happen.
- Use *don't / doesn't* to make negative sentences, and *do / does* to make questions.

spelling rules for the 3rd person -s (he, she, it)

infinitive	3rd person	spelling
work	works	add -s
study	studies	consonant + y > ies
finish	finishes	add -es after sh, ch, s, x
go / do	goes / does	add -es
have	has	change to -s

adverbs and expressions of frequency

1. We **often** go out on Friday night.
   She doesn't **usually** study at weekends.
   I'm **never** ill.
   He's **always** late for work.
2. She gets up early **every day**.
   We have English classes **twice a week**.

1. We often use the present simple with adverbs of frequency (*always, usually, often, sometimes, hardly ever, never*).
   - Adverbs of frequency go <u>before</u> the main verb.
   - Adverbs of frequency go <u>after</u> *be*.
     She's **never** ill. NOT ~~She's ill never.~~
   - Remember to use a + verb with *never*.
     It never rains. NOT ~~It doesn't never rain.~~
2. Expressions of frequency (*every day, once a week*, etc.) usually go at the end of a sentence.

1C present continuous: be + verb + -ing

1. **A** What **are you doing**?
   B I'**m sending** a message to Sarah.
2. My brother **is doing** a two-month course in the UK.
3. In this picture the woman **is standing** near the window.

- Use the present continuous:
  1. for things that are happening now, at this moment.
  2. for temporary things that are happening now, this week, etc.
  3. to describe a picture.

	I	you / we / they	he / she / it
+ −	I'm working I'm not working	You We They	're working aren't working	He She It	's working isn't working
? ✓ ✗	Are you working?	Yes, I am. / No, I'm not.		
	Is he working?	Yes, he is. / No, he isn't.		

spelling rules for the -ing form

infinitive	-ing form	spelling
cook study	cooking studying	add -ing
live	living	cut the final *e* and add -ing
run	running	double the final consonant and add -ing

present simple or present continuous?

A What **do you do**? **B** I **work** for Microsoft.
A What **are you doing**? **B** I'**m checking** my emails.

- Use the present simple for things that are generally true or always happen.
- Use the present continuous for an action happening now or at this moment.
- We normally use verbs which describe states or feelings (non-action verbs), e.g. *want, need, like*, in the present simple, not continuous.

GRAMMAR BANK

1A

a Put the word or phrase in the right place in the question.

How *old* are you? (old)
1 Where do you from? (come)
2 Where the train station? (is)
3 How often you read magazines? (do)
4 Where your friends from? (are)
5 Why you write to me? (didn't)
6 Do you often to the cinema? (go)
7 What this word mean? (does)
8 What time did arrive? (your friends)
9 Does finish at 8.00? (the class)
10 Where were born? (you)

b Put the words in the right order to make questions.

you live where do ?   *Where do you live?*
1 you a do have car ?
2 older is brother your you than ?
3 often he how to write does you ?
4 this time start does what class ?
5 Brazil from is friend your ?
6 languages how you many do speak ?
7 she born where was ?
8 last go where you summer did ?
9 father doctor your is a ?
10 come bus to you by school did ?

◄ p.5

1B

a Write sentences and questions with the present simple.

he / usually get up late ⊞   *He usually gets up late.*
1 Anna / like music ?
2 my sister / have a lot of hobbies ⊞
3 I / get on very well with my parents ⊟
4 my brother / study at university ⊞
5 my neighbours / have any children ⊟
6 when / the film start ?
7 he / go out twice a week ⊞
8 we / often talk about politics ⊟
9 how often / you email your brother ?
10 I / go on Facebook very often ⊟

b Put the words in the right order.

go cinema we often the to   *We often go to the cinema.*
1 always before go I bed 11.00 to
2 ever her Kate sees family hardly
3 Saturdays never shopping on go we
4 a to I dentist's year go twice the
5 in they breakfast the sometimes garden have
6 usually morning the we the listen in radio to
7 in day park every Alan the runs
8 after drink I coffee 4.00 never
9 often John to go doesn't cinema the
10 visit I once my month a mum

◄ p.7

1C

a Write sentences with the present continuous.

It / rain ⊟   *It isn't raining.*
1 John / wear a shirt today! ⊞
2 It's hot. Why / wear a coat ?
3 Anna / sit next to Jane today ⊟
4 Hey! You / stand on my foot! ⊞
5 what book / you read ?
6 we / think of you at the moment ⊞
7 she / wear make-up ?
8 they / make a big mistake ⊞
9 your mother / shop in town ?
10 she / live with her parents at the moment ⊟

b Complete the sentences with the present simple or present continuous.

The girl in the painting *is playing* the guitar. (play)
1 My dog's not dangerous. He _____. (not bite)
2 Why _____ you _____ sunglasses? It _____! (wear, rain)
3 You can turn off the radio. I _____ to it. (not listen)
4 I _____ to go to the bank. I _____ any money. (need, not have)
5 Be careful! The baby _____ that pen in her mouth! (put)
6 A _____ you usually _____ at weekends? (cook)
   B No, we normally _____ out. (eat)
7 A What _____ you _____ here? (do)
   B I _____ for Emma. She's late, as usual. (wait)
8 I usually drink tea, but I _____ a coffee today. (want)
9 My sister _____ from 9.00 to 5.00. She's a secretary. (work)
10 We _____ in Paris, but we _____ in Nice at the moment. (live, stay)

◄ p.8

2A past simple: regular and irregular verbs

	regular	irregular 1 36))
+	I **stayed** with friends.	We **went** to Brazil on holiday.
–	I **didn't stay** in a hotel.	We **didn't go** to São Paulo.
?	**Did** you **stay** for the weekend?	**Did** you **go** to Rio?
✓ ✗	Yes, I **did**.	No, we **didn't**.
Wh ?	Where **did** you **stay**?	Why **did** you **go** there?

- Use the past simple to talk about finished actions in the past.
- The form of the past simple is the same for all persons.
- To make the past simple + of regular verbs add *-ed*. See the spelling rules in the chart.
- Many common verbs are irregular in the + past simple, e.g. *go > went, see > saw*. See **Irregular verbs** p.164.

- Use the infinitive after *didn't* for negatives and *Did…?* for questions.
- Use **ASI** and **QUASI** to remember word order in questions.

spelling rules for regular verbs		
infinitive	past	spelling
work stay	work**ed** stay**ed**	add *-ed*
like	lik**ed**	add *-d* if verb finishes in *e*
study	stud**ied**	*y > ied* after a consonant
stop	stop**ped**	if verb finishes in consonant–vowel–consonant, double the final consonant

---

2B past continuous: was / were + verb + -ing

At 8.45 last Saturday I **was working** in my office. 1 39))
I **wasn't doing** anything important.
My friends **were having** breakfast. They **weren't working**.
A **Was** it **raining** when you got up? B No, **it wasn't**.
A What **were** you **doing** at 11 o'clock last night? B I **was watching** TV.

+	I / He / She / It	was working	You / We / They	were working
–	I / He / She / It	wasn't working	You / We / They	weren't working
? ✓ ✗	**Was** he **working**?	**Yes**, he **was**. / **No**, he **wasn't**.		
	Were they **working**?	**Yes**, they **were**. / **No**, they **weren't**.		

- Use the past continuous to describe an action in progress at a specific moment in the past.
- We often use the past continuous to describe the situation at the beginning of a story or narrative.

past simple or past continuous?

I **was working** in my office when the 1 40))
boss **walked in**.
I **was having** lunch when my sister **arrived**.

- Use the past simple for a completed action in the past.
- Use the past continuous for an action in progress before or at the time of the past simple action.

2C time sequencers

On our first date we went to the cinema. **After that** we started 1 46))
meeting every day.
On Thursday I had an argument with my boss. **Next day** I decided to look for a new job.
We sat down to eat. **Two minutes later** the phone rang.
When I came out of the club he was waiting for me.
The accident happened **when** I was crossing the road.

- We use time sequencers to say when or in what order things happen.
- We use *when* as a time sequencer and also to join two actions.
I *was watching* TV *when* the phone *rang*. (two verbs joined by *when*)

 then, after that
The most common way of linking consecutive actions is with *then* or *after that*, but **NOT** with *after*, e.g. *I got up and got dressed.* **Then** / **After that** *I made a cup of coffee.* **NOT** ~~After I made a cup of coffee.~~

connectors: because, so, but, although

because and so

She was driving fast **because** she was in 1 47))
a hurry. (reason)
She was in a hurry, **so** she was driving fast. (result)

- Use *because* to express a reason.
- Use *so* to express a result.

but and although

She tried to stop the car, **but** she hit the man. 1 48))
Although she tried to stop the car, she hit the man.
She was very tired, **but** she couldn't sleep.
She couldn't sleep, **although** she was very tired.

- Use *but* and *although* to show a contrast.
- *Although* can go at the beginning or in the middle of a sentence.

GRAMMAR BANK

2A

a Put the verbs in brackets in the past simple.

Two summers ago we _had_ (have) a holiday in Scotland. We ¹_____ (drive) there from London, but our car ²_____ (break) down on the motorway and we ³_____ (spend) the first night in Birmingham. When we ⁴_____ (get) to Edinburgh we ⁵_____ (not can) find a good hotel – they ⁶_____ (be) all full. We ⁷_____ (not know) what to do, but in the end we ⁸_____ (find) a Bed and Breakfast and we ⁹_____ (stay) there for the week. We ¹⁰_____ (see) the castle, ¹¹_____ (go) to the Arts Festival, and we ¹²_____ (buy) a lot of souvenirs. We ¹³_____ (want) to go to Loch Ness, but we ¹⁴_____ (not have) much time and it ¹⁵_____ (be) quite far away. The weather ¹⁶_____ (not be) very good, and it ¹⁷_____ (start) raining the day we ¹⁸_____ (leave).

b Complete the questions in the past simple.

Where did you go on holiday last year?
We went to Vancouver.
1 _____ a good time?
Yes, we had a great time.
2 _____ with?
I went with my family.
3 _____?
We stayed in a hotel.
4 _____ the plane ticket _____?
It cost £500.
5 _____ the weather like?
It was hot and sunny.
6 _____ at night?
We went to bars and restaurants. ◀ p.13

2B

a Complete the sentences with a verb in the past continuous.

I _was eating_ dinner, so I didn't answer the phone. (eat)
1 I took this photo when my wife _____ in the garden. (work)
2 He met his wife when he _____ in Japan. (live)
3 They _____ for us when we arrived. (not wait)
4 _____ she _____ a coat when she went out? (wear)
5 The sun _____ when I left for work. (shine)
6 What _____ you _____ at 7.30 last night? (do)
7 I _____ when you gave the instructions. (not listen)
8 We _____ TV when you phoned. (not watch)

b Put the verbs into the past simple or past continuous.

She _arrived_ when we _were having_ dinner. (arrive, have)
1 I _____ my arm when I _____ football. (break, play)
2 _____ you _____ fast when the police _____ you? (drive, stop)
3 It _____ when we _____ the pub. (snow, leave)
4 I _____ the match because I _____. (not see, work)
5 When you _____ me, I _____ to my boss. (call, talk)
6 We _____ in Cambridge when we _____. (study, meet)
7 _____ they _____ in Rome when they _____ their first baby? (live, have)

◀ p.14

2C

a Put the sentences in the right order.

a ☐ He told me he was a policeman and that they were looking for a thief.
b ☐ Then another man tried to do the same.
c ☐ 1 ☐ One day in 2011 I was standing in the queue for a bus.
d ☐ Next day I read the story in a newspaper.
e ☐ When the second man went in front of me, I told him to go and stand in the queue.
f ☐ A few seconds later, the first policeman got off the bus with a man.
g ☐ Suddenly a man ran in front of me and got on the bus.
h ☐ After that, a police car came and took the men away.

b Complete the sentences with _so_, _because_, _but_, or _although_.

We couldn't find a taxi, _so_ we walked home.
1 _____ it was very cold, she wasn't wearing a coat.
2 I woke up in the night _____ there was a noise.
3 I called him, _____ his mobile was turned off.
4 _____ she's very nice, she doesn't have many friends.
5 There was nothing on TV, _____ I went to bed.
6 All the cafés were full _____ it was a public holiday.
7 She wanted to be a doctor, _____ she failed her exams.
8 The garden looked very beautiful, _____ I took a photograph.
9 _____ the team played well, they didn't win.

◀ p.16

3

3A be going to

1 I'**m going to** work for an NGO. 🔊 1 57
  He'**s going to** meet me at the airport.
2 I'm sure England **are going to lose** tomorrow.
  It'**s going to** rain tonight.

	I	you / we / they		he / she / it		
+	I'**m going to**	You We They	'**re going to**	He She It	'**s going to**	work for an NGO.
−	I'**m not going to**	You We They	**aren't going to**	He She It	**isn't going to**	work for an NGO.

?	✓ ✗
Are you **going to** work for an NGO? **Is** he **going to** work for an NGO?	Yes, I **am**. / No, I'**m not**. Yes, he **is**. / No, he **isn't**.

1 Use *be going to* + infinitive to talk about future plans or intentions.
2 We use *be going to* + infinitive to make a prediction when we know or can see that something is going to happen.
*It's winter there so it'**s going to be** cold.*
*Look at that car! It'**s going to crash**.*

3B present continuous (future arrangements)

| + | I'**m seeing** a friend tonight. 🔊 1 64 |
| She'**s arriving** at lunchtime. |
| − | She **isn't leaving** until Friday. |
| They **aren't coming** to the party. |
| ? | What **are** you **doing** this evening? |
| **Is** she **meeting** us at the restaurant? |

- We often use the present continuous with a future meaning, especially for future arrangements, i.e. for plans we have made at a fixed time or place in the future. <u>Don't</u> use the present simple for this. **NOT** ~~I see some friends tonight~~.

> 🔍 **be going to** or present continuous?
> We can often use either with no difference in meaning, e.g. *I'm going to see Anna on Tuesday.* **OR** *I'm seeing Anna on Tuesday.*
> It's very common to use the present continuous with the expressions *tonight, tomorrow, this weekend*, etc. and with verbs describing travel arrangements, e.g. *go, come, leave, arrive.*
> *I'm leaving on Monday* is more common than *I'm going to leave on Monday.*

3C defining relative clauses with *who, which, where*

A cook is a person **who** makes food.   2 5
That's the woman **who** won the lottery last year.
A clock is something **which** tells the time.
Is that the book **which** everybody's reading?
A post office is a place **where** you can buy stamps.
That's the restaurant **where** I had dinner last week.

- Use defining relative clauses to explain what a person, thing or place is or does.
- Use *who* for a person, *which* for a thing and *where* for a place.

> 🔍 **that**
> You can use *that* instead of *who* or *which*.
> *She's the girl **who / that** works with my brother.*
> *It's a thing **which / that** connects two computers.*

GRAMMAR BANK

3A

a Complete with *going to* + a verb.

be	cook	do	get	not go
learn	not listen	see	stay	

What film *are* you *going to see* tonight?
1. _____ your sister _____ Chinese?
2. You _____ in class 3 next year.
3. We _____ camping next summer. We _____ in a hotel.
4. We _____ a taxi to the airport.
5. I _____ a wonderful meal tonight.
6. You can talk, but I _____ to you.
7. What _____ you _____ when you leave school?

b Look at the pictures. Make sentences with *going to* + a verb.

be (x2)   love   ~~rain~~

It*'s going to rain*.

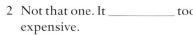

2 Not that one. It _____ too expensive.

1 We _____ late for work!   3 You _____ this book!

◀ p.21

3B

a Read the sentences. Write **N** for now, **F** for future.

- [F] I'm meeting Joe at two o'clock.
1. [ ] I'm living in a flat with two Swedish boys.
2. [ ] We're coming back on Monday.
3. [ ] She's moving to Canada soon.
4. [ ] I'm waiting for the postman.
5. [ ] I'm reading a really good book about science.
6. [ ] We're meeting Sally and James for lunch on Sunday.
7. [ ] Karl is arriving at 6 o'clock.
8. [ ] I'm studying for my maths exam.

b Complete the dialogue between two flatmates.

A What *are you doing* (do)?
B I ¹_____ (pack) my suitcase.
A Why?
B Because I ²_____ (fly) to Vienna at 8 o'clock tonight.
A Oh, I didn't know. Why ³_____ (go) to Vienna?
B I ⁴_____ (see) the boss of *VTech Solutions* tomorrow.
A Why ⁵_____ (meet) him?
B I ⁶_____ (work) on a project for him at the moment and I need to discuss it with him.
A Oh, well have a good trip!

◀ p.23

3C

a Complete the definitions with *who*, *which*, or *where*.

A postman is the person *who* brings you your letters.
1. An octopus is an animal _____ lives in the sea and has eight legs.
2. A lawnmower is a machine _____ cuts the grass.
3. A waiter is the person _____ serves you in a café.
4. A changing room is a room _____ people try on clothes.
5. A porter is the person _____ helps you with your luggage.
6. Garlic is a kind of food _____ keeps vampires away.
7. A garage is a place _____ people fix cars.

b Write sentences with *who*, *which*, or *where*.

She / the woman / catch the same bus as me
She's the woman who catches the same bus as me.
1. That / the dog / always barks at night
2. That / the shop / I bought my wedding dress
3. That / the actor / was in *Glee*
4. They / the children / live next door to me
5. This / the restaurant / they make great pizza
6. That / the switch / controls the air conditioning
7. He / the teacher / teaches my sister
8. That / the room / we have our meetings
9. This / the light / is broken

◀ p.24

4A present perfect

I**'ve finished** my homework. 🔊 2 16
She**'s cleaned** the kitchen.
He **hasn't done** the washing up.
A **Has she turned off** her phone?   B No, **she hasn't**.

- We often use the present perfect to talk about the recent past, not saying exactly when things happened.
- We often use the present perfect to give news.
  Mary**'s had** her baby! A parcel **has arrived** for you.

full form	contraction	negative	past participle
I **have**	I**'ve**	I **haven't**	
You **have**	You**'ve**	You **haven't**	
He / She / It **has**	He / She / It**'s**	He / She / It **hasn't**	**finished** the exercise.
We **have**	We**'ve**	We **haven't**	
They **have**	They**'ve**	They **haven't**	

Have you **finished** the exercise?   Yes, I **have**. / No, I **haven't**.
Has he **done** the homework?   Yes, he **has**. / No, he **hasn't**.

- For regular verbs the past participle is the same as the past simple (+ -ed). For irregular verbs the past participle is sometimes the same as the past simple (e.g. buy, bought, bought) and sometimes different (e.g. do, did, done). See **Irregular verbs** p.164.

yet, just, already

1 A Have you done your homework **yet**? 🔊 2 17
  B No, not **yet**. I haven't finished **yet**.
2 My sister's **just** started a new job.
3 A Do you want to see this film?
  B No, I've **already** seen it three times.

- We often use yet, just and already with the present perfect.
  1 Use yet in ? and − sentences to ask if something has happened or to say if it hasn't happened. Put yet at the end of the sentence.
  2 Use just in + sentences to say that something happened very recently. Put just before the main verb.
  3 Use already in + sentences to say that something happened before now or earlier than expected. Put already before the main verb.

4B present perfect or past simple? (1)

Have you ever been to a fancy dress party? 🔊 2 24
She**'s seen** that film twice.
I**'ve never met** Nina's husband.

- We often use the present perfect to talk about past experiences in our lives when we don't specify a time.

🔍 **been and gone**
Compare the present perfect of be and go.
Mike has **been** to Paris. = He went to Paris and came back.
Mike has **gone** to Paris. = He's in Paris now.

present perfect or past simple?

A **Have you ever been** to Mexico? 🔊 2 25
B Yes, I **have**.
A When **did you go** there?
B I **went** last year.

A **Have you seen** his new film?
B Yes, I **have**.
A What **did you think** of it?
B I **loved** it.

- Conversations often begin in the present perfect (with a general question) and then change to the past simple to ask for or give specific details, e.g. when, what, where, who with, etc.

4C something, anything, nothing, etc.

people 🔊 2 34

+	**Somebody / Someone** has taken my pen!
−	I didn't speak to **anybody / anyone**.
?	Did **anybody / anyone** phone?
✗	No, **nobody / no one**. **Nobody / No one** phoned.

things

+	I bought **something** for dinner.
−	I didn't do **anything** at the weekend.
?	Is there **anything** in the fridge?
✗	No, **nothing**. There's **nothing** in the fridge.

places

+	Let's go **somewhere** this weekend.
−	We didn't go **anywhere** this summer.
?	Is there **anywhere** to park?
✗	No, **nowhere**. There's **nowhere** to park.

- Use somebody / someone, something, somewhere with a + verb when you don't say exactly who, what, or where.
- Use anybody / anyone, anything, anywhere in questions or with a − verb.
  I **didn't do anything** last night. NOT ~~I didn't do nothing~~.
- Use nobody / no one, nothing, nowhere in short answers or in sentences with a + verb.

GRAMMAR BANK

4A

a Write sentences in the present perfect.

He / clean the car [+] He's cleaned the car.
1 She / buy a new jacket [+]
2 He / find a job yet [−]
3 / you speak to Mr Jackson [?]
4 We / find a fantastic hotel [+]
5 They / finish eating [−]
6 / you see Peter this morning [?]
7 / you do your homework this week [?]
8 We / reply to Mr Jones's email yet [−]

b Write sentences or questions with *already*, *just*, or *yet*.

He / arrive. (already) He's already arrived.
1 I / have / breakfast. (just)
2 / you / finish / your homework? (yet)
3 The film / start. (already)
4 I / not meet / his girlfriend. (yet)
5 They / get married. (just)
6 You're too late. He / go / home. (already)
7 / you speak / to him? (yet)
8 I / not read / his new book. (yet)

◀ p.29

4B

a Complete with the verb in the present perfect.

<u>Have</u> you <u>done</u> the shopping today? (do)
1 _____ you ever _____ clothes from that shop? (buy)
2 I _____ always _____ a pair of designer shoes. (want)
3 I _____ the newspaper today. (not read)
4 We _____ to the new shopping centre yet. (not be)
5 _____ your brother _____ abroad all his life? (live)
6 They _____ to live in South America. (go)
7 She _____ before. (not fly)
8 James _____ his girlfriend's family yet. (not meet)
9 _____ you _____ in this restaurant before? (eat)
10 Jane _____ to the gym – she'll be back in an hour. (go)

b Complete the dialogue with the present perfect or past simple.

A Oh no! I<u>'ve seen</u> this film before! (see)
B Really? When ¹_____ it? (see)
A I ²_____ to the cinema in March and it was on then. (go)
B Oh, never mind. I ³_____ to the cinema in ages. The last film I ⁴_____ was *Mamma Mia!* (not be, see)
A ⁵_____ it? (enjoy)
B Of course! I ⁶_____ it! (love)

c Complete with *been* or *gone*.

'Where's Rob?' 'He's <u>gone</u> to the football match.'
1 The kids aren't here. They've all _____ out.
2 Have you ever _____ to the swimming pool in town?
3 I haven't _____ to Sue's new flat yet.
4 My sister has _____ to teach in France.
5 Oh good. Dad's _____ to the shop – the fridge is full.

◀ p.31

4C

a Complete with *something*, *anything*, *nothing*, etc.

Are you doing <u>anything</u> tonight?
1 Did you meet _____ last night?
2 _____ phoned when you were out. They're going to call back later.
3 I've seen your wallet _____, but I can't remember where.
4 There's _____ interesting on TV tonight. Let's go out.
5 Did _____ call while I was out?
6 Did you go _____ exciting at the weekend?
7 I've bought you _____ really nice for Christmas!
8 I rang the doorbell, but _____ answered.
9 We went shopping, but we didn't buy _____.
10 There's _____ more expensive than London!

b Answer with *Nobody*, *Nowhere*, or *Nothing*.

1 What did you do last night? _____
2 Where did you go yesterday? _____
3 Who did you see? _____

c Answer the questions in **b** with a full sentence.

1 I didn't do _____.
2 _____.
3 _____.

◀ p.32

133

5A comparatives

1 My brother's **older than** me. (2 40))
  It's **more dangerous** to cycle **than** to drive.
2 People walk **more quickly than** in the past.
3 I'm **less relaxed** this year **than** I was last year.
4 The service in this restaurant isn't **as good as** it was.
  She doesn't drive **as fast as** her brother.

- To compare two people, places, things or actions use:
  1 comparative adjectives.
  2 comparative adverbs (for actions).
  3 *less* + adjective or adverb.
  4 (*not*) *as* + adjective / adverb + *as*.

comparative adjectives: regular

adjective	comparative	
short	short**er**	one syllable: add *-er*
big	big**ger**	one vowel + one consonant: double final consonant
busy	bus**ier**	consonant + *y*: *y* +*-ier*
relaxed	**more** relaxed	two or more syllables: *more* + adjective

comparative adjectives: irregular

adjective	comparative
good	better
bad	worse
far	further

adjective	comparative
stressed	more stressed
tired	more tired
bored	more bored

pcomparative adverbs: regular   irregular

quickly	**more** quickly
slowly	**more** slowly

hard	harder
well	better
badly	worse

> **Comparatives with pronouns**
> After comparative + *than* or *as...as* we use an object pronoun (*me*, *her*, etc.) or a subject pronoun + auxiliary verb, e.g.
> My brother's taller than **me**. My brother's taller than **I am**.
> He's not as intelligent as **her**. He's not as intelligent as **she is**.

5B superlatives

1 It's **the dirtiest** city in Europe. (2 43))
  It's **the most popular** holiday destination in the world.
2 It's **the most beautiful** city **I've ever been to**.
  It's **the best** film **I've seen** this year.

adjective	comparative	superlative
cold	cold**er**	the cold**est**
hot	hot**ter**	the hot**test**
pretty	pret**tier**	the pret**tiest**
beautiful	**more** beautiful	**the most** beautiful
good	better	the best
bad	worse	the worst
far	further	the furthest

1 Use *the* + superlative adjective to say which is the biggest, etc. in a group.
- After superlatives we use *in* + names of places or singular words for groups of people, e.g.
  It's **the noisiest** city **in** the world.
2 We often use *the* + superlative adjective with the present perfect + *ever*.

5C quantifiers

too much, too many, too

1 I'm stressed. I have **too much** work. (2 52))
  He talks **too much**.
2 My diet is unhealthy. I eat **too many** cakes and sweets.
3 I don't want to go out. I'm **too** tired.

- Use *too much*, *too many*, *too* to say 'more than is good'.
  1 Use *too much* + uncountable noun (e.g. *coffee*, *time*) or after a verb.
  2 Use *too many* + countable noun (e.g. *cakes*, *people*).
  3 Use *too* + adjective **NOT** ~~I'm too much tired~~.

enough

1 Do you eat **enough** vegetables? (2 53))
  I don't drink **enough** water.
2 She doesn't sleep **enough**.
3 My fridge isn't big **enough**.
  I don't go to bed early **enough**.

1 Use *enough* <u>before</u> a noun to mean 'all that is necessary'.
2 Use *enough* <u>after</u> a verb with no object.
3 Use *enough* <u>after</u> an adjective or adverb.

GRAMMAR BANK

5A

a Write sentences with a comparative adjective or adverb + *than*.

New York is <u>more expensive than</u> Miami. (expensive)
1 Modern computers are much _____ the early ones. (fast)
2 My sister is _____ me. (tall)
3 I'm _____ this week _____ last week. (busy)
4 Newcastle is _____ from London _____ Leeds. (far)
5 I thought the third *Men in Black* film was _____ the first two. (bad)
6 Manchester United played _____ Arsenal. (good)
7 The French exam was _____ the German. (hard)
8 My new job is _____ my old one. (boring)
9 My new apartment is _____ my old one. (big)
10 I'm not lazy – I just work _____ you! (slowly)

b Rewrite the sentences so they mean the same. Use *as… as*.

James is stronger than Clive.
Clive isn't <u>as strong as James</u>.
1 Adam is shorter than Jerry.
Jerry isn't _____.
2 Your bag is nicer than mine.
My bag isn't _____.
3 Tokyo is bigger than London.
London isn't _____.
4 Tennis is more popular than cricket.
Cricket isn't _____.
5 Children learn languages faster than adults.
Adults don't _____.
6 I work harder than you.
You don't _____.
7 England played better than France.
France didn't _____.

◀ p.37

5B

a Complete the sentences with the superlative.

Is this <u>the biggest</u> city in the world? (big)
1 Thais are _____ people I've ever met. (polite)
2 Yesterday was _____ day of the year. (hot)
3 This is _____ time to drive to the city. (bad)
4 She's _____ girl at school. (friendly)
5 This is _____ part of the exam. (important)
6 _____ time to visit New England is autumn. (good)
7 Ulan Bator is one of _____ cities in the world. (polluted)
8 _____ I've ever flown is to Bali. (far)
9 That's definitely _____ film I've ever seen. (funny)
10 Rob's daughters are all pretty, but I think Emily is _____. (pretty)

b Write sentences with a superlative + *ever* + the present perfect.

It / good film / I / see
It's the best film I've ever seen.
1 It / hot country / I be to
2 She / unfriendly person / I / meet
3 It / easy exam / he / do
4 They / expensive trousers / I / buy
5 It / long film / I / watch
6 He / attractive man / I / see
7 It / bad meal / I / eat
8 He / interesting teacher / I / have
9 It / exciting job / we / do

◀ p.38

5C

a Circle the correct form.

How (much) / many milk do you drink?
1 I eat *too / too much* chocolate.
2 I eat *too much / too many* crisps.
3 I don't drink *enough water / water enough*.
4 I can't come. I am *too busy / too much busy*.
5 You work *too much / too many*.
6 I don't have *enough time / time enough*.
7 I don't *go out enough / enough go out*.
8 She's *too lazy / too much lazy*.

b Complete the sentences with *too*, *too much*, *too many*, or *enough*.

You eat <u>too much</u> red meat. It isn't good for you.
1 I'm not very fit. I don't do _____ exercise.
2 I can't walk to school. It's _____ far.
3 There are _____ cars on the roads today.
4 I spend _____ time on the computer – it gives me headaches.
5 I don't sleep _____ – only five or six hours, but I really need eight.
6 I was _____ ill to go to work yesterday.
7 There were _____ people at the party, so it was impossible to dance.
8 I always have _____ work and not _____ free time.

◀ p.41

6

6A will / won't (predictions)

A I'm seeing Jane at six.   B **She'll be** late.
The film's in French. **We won't understand** anything.
It's a great book. I'm sure **you'll like** it.
I don't think **it'll rain** tomorrow.

+	
I / You / He / She / It / We / They	**'ll be** late.

−	
I / You / He / She / It / We / They	**won't be** late.

Contractions: 'll = will; won't = will not

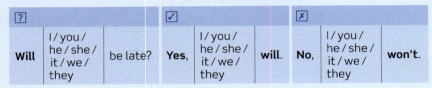

- We often use *will / won't* + infinitive for future predictions, i.e. to say things we think, guess or know about the future.
- We often use *I think / I don't think* + *will*.
  I think he'll **fail** the exam. **I don't think** he'll **pass** the exam. NOT *I think he won't pass.*

> **be going to for predictions**
> We can also use *be going to* to predict something you know or can see is going to happen (see **3A**), e.g.
> *Look at the clouds. It's going to rain.*
> *They're playing very well. I'm sure they're going to win.*

6B will / won't (decisions, offers, promises)

decisions
I **won't stay** for dinner. I think **I'll go** home early.
offers
I'll help you with your homework.   **Shall I open** the window?
promises
I'll always **love** you.   I **won't tell** anybody.

- Use *will / won't* + infinitive for making decisions, offering and promising.
  I'll help you with those bags. NOT *Help you.*
- When an offer is a question, we use *Shall I…?* or *Shall we…?*
  Shall I pay?   **Shall we** do the washing-up?

6C review of tenses: present, past and future

tense	example	use
present simple	I **live** in the city centre. She **doesn't smoke**.	things that happen always or usually
present continuous	He**'s looking** for a new job.	things that are happening now or in the near future
	I**'m leaving** tomorrow.	things that we have arranged for the future
past simple	We **saw** a good film last night. We **didn't do** anything yesterday.	finished actions in the past
past continuous	He **was working** in Paris. What **were** you **doing** at 7.00?	actions that were in progress at a past time
be going to + infinitive	I**'m going to see** Tom tonight.	future plans
	Look! It**'s going to rain**.	predictions when we know / can see what's going to happen
will / won't + infinitive	You**'ll love** New York.	predictions
	I**'ll phone** her later.	instant decisions
	I**'ll help** you.	offers
	I**'ll pay** you back tomorrow.	promises
present perfect	I**'ve finished** the book.	recently finished actions (we don't say when)
	Have you **ever been** to Iran?	past experiences

GRAMMAR BANK

6A

a Write sentences and questions with *will / won't*. Use contractions where you can.

⊟ it / be easy to pass *It won't be easy to pass.*
1 ⊞ I think they / lose the match
2 ❓ the meeting / be long
3 ⊟ she / get the job – she's not qualified
4 ❓ you / see him at work later
5 ⊞ I don't want to go. it / be impossible to park
6 ⊟ you / like that book
7 ⊞ I think she / love the present I bought her
8 ⊟ there / be a lot of traffic in the morning
9 ⊞ you / find a good job, I'm sure
10 ⊞ everything / be OK, so there's no need to worry

b Complete with *will* + a verb from the list.

be (2) get like pass snow

A Do you think the traffic *will be* bad?
B No, because it's a holiday today.
1 A Do you like this band?
B Yes, I think they _____ famous one day.
2 A Is this a good film?
B Yes, I'm sure you _____ it.
3 A Do you think it _____ ?
B No, it's not cold enough.
4 A What do you think I _____ for Christmas?
B I don't know. What did you ask for?
5 A I'm so worried about the exam!
B Don't worry. I'm sure you _____ . ◀ p.44

6B

a Match the sentences.

It's hot in here. [G]
1 I'm thirsty. ☐
2 I have a headache. ☐
3 This exercise is hard. ☐
4 I'm hungry. ☐
5 These bags are heavy. ☐
6 I left my wallet at home. ☐
7 I need that photo urgently. ☐
8 We haven't got any milk. ☐

A I'll help you to do it.
B Shall I make you a sandwich?
C Shall I carry one for you?
D I'll lend you some money.
E I'll buy some on my way home.
F I'll send it by email now.
G Shall I open the window?
H Shall I turn off the music?
I I'll get you a glass of water.

b Complete the sentences with *will / won't* (or *shall*) + a verb.

buy call forget get have help pay take tell

A What would you like? B *I'll have* the fish.

1 A I can't do this crossword.
B _____ you?
2 A It's a secret.
B I _____ anyone, I promise.
3 A When will I hear from you again?
B I _____ you tonight.
4 A Can I borrow €50?
B When _____ you _____ me back?
5 A It's my birthday next week.
B Don't worry. I _____ .
6 A I feel ill.
B _____ I _____ you home?
7 A This chocolate you bought isn't very nice.
B Yes, I know. I _____ it again.
8 A These shoes are too small.
B I _____ a bigger pair for you, madam.

◀ p.46

6C

a Complete the questions with one word.

Where *do* you usually have lunch?
I didn't see you at work last week. *Were* you ill?
1 _____ you often remember your dreams?
2 _____ you listen to the match on the radio last night?
3 Who do you think _____ win the election next year?
4 _____ your brother like rock music?
5 What _____ you going to watch on TV tonight?
6 _____ it snowing when you left?
7 Were you at the party last night? I _____ see you.
8 _____ you been to the supermarket?
9 _____ the film finished yet?

b Put the verb in the right form.

A What *are* we *doing* tonight? (do)
B We ¹_____ dinner with Jack and Mary. (have)
A But we ²_____ dinner with them last week! (have)
B Yes, but they ³_____ to tell us some good news. (want)
A Oh, OK then. ⁴_____ I _____ some champagne? (buy)
B It's 8 o'clock! Where ⁵_____ you _____ ? (be)
A I'm sorry. When I ⁶_____ home I ⁷_____ to buy the champagne. And then I ⁸_____ Mark in the shop… (walk, stop, see)
B Well, hurry up. We ⁹_____ late! (be)
A It's OK. I ¹⁰_____ a taxi and I'll be ready in five minutes. (already order)

◀ p.49

7

7A uses of the infinitive with *to*

1 I need **to buy** some new clothes. (3 24))
  Try **not to talk** about politics.
2 It'll be nice **to meet** your parents.
  It's important **not to be** late.
3 I don't know where **to go** or what **to do**.
4 **A** Why did you go to the party?
  B **To meet** new people.
    I went to the party **to meet** new people.

- The infinitive is the base form of the verb. It is often used with *to*. It can be positive (e.g. *to be*) or negative (e.g. *not to be*).
- Use the infinitive with *to*:
  1 after some verbs, e.g. *want, need, would like*, etc. See **Verb forms** *p.158*.
  2 after adjectives.
  3 after question words, e.g. *what, where, when*, etc.
  4 to say why you do something.
     *I came to this school **to learn** English.* **NOT** *for learn English.*

> **Infinitive without *to***
> Remember that we use the infinitive <u>without</u> *to* after auxiliary verbs (*do / does / didn't*) and after most modal verbs (*can, could, will, would*, etc.), e.g. **Do** you **live** near here? **Can** you **help** me? I **won't forget**. What **would** you **do**?

7B uses of the gerund (verb + *-ing*)

1 **Eating** outside in the summer makes me feel good. (3 28))
  My idea of happiness is **getting up** late and **not going** to work.
2 I love **reading** in bed.
  I hate **not getting** to the airport early.
3 I'm thinking of **buying** a new car.
  He left without **saying** goodbye.

- The gerund is the base form of the verb + *ing*. It can be positive (e.g. *going*) or negative (e.g. *not going*).
- Use the gerund:
  1 as the subject or object of a sentence.
  2 after some verbs, e.g. *like, love, hate, enjoy*, etc. See **Verb forms** *p.158*.
  3 after prepositions.
- Remember the spelling rules for the *-ing* form. See **1C** *p.126*.

7C *have to, don't have to, must, mustn't*

have to, don't have to

| + | I **have to** get up at seven every day. (3 34))
    She **has to** speak English at work.
| − | We **don't have to** wear a uniform at this school.
    He **doesn't have to** work on Saturdays.
| ? | **Do** I **have to** buy a grammar book?
    What time **does** she **have to** get up in the morning?

- Use *have to* + verb (infinitive) to talk about rules and obligations.
- Use *don't have to* + verb (infinitive) to say that there is no obligation, or that something is not necessary.
- Use *do / does* to make questions and negatives. **Do** I have to go? **NOT** *Have I to go?*
- Don't contract *have* or *has*. I **have to** go. **NOT** *I've to go.*

must / mustn't

| + | You **must** do your homework tonight. (3 35))
    She **must** tidy her room before she goes out.
| − | You **mustn't** leave your bags here.
    I **mustn't** forget to call her tonight.
    (**mustn't** = **must not**)
| ? | **Must** I buy a grammar book?
    When **must** we register for the exam?

- Use *must* + verb (infinitive without *to*) to talk about rules and obligations.
- *must / mustn't* is the same for all persons.
- Use *mustn't* + verb (infinitive without *to*) to say something is prohibited.

> **must and have to**
> *Must* and *have to* are very similar, but there is a small difference. We normally use *have to* for a **general** obligation (a rule at work / school or a law). We normally use *must* for a **personal** obligation (one that the speaker imposes), e.g. a teacher to students or a parent to a child. But often you can use either *must* or *have to*.
>
> **mustn't and don't have to**
> *Mustn't* and *don't have to* have completely different meanings. Compare:
> You **mustn't** go. = It's prohibited. Don't go.
> You **don't have to** go. = You can go if you want to, but it's not obligatory / necessary.
>
> **Impersonal *you***
> We often use *have to* and *must* with impersonal *you* (*you* = people in general), e.g.
> *You **have to** wear a seatbelt in a car. You **mustn't** take photos in the museum.*

GRAMMAR BANK

7A

a Match the sentence halves.

Be ready `B`
1. Do we need
2. In some countries it's important
3. I know you're tired, but try
4. We were late, so Simon offered
5. It's difficult

A to give us a lift to the station.
B ~~to show your passport at check-in.~~
C not to forget people's names in a big class.
D to dress correctly in public.
E to buy some dollars at the airport?
F not to fall asleep during the film!

b Complete the sentences with a positive or negative infinitive.

| do | not drive | go | have | learn | look for | not make | meet |

I'm planning *to have* a party next week.
1. **A** Hi, I'm Donatella.
   B I'm Renée. Nice _____ you.
2. What do you want _____ tonight?
3. I need _____ to the shop. I don't have any bread or milk.
4. Try _____ a noise. Your father's asleep.
5. I'd really like _____ how to drive.
6. Be careful _____ too fast on the way home – the roads are icy.
7. He's decided _____ a new job.

◀ p.53

7B

a Complete the sentences with a verb in the list in the *-ing* form.

| be | do | practise | remember | study | swim | teach | text | travel |

I really enjoy *doing* exercise. It makes me feel great!
1. One thing that always makes me happy is _____ in the sea.
2. You can't learn to play a musical instrument well without _____ regularly.
3. My mother's very bad at _____ names.
4. _____ teenagers is very hard work.
5. My sister spends hours on the phone _____ her friends.
6. I hate _____ the first to arrive at parties.
7. _____ by train is usually cheaper than by plane.
8. I'll go on _____ for as long as I can – I love being a student!

b Put the verbs in the *-ing* form or infinitive.

I like *listening* to the radio in the mornings. (listen)
1. _____ Pilates is good for your health. (do)
2. We've decided _____ a holiday this year. (not have)
3. We won't take the car. It's impossible _____. (park)
4. I'm not very good at _____ maps. (read)
5. You can borrow the car if you promise _____ slowly. (drive)
6. Has it stopped _____? (rain)
7. I don't mind _____, but I don't like _____ the washing-up. (cook, do)
8. I hate _____ early in the morning. (get up)

◀ p.54

7C

a Complete the sentences with the correct form of *have to*.

I *don't have to* go to school on Saturdays
1. Janice _____ study very hard – she has exams soon.
2. You _____ stop your car at a red light.
3. _____ your sister _____ go to London for her job interview?
4. You _____ wear a uniform if you are a policeman.
5. We _____ get up early tomorrow. Our flight leaves at 6.30.
6. Harry _____ work today – his shop is closed.
7. I _____ go now. It's very late.
8. _____ we _____ go to bed? It's only 10 o'clock!

b Circle the correct form, *have to* / *must*, *don't have to*, or *mustn't*. Tick ✓ if both forms are possible.

We (*don't have to*) / *mustn't* go to work next week. It's a holiday.
1. You *don't have to* / *mustn't* touch the oven. It's hot.
2. Do you *have to* / *must* send a photo with your passport form?
3. The concert is free. You *don't have to* / *mustn't* pay.
4. I'm late for a meeting. I *have to* / *must* go now.
5. You *don't have to* / *mustn't* leave the door open – the dog will get out.
6. We *have to* / *must* try that new restaurant in town.
7. In Britain you *have to* / *must* drive on the left.
8. *Do you have to* / *Must you* be tall to be good at tennis?

◀ p.56

8

8A should / shouldn't

You **should** wear a suit to the interview.
I think you **should** change your job.
I don't think you **should** speak to her.
He's very stressed. He **shouldn't** work so hard.
You **shouldn't** drink coffee in the evening. It'll keep you awake.

- Use *should | shouldn't* + verb (infinitive without *to*) to give somebody advice or say what you think is the right thing to do.
- *should | shouldn't* is the same for all persons.
- We often use *I think you should…* or *I don't think you should…* NOT ~~I think you shouldn't…~~

> **ought to**
> You can also use *ought to / ought not to* instead of *should / shouldn't*, e.g.
> You **ought to** wear a suit. He **ought not to** work so hard.

8B first conditional: *if* + present, *will / won't*

1 If I **miss** the last bus, I'**ll get** a taxi.
   If you **tell** her the truth, she **won't believe** you.
   What **will** you **do** if he **doesn't call** you?
2 If you **don't go**, she **won't be** very pleased.
   She **won't be** very pleased if you **don't go**.
3 If you **miss** the last bus, **get** a taxi.
   If you **miss** the last bus, you **can get** a taxi.

1 Use *if* + present to talk about a possible situation and *will / won't* + verb to talk about the consequence.
2 The *if*-clause can come first or second. If the *if*-clause comes first, we usually put a comma before the next clause.
3 You can also use the imperative or *can* + infinitive instead of *will* + infinitive in the other clause.

If I miss the last bus, I'll get a taxi.

8C possessive pronouns

Whose coat is it? It's my coat.
   It's **mine**.
Whose jacket is it? It's your jacket.
   It's **yours**.
Whose phone is it? It's his phone.
   It's **his**.
Whose bag is it? It's her bag. It's **hers**.
Whose dog is it? It's our dog. It's **ours**.
Whose house is it? It's their house.
   It's **theirs**.

- Use possessive pronouns to talk about possession. *Is it **yours**? Yes, it's **mine**.*
- Use *Whose* to <u>ask</u> about possession. ***Whose** book is it? **Whose** is that bag?*

- Don't use possessive pronouns with a noun. **NOT** ~~It's mine book.~~
- Don't use *the* with possessive pronouns, e.g. *Is this **yours**?* **NOT** ~~Is this the yours?~~

pronouns and possessive adjectives overview

subject pronouns		object pronouns		possessive adjectives		possessive pronouns	
I	can come.	She loves	me.	This is	my	seat. It's	mine.
You			you		your		yours
He			him		his		his
She			her		her		hers
It			it		its		its
We			us		our		ours
They			them		their		theirs

GRAMMAR BANK

8A

a Complete with *should* or *shouldn't*.

You *should* stop smoking.
1 You _____ work really long hours every day.
2 You _____ lose a bit of weight.
3 You _____ eat more fruit and vegetables.
4 You _____ put so much sugar in your coffee.
5 You _____ start doing some exercise.
6 You _____ drink less alcohol.
7 You _____ drink more water.
8 You _____ go to bed so late.

b Complete the sentences with *should* or *shouldn't* + a verb in the list.

| drive | have | go | ~~leave~~ | relax | spend | study | walk | wear |

We *should leave* early. It's going to start snowing soon.
1 You _____ a scarf. It's really cold today.
2 I _____ this afternoon. I have an exam tomorrow.
3 You _____ alone in that part of the city. Get a taxi.
4 She _____ more. She's very stressed.
5 You _____ so fast at night – the roads are dangerous.
6 You _____ to bed. You look tired.
7 Parents _____ more time with their children.
8 We _____ a break yet – we only started work at 10.00.

◀ p.61

8B

a Match the sentence halves.

If you leave now, [C]
1 The ticket will be cheaper ☐
2 If I don't see you this afternoon, ☐
3 You'll learn more quickly ☐
4 If you get that new job, ☐
5 You won't pass your driving test ☐
6 If I lend you this book, ☐

A if you don't have enough lessons.
B will you give it back to me soon?
C ~~you'll catch the 8.00 train.~~
D if you travel after 9.00.
E if you come to every class.
F will you earn more money?
G I'll call you this evening.

b Complete with the correct form of the verbs.

If we *start* walking, the bus *will come*. (start, come)
1 If you _____ me your secret, I _____ anybody else. (tell, not tell)
2 If I _____ it down, I _____ it. (not write, not remember)
3 _____ you _____ me if you _____ any news? (call, get)
4 She _____ you if you _____ her nicely. (help, ask)
5 I _____ you if I _____ from Alex. (phone, hear)
6 You _____ your friends if you _____ to Paris. (miss, move)
7 If you _____ carefully, you _____ everything. (listen, understand)
8 The boss _____ very pleased if you _____ late for work. (not be, be)
9 I _____ you home if you _____ me directions. (drive, give)

◀ p.62

8C

a (Circle) the correct form.

Whose car is that? It's *her* / (*hers*).
1 This isn't *my* / *mine* pen, it's Susan's.
2 I think this book is *your* / *yours*.
3 This isn't your suitcase, it's *ours* / *our*.
4 Where's Mary? I think these are *her* / *hers* gloves.
5 These keys are *mine* / *the mine*.
6 They showed us all *theirs* / *their* holiday photographs.
7 These seats are *theirs* / *their*, not ours. We're over there.
8 Is this *yours* / *your* bag?
9 This isn't my jacket. It's *her* / *hers*.

b Complete the sentences with a pronoun or possessive adjective.

This isn't my coffee, it's yours. Where's *mine*?
1 **A** Is that her car?
   B No, it's her boyfriend's. _____ is a white Peugeot.
2 Maya has a new boyfriend, but I haven't met _____ yet.
3 Look. Here's a photo of Alex and Kim with _____ new baby.
4 We've finished paying for our house, so it's _____ now.
5 These are our tickets. Can you give Maria and Marta _____?
6 We're very lucky. Our parents bought this dog for _____.
7 We both love gardening. Would you like to see _____ garden?
8 London is famous for _____ parks.

◀ p.65

141

9

9A second conditional: *if* + past, *would* / *wouldn't*

1 If a bull **attacked** me, **I'd run** away.   4)) 16
   If you **didn't go** to bed so late, you **wouldn't be** so tired in the morning.
   Would you **take** the manager's job **if** they **offered** it to you?
2 If I **had** more time **I'd do** more exercise.
   I'd do more exercise **if** I **had** more time.
3 If we **went** by car, we **could stop** at places on the way.

1 Use *if* + past to talk about an imaginary or hypothetical future situation and *would* / *wouldn't* + verb to talk about the consequence.
- *would* / *wouldn't* is the same for all persons.
- Contractions: *'d* = *would* (*I'd*, *you'd*, *he'd*, etc.); *wouldn't* = *would not*.
2 The *if*-clause can come first or second. If the *if*-clause comes first, we usually put a comma before the next clause.
3 You can also use *could* + infinitive instead of *would* + infinitive in the other clause.

🔍 **be in second conditionals**
With the verb *be* you can use *were* (instead of *was*) after *I* / *he* / *she* / *it*, e.g.
If Jack **was** / **were** here, he'd know what to do.
Use *were* (not *was*) in the expression *If I* **were** *you,...*
We often use this expression for advice, e.g. **If I were you**, I wouldn't take that job.

first or second conditional?

Compare the first and second conditionals.
- Use the **first conditional** for **possible** future situations.
  If I **don't have to** *work tomorrow,* **I'll help** *you.*
  (= It's a possibility. Maybe I will help you.)
- Use the **second conditional** for **imaginary** or **hypothetical** situations.
  If I **didn't have to** *work tomorrow,* **I'd help** *you.*
  (= It's a hypothetical situation. I have to work, so I can't help you.)

9B present perfect + *for* or *since*

A Where do you live now?   4)) 21
B In Manchester.
A How long **have** you **lived** there?
B **I've lived** there **for** twenty years.
A Where do you work?
B In a primary school.
A How long **have** you **worked** there?
B **I've worked** there **since** 2005.

- Use the present perfect + *for* or *since* to talk about actions and states which started in the past and are still true now.
  I've lived in Manchester **for** twenty years. = I came to live in Manchester twenty years ago and I live in Manchester now.
- Don't use the present simple in this type of sentence, e.g. **NOT** I live in Manchester for twenty years.
- Use *How long...?* to ask questions about the duration of an action or a state.

for or since?
- Use *for* + a period of time, e.g. **for** two weeks, **for** ten years, **for** a long time, etc.
  I've had this car **for** three months.
- Use *since* with the beginning of a period of time, e.g. **since** 1980, **since** last June, etc.
  I've been afraid of spiders **since** I was a child.

9C present perfect or past simple? (2)

1 A How long **was** Bob Marley a musician?   4)) 28
  B He **was** a musician for twenty years.
  A How many Grammys **did** he **win**?
  B He **didn't win** any.
2 A How long **has** Ziggy Marley **been** a musician?
  B **He's been** a musician since he was ten.
  A How many Grammys **has** he **won**?
  B **He's won** four.

1 Use the **past simple** to talk about a finished period of time in the past.
2 Use the **present perfect** to talk about a period of time from the past until now.
- Compare the past simple and present perfect.
  Jack **was** *married for ten years.* = Jack is not married now. He's divorced or dead.
  Jack **has been** *married for ten years.* = Jack is married now.

GRAMMAR BANK

9A

a Match the sentence halves.

You'd feel much better A
1 I'd enjoy the weekend more ☐
2 If it's sunny tomorrow, ☐
3 Would you wear it ☐
4 If we learned Portuguese, ☐
5 I wouldn't work ☐
6 If I went to live in London, ☐

A if you did some exercise.
B would you come to visit me?
C if I bought it for you?
D we could go to the beach.
E if I didn't have to work on Saturday.
F we could go and work in Brazil.
G if I didn't need the money.

b Complete with the correct form of the verbs.

If I _found_ a good job, I _would move_ to the USA. (find, move)
1 We _____ the house if it _____ a garden. (buy, have)
2 If you _____ Indian food, I'm sure you _____ it. (try, like)
3 You _____ more if you _____ harder. (learn, work)
4 If we _____ a car, we _____ drive up to the mountains. (rent, can)
5 We _____ our son more often if he _____ nearer. (see, live)
6 I _____ to that restaurant if I _____ you – it's very expensive. (not go, be)
7 I _____ you to the airport if my mum _____ the car. (take, not have)
8 I quite like cycling, but I _____ to work if I _____ a car. (not cycle, have)
9 _____ you _____ your country if you _____ a well-paid job abroad? (leave, get)
10 I love living here. I _____ happy if I _____ leave. (not be, have to)

◀ p.68

9B

a Write questions with *How long* and the present perfect.

you / be married   How long have you been married?
1 you / be frightened of clowns _____?
2 your sister / have her car _____?
3 you / live here _____?
4 your dad / be a teacher _____?
5 you / know your boyfriend _____?
6 Britain / be in the EU _____?
7 you / have your cat _____?
8 he / work for the same company _____?

b Answer the questions in **a**. Use the present perfect + *for* or *since*.

I've been married for 20 years.
1 I _____ I was a child.
2 She _____ three years.
3 I _____ a long time.
4 He _____ 1990.
5 I _____ May.
6 It _____ 1973.
7 We _____ about two years.
8 He _____ 2008. ◀ p.71

9C

a Circle the correct form.

She is / *She's been* single since last summer.
1 *He left* / *He has left* school two years ago.
2 *I lived* / *I've lived* in Cardiff for two years, but then I moved to Swansea.
3 *She lives* / *She's lived* in Florida since 2010.
4 *My sister had* / *My sister has had* her baby yesterday!
5 I work in an office. *I work* / *I've worked* there for 20 years.
6 *The city changed* / *The city has changed* a lot since I was a child.
7 They're divorced now. *They were* / *They have been* married for ten years.
8 *I met* / *I've met* Sandra when I *was* / *have been* at university.

b Complete with the present perfect or past simple.

1 A Where does Rob live now?
  B In Madrid.
  A How long _____ there? (he / live)
  B For three months. He _____ there in September. (move)
2 A When _____? (Picasso / die)
  B In 1977, in Paris I think.
  A How long _____ in France? (he / live)
  B For a long time. He _____ Spain when he was 25. (leave)
3 A My brother and his wife get on very well.
  B How long _____ married? (they / be)
  A They _____ married since 1995. They _____ at university. (be, meet)
  B Really? _____ that in Paris? (be)

◀ p.72

10

10A passive: be + past participle

Present: *am / is / are* + past participle   38

[+] Kevlar **is used** to make bullet-proof vests.
[–] Tippex **isn't used** very much today.
[?] **Are** disposable nappies **used** all over the world?

Past: *was / were* + past participle

[+] The dishwasher **was invented** by Josephine Cochrane.
[–] Windscreen wipers **weren't invented** until 1903.
[?] When **was** the washing machine **invented**?

- You can often say things in two ways, in the active or in the passive.
  Josephine Cochrane **invented** the dishwasher. (**active**)
  The dishwasher **was invented** by Josephine Cochrane. (**passive**)
- In the **active** sentence, the focus is more on **Josephine Cochrane**.
- In the **passive** sentence the focus is more on **the dishwasher**.
- You can also use the passive when it isn't known or isn't important who does or did the action.
  My car **was stolen** last week.
  Volvo cars **are made** in Sweden.
- Use *by* to say who did the action.
  The Lord of the Rings *was written* **by** Tolkien.

10B used to / didn't use to

[+] When I was a child, I **used to** play in the street.   43
    My brother **used to** have very long hair.
[–] Children **didn't use to** watch much TV when my father was young.
    My daughter **didn't use to** like vegetables, but now she loves them.
[?] **Did** you **use to** wear a uniform at school? Yes, I did.
    Did you **use to** like your teachers? No, I didn't.

> 🔍 **used to or usually?**
> *used to* only exists in the past.
> For habits in the present, use *usually* + present simple, **NOT** ~~use to~~
> *I usually cook in the evenings.*
> **NOT** ~~I use to cook in the evenings.~~

- Use *used to / didn't use to* + verb to talk about things that happened repeatedly or were true for a long period of time in the past, but are usually <u>not</u> true now, e.g. things that happened when you were a child.
- *used to / didn't use to* is the same for all persons.
- Instead of *used to* you can use the past simple with an adverb of frequency.
  When I was a child, I **often played** in the street.

10C might / might not (possibility)

We **might** have a picnic tomorrow, but it depends on the weather.   50
She **might** come with us, but she's not sure yet.
I **might not** go to the party. I haven't decided yet.
You **might not** see him today. He's coming home late.

> 🔍 **may / may not**
> You can also use *may* instead of *might* for possibility, e.g.
> We **may** have a picnic tomorrow.
> I **may not** go to the party.

- Use *might / might not* + verb (infinitive without *to*) to say that perhaps you will or won't do something.
  We **might** have a picnic tomorrow. = Perhaps we will have a picnic tomorrow.
- *might / might not* is the same for all persons.
- *might not* is not usually contracted.

GRAMMAR BANK

10A

a Complete with present or past passive.

The Eiffel Tower *was completed* in 1889. (complete)
1 Many of the things we use every day _____ by women. (invent)
2 In the UK most children _____ in state schools. (educate)
3 Australia _____ by Captain Cook in 1770. (discover)
4 This morning I _____ up by the neighbour's dog. (wake)
5 Cricket _____ in the summer in the UK. (play)
6 The songs on this album _____ last year. (record)
7 Nowadays a lot of toys _____ in China. (make)
8 Carols are songs which _____ at Christmas. (sing)
9 These birds _____ in northern Europe. (not usually see)
10 'Rome _____ in a day.' (not build)

b Rewrite the sentences in the passive, beginning with the highlighted words.

Shakespeare wrote Hamlet in 1603.
Hamlet was written by Shakespeare in 1603.
1 Jonathan Ive designed the iPod and the iPhone.
2 Most Mediterranean countries produce olive oil.
3 Herschel discovered Uranus in 1781.
4 Barry Sonnenfeld directed the Men in Black films.
5 David Hockney painted Mr and Mrs Clark and Percy in 1970–1971.
6 Elvis Presley didn't write Blue Suede Shoes.
7 JK Rowling wrote the Harry Potter books.
8 They make Daihatsu cars in Japan.

 p.76

10B

a Look at how John has changed. Write five sentences about how he was **IN THE PAST**.

He used to be slim.
1 _____ long hair.
2 _____ glasses.
3 _____ a beard.
4 _____ football.
5 _____ a tie.

b Make sentences with *used to*, *didn't use to*, or *did … use to?*

[?] you / have long hair
Did you use to have long hair?
1 [+] my sister / hate maths, but she loves it now
2 [?] where / you / work
3 [−] I / like vegetables when I was a child
4 [?] what / you / do in the summer holidays when you were young
5 [−] The British / drink a lot of coffee
6 [+] this building / be a cinema
7 [?] your brother / teach here
8 [−] I / be a Manchester United fan
9 [?] Jeff / have a motorbike
10 [+] telegrams / be a way of sending important messages

◀ p.79

10C

a Match the sentences.

Take some sun cream. [D]
1 Let's buy a lottery ticket. [ ]
2 Phone the restaurant. [ ]
3 Don't stand on the wall. [ ]
4 Let's take a map. [ ]
5 Try the shirt on. [ ]
6 Don't wait for me. [ ]
7 Be careful with that knife! [ ]
8 Ask how much it costs. [ ]

A You might fall.
B It may not be your size.
C We might get lost.
D ~~It might be really sunny.~~
E We may not have enough money.
F You might cut yourself.
G It may be closed on Sundays.
H We might win.
I I may be late.

b Complete the sentences with *might* + a verb phrase.

| be cold   be ill   be in a meeting   ~~go to the cinema~~ |
| not have time   not like it   have fish and chips |

I'm not sure what to do tonight. I *might go to the cinema.*
1 Kim wasn't at school today. She _____
2 His phone is turned off. He _____
3 It's an unusual book. You _____
4 I don't know if I'll finish it. I _____
5 I'm not sure what to order. I _____
6 Take a jacket. It _____

 p.80

11

11A expressing movement

The man **went up** the steps and **into** the church.
He **drove out of** the garage and **along** the street.
I **ran over** the bridge and **across** the park.

- To express movement use a verb of movement, e.g. *go, come, run, walk,* etc. and a preposition (or adverb) of movement e.g. *up, down, away,* etc.

> **in** or **into**? **out** or **out of**?
> Remember, use *into / out of* + noun, and *in / out* if there isn't a noun.
> Come **into** the living room. Come **in**.
> He went **out of** the house. He went **out**.
> See **Expressing movement** p.162.

11B word order of phrasal verbs

1 What time do you **get up**?
  I don't usually **go out** during the week.
2 **Put on** your coat. **Put** your coat **on**. **Put** it **on**.
  Turn off the TV. **Turn** the TV **off**. **Turn** it **off**.
3 I'm **looking for** my glasses.
  Have you found your glasses? No, I'm still **looking for** them.

- A phrasal verb = verb + particle (preposition or adverb), e.g. *get up, turn on, look for*.
  1 Some phrasal verbs don't have an object, e.g. *get up, go out*.
  2 Some phrasal verbs have an object and are separable. With these phrasal verbs you can put the particle (*on, off,* etc.) before **or** after the object.
- When the object is a pronoun (*me, it, him,* etc.) it <u>always</u> goes between the verb and particle.
  Here's your coat. **Put it on**. NOT ~~Put on it.~~
  3 Some phrasal verbs have an object and are inseparable, e.g. *look for*. With these phrasal verbs the verb (e.g. *look*) and the particle (e.g. *for*) are never separated.
  I'm **looking for** *my glasses.* NOT ~~I'm looking my glasses for.~~
See **Phrasal verbs** p.163.

11C so, neither + auxiliaries

1 A I love classical music.
  B **So do I**.
  A I went to a classical concert last night.
  B **So did I**.
2 A I'm not married.
  B **Neither am I**.
  A I don't want to get married.
  B **Neither do I**.

present simple	I don't like classical music.	Neither **do** I.
present continuous	I'm having a great time.	So **am** I.
can / can't	I can swim.	So **can** I.
past simple	I didn't like the film.	Neither **did** I.
	I was very tired.	So **was** I.
would / wouldn't	I wouldn't like to go there.	Neither **would** I.
present perfect	I've been to Brazil.	So **have** I.

- Use *So do I, Neither do I,* etc. to say that you have something in common with somebody.
  1 Use *So* + auxiliary + *I* to respond to positive sentences.
  2 Use *Neither* + auxiliary + *I* to respond to negative sentences.
- The auxiliary you use depends on the tense.

- Be careful with the word order.
  So do I. | Neither do I. NOT ~~So I do. | Neither I do.~~

> **neither** and **nor**
> You can also use *nor* instead of *neither*, e.g.
> A *I didn't like the film.*
> B **Nor** / **Neither** *did I.*
> *Neither* is usually pronounced /ˈnaɪðə/, but can also be pronounced /ˈniːðə/.

146

GRAMMAR BANK

11A

a Circle the correct preposition.

I lost my mobile phone signal when we went *across* / *through* a tunnel.
1 We ran *to* / *down* the sea, and jumped *into* / *out of* the water.
2 If you go *over* / *past* the bank, you'll see the supermarket on the right.
3 He walked *along* / *across* the street until he got to the park.
4 The plane flew *on* / *over* the town and then landed.
5 The dog ran *towards* / *to* me, but then it stopped.
6 We cycled *over* / *out of* the bridge and *in* / *into* the city centre.
7 The racing cars went *round* / *under* the track 12 times.
8 The little boy suddenly ran *across* / *through* the road.

b Complete the sentences with the correct preposition.

He jumped *into* his car and drove away.
1 As I cycled under the bridge, a train went _____ it.
2 Come _____. The door's open.
3 This is the 3rd floor. Go _____ those stairs and you'll come to the 2nd floor.
4 He walked _____ the bar and ordered a drink.
5 I like going _____ on a Saturday night.
6 He took his passport _____ his bag.
7 I'm exhausted. I've just cycled _____ a huge hill.   ◀ p.85

11B

a Circle the correct form. If both are correct, tick ✓ the box.

Turn off your mobile / *Turn your mobile off* before the film starts. ✓
1 Tonight I have to *look my sister after* / *look after my sister*. ☐
2 Let's *go out this evening* / *go this evening out*. ☐
3 *Turn down the radio* / *Turn the radio down*. It's too loud. ☐
4 My brother is *looking for a new job* / *looking a new job for*. ☐
5 You should *throw away those old jeans* / *throw those old jeans away*. ☐
6 I don't like shopping for clothes online – I prefer to *try them on* / *try on them* before I buy them. ☐
7 *Take off your shoes* / *Take your shoes off* before you come in. ☐
8 That's my sister – I think you'd really *get on with her* / *get on her with*. ☐
9 If it doesn't fit, you should *take back it* / *take it back* to the shop. ☐
10 What time do you *get up in the morning* / *get in the morning up*? ☐

b Complete the sentences with *it* or *them* and a word from the list.

| back   in   on (x2)   up (x3)   down |

I can't hear the radio. Turn *it up*.
1 Your clothes are all over the floor. Pick _____ _____.
2 Here's your coat. Put _____ _____.
3 'What does this word mean?' 'Look _____ _____.'
4 To get your passport there are three forms. Please fill _____ _____ now.
5 You remember that money I lent you? When can you give _____ _____?
6 Is there anything on TV? Let's turn _____ _____ and see.
7 You won't remember my address. Write _____ _____.

◀ p.87

11C

a Complete B's answers with an auxiliary verb.

A I like chocolate.   B So *do* I.
1 A I'm really thirsty.   B So _____ I.
2 A I didn't go out last night.   B Neither _____ I.
3 A I was born in Rome.   B So _____ I.
4 A I don't eat meat.   B Neither _____ I.
5 A I've been to Moscow.   B So _____ I.
6 A I can't sing.   B Neither _____ I.
7 A I'd like to go to Bali.   B So _____ I.
8 A I saw a film last week.   B So _____ I.
9 A I wouldn't like to eat that.   B Neither _____ I.
10 A I can play chess.   B So _____ I.

b Respond to A. Say you are the same. Use *So…I* or *Neither…I*.

A I don't like cabbage.   *Neither do I.*
1 A I live near the supermarket.   _____
2 A I'm not afraid of snakes.   _____
3 A I went to bed late last night.   _____
4 A I haven't been to Canada.   _____
5 A I don't have any pets.   _____
6 A I can speak three languages.   _____
7 A I always drink coffee in the morning.   _____
8 A I'm waiting for the bus to the airport.   _____

◀ p.88

12

12A past perfect

+	When I woke up the garden was all white. (5 17) It **had snowed** during the night. I suddenly realized that **I'd left** my mobile in the taxi.
–	We got home just in time – the match **hadn't started**. When she got to class, she realized that she **hadn't brought** her book.
?	A I went to Paris last weekend. I really loved it. B **Had** you **been** there before? A No, I **hadn't**.

- Use the past perfect when you are already talking about the past and want to talk about an earlier past action.
  *When I woke up the garden was all white. It **had snowed** during the night.* = It snowed <u>before</u> I woke up.
- Make the past perfect with *had | hadn't* + past participle.
- The form of the past perfect is the same for all persons.
- *had* is sometimes contracted to *'d*.

> 🔍 **had or would?**
> Be careful: *'d* can be *had* or *would*.
> *I didn't know that you'**d** found a new job.* (*'d = had*)
> *If you went by taxi, you'**d** get there more quickly.*
> (*'d = would*)

12B reported (or indirect) speech

direct speech	reported speech (5 23)
'I love you.'	He said (that) **he loved me**.
'I've just arrived.'	She said (that) **she had just arrived**.
'We'll come at eight.'	He told me (that) **they would come** at eight.
'I don't want to go to the party.'	Jack told Anna (that) **he didn't want** to go to the party.

- Use reported speech to report (to tell somebody) what another person said.
- We often introduce reported speech with *said* or *told* (+ person)
- After *said* or *told* **that** is optional, e.g. *He said (**that**) he loved me.*
- Pronouns often change in reported speech, e.g. *I* changes to *he* or *she*.
  'I'm tired.' **She** told me (that) **she** was tired.

- Verb tenses change like this:

direct speech	reported speech
'I **can** help you.' (present simple)	He said (that) he **could** help me. (past simple)
'I'**m watching** TV.' (present continuous)	She said (that) she **was watching** TV. (past continuous)
'I'**ll** phone you.' (will)	He told me (that) he **would** phone me. (would)
'I **met** a girl.' (past simple)	John told me (that) he **had met** a girl. (past perfect)
'I'**ve broken** my leg.' (present perfect)	Sara said (that) she **had broken** her leg. (past perfect)

> 🔍 **say or tell?**
> You <u>can</u> use *said* or *told* in reported speech but they are used differently.
> You <u>can't</u> use *said* with an object or pronoun.
> *He **said** (that) he loved me.* **NOT** ~~He said me (that) he loved me.~~
> You <u>must</u> use *told* with an object.
> *He **told me** (that) he loved me.* **NOT** ~~He told (that) he loved me.~~

12C questions without auxiliaries

subject	verb	(5 27)
Who	painted	*Mr and Mrs Clark and Percy*?
Which singer	made	reggae popular all over the world?
How many people	live	near the school?
Who	wants	a cup of coffee?

- When the question word (*Who?*, *What?*, *Which?*, *How many?*, etc.) is the <u>subject</u> of the verb in the question, we <u>don't</u> use an auxiliary verb (*do | does | did*).
  Who painted *Mr and Mrs Clark and Percy*?
  NOT ~~Who did paint…?~~
- In most other questions in the present and past simple we use the auxiliary verb *do | does | did* + the infinitive.
  *What music **do** you like?* **NOT** ~~What music you like?~~
  See **1A** *p.126*.

GRAMMAR BANK

12A

a Match the sentence halves.

I couldn't get into my flat because [C]
1 When our friends arrived [ ]
2 I took the jacket back because [ ]
3 Jill didn't come with us because [ ]
4 I turned on the TV news [ ]
5 Johnny was nervous because [ ]
6 When I got to the supermarket checkout [ ]

A she'd made other plans.
B I realized that I'd left my wallet at home.
C I'd lost my keys.
D I had bought the wrong size.
E it was the first time he had flown.
F to see what had happened.
G we hadn't finished cooking the dinner.

b Complete the sentences. Put the verbs in the past simple and past perfect.

We _didn't get_ a table in the restaurant because we _hadn't booked_. (not get, not book)
1 I _____ Caroline because she _____ a lot. (not recognize, change)
2 My friend _____ to tell me that I _____ my wallet in his car. (phone, leave)
3 When I _____ the radio, the news _____. (turn on, already finish)
4 She _____ me the DVD because she _____ it yet. (not lend, not watch)
5 The bar _____ by the time we _____. (close, arrive)
6 When we _____ home we saw that somebody _____ the kitchen window. (get, break)
7 Luckily it _____ snowing when we _____ work. (stop, leave)

◀ p.93

12B

a Write the sentences in reported speech.

'I love you.'   He told her that he _loved her_.
1 'I'm hungry.'   She said that she _____.
2 'I don't like sad films.'
   He told her he _____.
3 'I'll call the doctor.'   He said he _____.
4 'I've bought a new phone.'
   Paul told us that he _____.
5 'I live in the city centre.'
   She said that she _____.
6 'We can't do it!'
   They said that they _____.
7 'I saw Eclipse at the cinema.'
   Julie said that she _____.

b Write the sentences in direct speech.

He told her that he was a doctor.   He said: '_I'm a doctor._'
1 She said that she was studying German.
   She said: '_____.'
2 Tony told me that his car had broken down.
   Tony said: '_____.'
3 Paul said that he would send me an email.
   Paul said: '_____.'
4 Wanda and Jack said they were in a hurry.
   Wanda and Jack said: '_____.'
5 He said he hadn't finished his essay yet.
   He said: '_____.'
6 She told us that she wouldn't arrive on time.
   She said: '_____.'
7 David said he had just arrived.
   David said: '_____.'

◀ p.94

12C

a Circle the correct question form.

What _you did_ / _did you do_ last night?
1 What _happened_ / _did happen_ to you?
2 What _means this word_ / _does this word mean_?
3 How many people _came_ / _did come_ to the meeting?
4 Which bus _goes_ / _does go_ to town?
5 Which film _won_ / _did win_ the Oscar this year?
6 What _said the teacher_ / _did the teacher say_?
7 Who _made_ / _did make_ this cake? It's fantastic!

b Write the questions. Do you know the answers?

How many Formula 1 championships _did Michael Schumacher win_? (Michael Schumacher / win)
1 When _____ president of the USA? (Barack Obama / become)
2 Which US state _____ with the letter 'H'? (start)
3 Which books _____? (J.R.R. Tolkien / write)
4 Who _____ the football World Cup in 2010? (win)
5 Which sport _____ the lightest ball? (use)
6 Where _____? (the 2008 Olympics / take place)
7 Which company _____? (Steve Jobs / start)

◀ p.96

Describing people

VOCABULARY BANK

1 APPEARANCE

a Match the sentences and pictures.

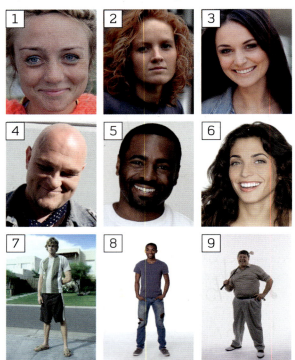

What does he / she look like?

- ☐ She has curly red hair.
- ☐ She has long straight hair.
- 1 She has big blue eyes.
- ☐ She has dark wavy hair.
- ☐ He has a beard and a mou<u>stache</u>.
- ☐ He's bald.
- ☐ He's very tall and thin.
- ☐ He's quite short and a bit over<u>weight</u>.
- ☐ He's <u>me</u>dium height and quite slim.

b 🔊 1 10 Listen and check.

> 🔍 **thin or slim? fat or overweight?**
> *Thin* and *slim* are both the opposite of *fat*, but *slim* = thin in an attractive way.
> *Fat* is not very polite. It is more polite to say someone is (*a bit*) *overweight*.
>
> **Using two adjectives together**
> We often use two adjectives together (without *and*) to describe hair or eyes, e.g. *She has long curly hair* or *He has big brown eyes*. Adjectives go in this order: **size** > **style** > **colour** noun.

2 PERSONALITY

a Match the adjectives with the definitions.

What's he like? What's she like?

clever /ˈklevə/   friendly /ˈfrendli/   funny /ˈfʌni/   generous /ˈdʒenərəs/
kind /kaɪnd/   lazy /ˈleɪzi/   shy /ʃaɪ/   talkative /ˈtɔːkətɪv/

		Adjective	Opposite
1	A person who is open and warm is	*friendly*	_____
2	A person who talks a lot is	_____	_____
3	A person who likes giving people things is	_____	_____
4	A person who is friendly and good to other people is	_____	_____
5	A person who doesn't want to work is	_____	_____
6	A person who makes people laugh is	_____	_____
7	A person who is quick at learning and understanding things is (synonym *intelligent*)	_____	_____
8	A person who can't talk easily to people he / she doesn't know is	_____	_____

b Complete the **Opposite** column with an adjective from the list.

extrovert /ˈekstrəvɜːt/   hard-working /hɑːd ˈwɜːkɪŋ/
mean /miːn/   quiet /ˈkwaɪət/   serious /ˈsɪəriəs/
stupid /ˈstjuːpɪd/   unfriendly /ʌnˈfrendli/   unkind /ʌnˈkaɪnd/

c 🔊 1 11 Listen and check.

d In pairs, ask and answer about a member of your family or a good friend.

A *What does your sister look like?*
B *She's quite tall and she has short dark hair.*
A *What's she like?*

> 🔍 **nice; funny or fun?**
> *Nice* is a very common ➕ adjective of personality, e.g. *He's a very nice person*. *Nice* describes a person who is friendly and kind.
> A person who is *funny* makes you laugh. A person who is *fun* is a person who you have a good time with.

◀ p.6

Things you wear

VOCABULARY BANK

a Match the words and pictures.

Clothes
- cardigan /ˈkɑːdɪɡən/
- coat /kəʊt/
- dress /dres/
- jacket /ˈdʒækɪt/
- jeans /dʒiːnz/
- shirt /ʃɜːt/
- 1 shorts /ʃɔːts/
- skirt /skɜːt/
- suit /suːt/
- sweater (synonym *jumper*) /ˈswetə/
- top /tɒp/
- tracksuit /ˈtræksuːt/
- trousers /ˈtraʊzəz/
- T-shirt /ˈtiːʃɜːt/

Footwear
- boots /buːts/
- flip-flops /ˈflɪp flɒps/
- sandals /ˈsændlz/
- shoes /ʃuːz/
- trainers /ˈtreɪnəz/

Accessories
- belt /belt/
- cap /kæp/
- hat /hæt/
- leggings /ˈleɡɪŋz/
- gloves /ɡlʌvz/
- scarf /skɑːf/
- socks /sɒks/
- tie /taɪ/
- tights /taɪts/

Jewellery
- bracelet /ˈbreɪslət/
- earrings /ˈɪərɪŋz/
- necklace /ˈnekləs/
- ring /rɪŋ/

b 1 19))) Listen and check.

c Cover the words and look at the pictures. Test yourself or a partner.

◀ p.8

> 🔍 **wear, carry, or dress?**
> Use *wear* for clothes and jewellery / glasses, etc.
> She's wearing a hat. He's wearing sunglasses.
> Use *carry* for bags, cases, etc.
> She's carrying a bag.
> Use *dress* (with no object) to describe the kind of clothes people wear.
> The Italians dress very well. Jane always dresses in black.

Holidays

VOCABULARY BANK

1 PHRASES WITH GO

a Match the phrases and pictures.

- go a<u>broad</u>
- *1* go away for the wee<u>kend</u>
- go by bus / car / plane / train
- go <u>camp</u>ing
- go for a walk
- go on <u>hol</u>iday
- go out at night
- go <u>sight</u>seeing
- go <u>ski</u>ing / <u>wal</u>king / <u>cyc</u>ling
- go <u>swim</u>ming / <u>sai</u>ling / <u>surf</u>ing

b 🔊 1 31 Listen and check.

c Cover the phrases and look at the pictures. Test yourself or a partner.

2 OTHER HOLIDAY ACTIVITIES

a Complete the verb phrases.

book	buy	have	hire	rent
spend	~~stay~~	sunbathe	take	

- _stay_ in a h<u>o</u>tel / at a <u>camp</u>site / with friends
- _____ <u>pho</u>tos
- _____ souve<u>nirs</u>
- _____ on the beach
- _____ a good time
- _____ <u>mo</u>ney / time
- _____ an a<u>part</u>ment
- _____ a <u>bi</u>cycle / skis
- _____ flights / h<u>o</u>tels on<u>line</u>

b 🔊 1 32 Listen and check.

> 🔍 **rent or hire?**
> *Rent* and *hire* mean the same but we normally use *rent* for a longer period of time, e.g. you rent a flat or apartment, and *hire* for a short time, e.g. you hire skis, a bike, a boat, etc. With a car you can use *hire* or *rent*.

c Test yourself. Cover the verbs. Remember the phrases.

3 ADJECTIVES

a Match the questions and answers.

1. What was the weather like? It was…
2. What was the hotel like? It was…
3. What was the town like? It was…
4. What were the people like? They were…
5. What was the food like? It was…

- ☐ [+] com<u>for</u>table, lu<u>xu</u>rious
  - [−] <u>ba</u>sic, <u>dir</u>ty, un<u>com</u>fortable
- ☐ [+] <u>friend</u>ly, <u>help</u>ful   [−] un<u>friend</u>ly, un<u>help</u>ful
- ☐ [+] <u>beau</u>tiful, <u>love</u>ly   [−] <u>nois</u>y, <u>crow</u>ded
- ☐ [+] de<u>li</u>cious   [−] <u>no</u>thing <u>spe</u>cial, dis<u>gust</u>ing
- ☐ [+] warm, <u>sun</u>ny   [−] <u>ve</u>ry <u>win</u>dy, <u>fog</u>gy, <u>cloud</u>y

b 🔊 1 33 Listen and check.

> 🔍 **General positive and negative adjectives**
> [+] <u>love</u>ly, <u>won</u>derful, fan<u>tas</u>tic, great
>   OK, not bad, al<u>right</u>
> [−] <u>aw</u>ful, <u>hor</u>rible, <u>ter</u>rible

◀ *p.12*

Prepositions

VOCABULARY BANK

1 AT / IN / ON

a Complete the chart with *at*, *in*, or *on*.

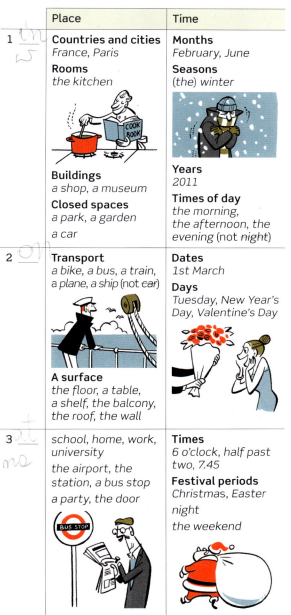

	Place	Time
1 in	**Countries and cities** France, Paris **Rooms** the kitchen **Buildings** a shop, a museum **Closed spaces** a park, a garden a car	**Months** February, June **Seasons** (the) winter **Years** 2011 **Times of day** the morning, the afternoon, the evening (not *night*)
2 on	**Transport** a bike, a bus, a train, a plane, a ship (not *car*) **A surface** the floor, a table, a shelf, the balcony, the roof, the wall	**Dates** 1st March **Days** Tuesday, New Year's Day, Valentine's Day
3 at	school, home, work, university the airport, the station, a bus stop a party, the door	**Times** 6 o'clock, half past two, 7.45 **Festival periods** Christmas, Easter *night* the weekend

b **1 42))** Listen and check.

c Look at the chart for a few minutes. Then test a partner:

 A Say a place or time word, e.g. *Paris*, *Tuesday*.
 B Close your books. Say the preposition (*at*, *in*, or *on*).

 Swap roles.

◀ p.14

2 VERBS + PREPOSITIONS

a Complete the **Prepositions** column with a word from the list.

about   at   for   in   of   on   to   with

	Prepositions
1 I arrived ___ Paris on Friday night.	in
2 I was very tired when I arrived ___ the hotel.	___
3 I hate waiting ___ people who are late.	___
4 **A** What are you going to do ___ the weekend? **B** I don't know. It depends ___ the weather.	___
5 I'm sorry, but I really don't agree ___ you.	___
6 I asked ___ a chicken sandwich, but this is tuna!	___
7 Let's invite Debbie and Tim ___ the party.	___
8 Who's going to pay ___ the meal?	___
9 I need to speak ___ Martin ___ the meeting.	___, ___
10 I don't spend much money ___ food.	___
11 Are you going to write ___ him soon?	___
12 Don't worry ___ the exam. It isn't very hard.	___
13 She fell ___ love ___ a man she met on the internet.	___, ___
14 You're not listening! What are you thinking ___?	___
15 **A** What do you think ___ Shakira? **B** I really like her. I think she's great.	___

b **1 68))** Listen and check.

c Cover the **Prepositions** column. Say the sentences.

🔍 **arrive in or arrive at?**
Remember we use *arrive in* + cities or countries and *arrive at* + buildings, stations, etc.

◀ p.23

153

Housework, *make* or *do*?

VOCABULARY BANK

1 HOUSEWORK

a Match the verb phrases and the pictures.

```
   clean the floor
   do the ironing
   do the shopping
   do the washing
   do the washing-up
 1 lay the table (opposite clear)
   make lunch
   make the beds
   pick up dirty clothes (from the floor)
   put away your clothes
   take out the rubbish
   tidy your room
```

b (2 13)) Listen and check.

c Cover the phrases and look at the pictures. Say the phrases.

2 MAKE OR DO?

a Write *make* or *do* next to the pictures.

  _do_   a course

  _____ a mistake

  _____ an exam / an exercise / homework

  _____ a noise

  _____ a phone call

  _____ housework

  _____ friends

  _____ lunch / dinner

  _____ sport / exercise

  _____ plans

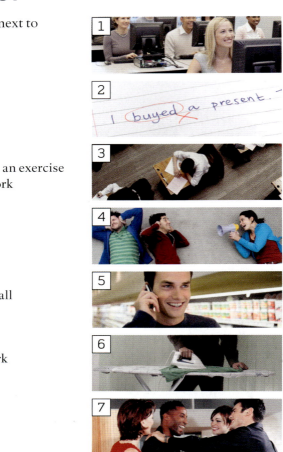

b (2 14)) Listen and check.

c Cover the phrases and look at the pictures. Say the phrases.

d Talk to a partner.
- What housework do *you* usually do? What have you done today?
- Who does the most housework in your family?
- Do you argue about housework in your family? Give examples.
- What housework do you hate doing? What don't you mind doing? Is there any housework you like doing?

◀ p.28

Shopping

VOCABULARY BANK

1 IN A SHOP OR STORE

a Match the words and pictures.

- ☐ changing rooms
- ☐ checkout
- ☐ customer
- ☐ receipt
- ☐ shop assistant
- 1 take sth back
- ☐ trolley / basket
- ☐ try sth on

b 🔊 2 28)) Listen and check.

c Cover the words and look at the pictures. Say the words.

> **fit or suit?**
> If clothes **don't fit** you, it means they are the wrong size (e.g. too big, too small, too tight, too loose).
> If clothes **don't suit** you, it means they don't look good on you.

2 ONLINE

a Read the text about shopping online. Then complete it with words from the list.

account /ə'kaʊnt/   auction /'ɔːkʃn/   basket /'bɑːskɪt/
checkout /'tʃekaʊt/   delivery /dɪ'lɪvəri/   item /'aɪtəm/
payment /'peɪmənt/   size /saɪz/   website /'websaɪt/

Shopping online

When you are shopping online, first you go to the ¹*website*. The first time you use a site you usually have to **create** an ²_____, where you give your personal details. You then choose what you want to buy, and **click on** each ³_____. If you are buying clothes, make sure you get the right ⁴_____! Everything you buy goes into your **shopping bag** or ⁵_____, usually at the top right of the page. When you are ready to pay you click on '**proceed** to ⁶_____'. You then have to give your ⁷_____ **address** where you want them to send your things, and give your ⁸_____ **details**, for example your credit card number and expiry date. Many people today also buy and sell things online at ⁹_____ **sites** like eBay.

b 🔊 2 29)) Listen and check.

◀ p.31

1
2
3
4
5
6
7
8

Describing a town or city

VOCABULARY BANK

1 WHERE IS IT? HOW BIG IS IT?

a Look at the map. Then read the description of Reading and circle the correct words or phrases.

> Reading is a town in the *south / north* of England, or *the River Thames / the South coast*. It is about 40 miles *east / west* of London. It is a *small / medium sized / large* town and it has a population of about 250,000. It is famous for its music festival, which is one of the biggest in the UK.

b 2 46)) Listen and check.

2 WHAT'S IT LIKE? adjectives to describe a town or city

a Match the adjectives and sentences 1–6.

		Opposite
	boring /ˈbɔːrɪŋ/	*exciting*
	crowded /ˈkraʊdɪd/	_____
	dangerous /ˈdeɪndʒərəs/	_____
	modern /ˈmɒdn/	_____
	noisy /ˈnɔɪzi/	_____
	polluted /pəˈluːtɪd/	_____

1 There are a lot of bars and clubs with loud music.
2 The air is very dirty.
3 There are too many people.
4 The buildings were all built quite recently.
5 There's nothing to do.
6 You have to be careful, especially at night.

b Match these adjectives with their opposites in **a**.

> clean /kliːn/   empty /ˈempti/
> exciting /ɪkˈsaɪtɪŋ/   interesting /ˈɪntrestɪŋ/
> old /əʊld/   quiet /ˈkwaɪət/   safe /seɪf/

c 2 47)) Listen and check your answers to **a** and **b**.

d Cover the words and look at the sentences. Remember the adjectives and their opposites.

3 WHAT IS THERE TO SEE?

a Put the words in the right column.

> castle /ˈkɑːsl/   cathedral /kəˈθiːdrəl/   church /tʃɜːtʃ/
> department store /dɪˈpɑːtmənt stɔː/   market /ˈmɑːkɪt/   mosque /mɒsk/
> museum /mjuˈziːəm/   palace /ˈpæləs/   shopping centre /ˈʃɒpɪŋ sentə/
> statue /ˈstætʃuː/   temple /ˈtempl/   town hall /taʊn ˈhɔːl/

Religious buildings	Places where you can buy things	Historic buildings and monuments
		castle

b 2 48)) Listen and check.

c Which of the places in **a** are there / aren't there in your city?

> There's a cathedral and some churches.
> There isn't a castle.

◀ p.39

Opposite verbs

VOCABULARY BANK

a Match the verbs and pictures.

	Opposite
arrive (*early*) /əˈraɪv/	leave
break (*your glasses*) /breɪk/	
buy (*a house*) /baɪ/	
find (*your keys*) /faɪnd/	
forget (*a name*) /fəˈget/	
lend (*money to somebody*) /lend/	
miss (*a train*) /mɪs/	
pass (*an exam*) /pɑːs/	
1 push (*the door*) /pʊʃ/	
send (*an email*) /send/	
start (*a race*) /stɑːt/	
teach (*English*) /tiːtʃ/	
turn on (*the TV*) /tɜːn ˈɒn/	
win (*a match*) /wɪn/	

b Find the opposite verbs in the list. Write them in the **Opposite** column.

borrow (*from somebody*) /ˈbɒrəʊ/
catch /kætʃ/
fail /feɪl/
get / receive /get/ /rɪˈsiːv/
learn /lɜːn/
leave /liːv/
lose (x2) /luːz/
mend / repair /mend/ /rɪˈpeə/
pull /pʊl/
remember /rɪˈmembə/
sell /sel/
stop / finish /stɒp/ /ˈfɪnɪʃ/
turn off /tɜːn ˈɒf/

c))) 3 2 Listen and check.

d Cover the verbs and look at the pictures. Remember the verbs and their opposites.

◀ p.44

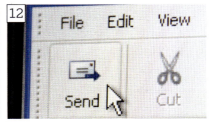

Verb forms

VOCABULARY BANK

1 VERBS + INFINITIVE

a Complete the **to + verb** column with *to* + a verb from the list.

| be bring buy catch drive find get married |
| go (x2) help pay rain see turn off |

			to + verb
1	decide	We've decided ___ to France for our holiday.	*to go*
2	forget	Don't forget ___ all the lights.	_____
3	hope	We hope ___ you again soon.	_____
4	learn	I'm learning ___. My test's next month.	_____
5	need	I need ___ to the supermarket. We don't have any milk.	_____
6	offer	He offered ___ me with my CV.	_____
7	plan	They're planning ___ soon.	_____
8	pretend	He pretended ___ ill, but he wasn't really.	_____
9	promise	He's promised ___ me back when he gets a job.	_____
10	remember	Remember ___ your dictionaries to class tomorrow.	_____
11	start	It was very cloudy and it started ___.	_____
12	try	I'm trying ___ a job, but it's very hard.	_____
13	want	I want ___ the six o'clock train.	_____
14	would like	I'd like ___ a new car next month.	_____

b ③ 25))) Listen and check.

c Cover the **to + verb** column. Say the sentences.

◀ p.53

2 VERBS + GERUND (VERB + -ING)

a Complete the **gerund** column with a verb from the list in the gerund.

| be cook do have make rain read talk tidy wake up work |

			gerund
1	enjoy	I enjoy ___ in bed.	*reading*
2	finish	Have you finished ___ your room?	_____
3	go on (= continue)	I want to go on ___ until I'm 60.	_____
4	hate	I hate ___ late when I'm meeting someone.	_____
5	like	I like ___ breakfast in a café.	_____
6	love	I love ___ on a sunny morning.	_____
7	(don't) mind	I don't mind ___ the ironing. It's quite relaxing.	_____
8	spend (time)	She spends hours ___ on the phone.	_____
9	start*	It started ___ at 5.30 in the morning.	_____
10	stop	Please stop ___ such a noise. I can't think.	_____
11	feel like	I don't feel like ___ today. Let's go out for lunch.	_____

* *start* can be used with a gerund or infinitive, e.g. *It started raining. It started to rain.*

b ③ 29))) Listen and check.

c Cover the **gerund** column. Say the sentences.

◀ p.55

get

VOCABULARY BANK

> **get**
> *get* is one of the most common verbs in English. It has several different meanings, e.g. *arrive*, *become*, and can also be used with many prepositions or adverbs with different meanings, e.g. *get up*, *get on with*.

a Match the phrases and the pictures.

get = become (+ adjective / past participle)
- get angry
- get divorced
- get fit
- get lost
- get married
- 1 get nervous

get = become (+ comparative)
- get better
- get colder
- get worse

get = buy / obtain
- get a job
- get a newspaper
- get a ticket

get + preposition (phrasal verbs)
- get on / off a bus
- get on (well) with
- get up

get (to) = arrive
- get home
- get to school
- get to work

get = receive
- get an email
- get a present
- get a (text) message

b 3 55))) Listen and check.

c Cover the phrases and look at the pictures. Test yourself or a partner.

◀ *p.61*

159

Confusing verbs

VOCABULARY BANK

a Match the verbs and pictures.

- **wear** /weə/
  jewellery
  clothes
- **carry** /ˈkæri/
  a bag
  a baby
- **win** /wɪn/
  a medal
  a prize
  a match
- **earn** /ɜːn/
  a salary
  money
- **know** /nəʊ/
  somebody well
  something
- **meet** /miːt/
  somebody for the first time
  at 11 o'clock
- 1 **hope** /həʊp/
  that something good will happen
  to do sth
- **wait** /weɪt/
  for a bus
  for a long time
- **watch** /wɒtʃ/
  TV
  a match
- **look at** /lʊk æt/
  a photo
  your watch
- **look** /lʊk/
  happy
  about 25 years old
- **look like** /lʊk laɪk/
  your mother
  a model
- **miss** /mɪs/
  the bus
  a class
- **lose** /luːz/
  a match
  your glasses
- **bring** /brɪŋ/
  your dictionary
  sth back from holiday
- **take** /teɪk/
  an umbrella
  your children to school
- **look for** /lʊk fɔː/
  your glasses
  a job
- **find** /faɪnd/
  your glasses
  a job
- **say** /seɪ/
  sorry
  hello
  something **to** sb
- **tell** /tel/
  a joke
  a lie
  somebody something
- **lend** /lend/
  money **to** sb
- **borrow** /ˈbɒrəʊ/
  money **from** sb

b 4 5))) Listen and check.

c Work with a partner. A say a verb, B say a possible continuation.

A Wait...   B for a bus

◀ p.63

> **hope and expect**
> hope = to want sth to happen and think it will happen, always for positive things, e.g. *I hope I'll pass the exam.*
> expect = to think sth will happen, usually for a reason (not necessarily a positive thing), e.g. *I expect I'll fail because I haven't worked very hard.*
>
> **look and look like**
> After *look* we use an adjective or an age.
> After *look like* we use a noun.

Animals

VOCABULARY BANK

a Match the words and pictures.

- ☐ bee /biː/
- ☐ butterfly /ˈbʌtəflaɪ/
- ☐ fly /flaɪ/
- ☐ mosquito /məˈskiːtəʊ/
- ☐ spider /ˈspaɪdə/

- 1 bull /bʊl/
- ☐ chicken /ˈtʃɪkɪn/
- ☐ cow /kaʊ/
- ☐ goat /ɡəʊt/
- ☐ horse /hɔːs/
- ☐ pig /pɪɡ/
- ☐ sheep /ʃiːp/

- ☐ bat /bæt/
- ☐ bear /beə/
- ☐ bird /bɜːd/
- ☐ camel /ˈkæml/
- ☐ crocodile /ˈkrɒkədaɪl/
- ☐ dolphin /ˈdɒlfɪn/
- ☐ elephant /ˈelɪfənt/
- ☐ giraffe /dʒəˈrɑːf/
- ☐ jellyfish /ˈdʒelifɪʃ/
- ☐ kangaroo /ˌkæŋɡəˈruː/
- ☐ lion /ˈlaɪən/
- ☐ monkey /ˈmʌŋki/
- ☐ mouse (plural *mice*) /maʊs/
- ☐ rabbit /ˈræbɪt/
- ☐ shark /ʃɑːk/
- ☐ snake /sneɪk/
- ☐ tiger /ˈtaɪɡə/
- ☐ whale /weɪl/

b **4 17**)) Listen and check.

c Cover the words and look at the pictures. Test yourself or a partner.

◀ p.68

Expressing movement

VOCABULARY BANK

a Match the words and pictures.

- under (*the bridge*) /ˈʌndə/
- along (*the street*) /əˈlɒŋ/
- round / around (*the lake*) /raʊnd/ /əˈraʊnd/
- through (*the tunnel*) /θruː/
- into (*the shop*) /ˈɪntuː/
- across (*the road*) /əˈkrɒs/
- over (*the bridge*) /ˈəʊvə/
- up (*the steps*) /ʌp/
- past (*the church*) /pɑːst/
- towards (*the lake*) /təˈwɔːdz/
- **1** down (*the steps*) /daʊn/
- out of (*the shop*) /ˈaʊt əv/

> 🔍 **in(to) and out (of)**
> After a verb of movement we use either *in / out* or *into / out of* + place, e.g.
> Come **in**. Come **into** my office.
> He ran **out**. He ran **out of** the room.

b 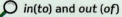 Listen and check.

c Cover the words. Where did Snowy go?

He went down the steps…

> 🔍 **away, off, and back**
>
> We use **away** to express movement to another place, e.g. **Go away**! I don't want to speak to you. The man **ran away** when he saw the policeman.
>
>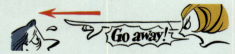
>
> We use **back** to express movement to the place where something or somebody was before, e.g. After dinner we **went back** to our hotel. Their dog ran away and never **came back**.
>
>
>
> We use **off** to express movement down or away, e.g. **Get off** the bus at the railway station. The man **ran off** when he saw the policeman.
>
>

◀ p.84

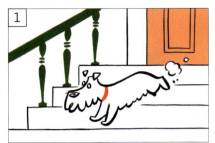

Phrasal verbs

VOCABULARY BANK

a Match the sentences and the pictures.

- [ ] The match will **be over** at about 5.30.
- [ ] I need to **give up** smoking.
- [1] Don't **throw away** that letter!
- [ ] **Turn down** the music! It's very loud.
- [ ] **Turn up** the TV! I can't hear.
- [ ] He **looked up** the words in a dictionary.
- [ ] Could you **fill in** this form?
- [ ] I want to **find out** about hotels in Madrid.
- [ ] It's bedtime – go and **put on** your pyjamas.
- [ ] Could you **take off** your boots, please?
- [ ] My sister's **looking after** Jimmy for me today.
- [ ] I'm really **looking forward to** the holidays.

b 5 2))) Listen and check.

c Cover the sentences and look at the pictures. Remember the phrasal verbs.

d Look at these other phrasal verbs from Files 1–10. Can you remember what they mean?

get up
come on
go away (for the weekend)
go out (at night)
stand up
sit down

turn on (the TV)
turn off (the TV)
try on (clothes)
give back (something you've borrowed)
take back (something to a shop)
call back (later)
pay back (money you've borrowed)
switch off (the air conditioning)
write down (the words)
put away (e.g. clothes in a cupboard)
pick up (something on the floor)

carry on (doing something)
look for (something you've lost)
get on / off (a bus)
get on with (a person)

◀ p.87

> **Type 1 = no object**
> The verb and the particle (*on, up,* etc.) are **never separated**.
> *I get up at 7.30.*
>
> **Type 2 = + object**
> The verb and the particle (*on, up,* etc.) **can be separated**.
> *Turn the TV on.* OR *Turn on the TV.*
>
> **Type 3 = + object**
> The verb and the particle (*on, up,* etc.) are **never separated**.
> *Look for your keys.* NOT *Look your keys for.*

163

Irregular verbs

🔊 5 29

Present	Past simple	Past participle
be /bi/	was /wɒz/ were /wɜː/	been /biːn/
become /bɪˈkʌm/	became /bɪˈkeɪm/	become
begin /bɪˈgɪn/	began /bɪˈgæn/	begun /bɪˈgʌn/
break /breɪk/	broke /brəʊk/	broken /ˈbrəʊkən/
bring /brɪŋ/	brought /brɔːt/	brought
build /bɪld/	built /bɪlt/	built
buy /baɪ/	bought /bɔːt/	bought
can /kæn/	could /kʊd/	–
catch /kætʃ/	caught /kɔːt/	caught
choose /tʃuːz/	chose /tʃəʊz/	chosen /ˈtʃəʊzn/
come /kʌm/	came /keɪm/	come
cost /kɒst/	cost	cost
cut /kʌt/	cut	cut
do /duː/	did /dɪd/	done /dʌn/
drink /drɪŋk/	drank /dræŋk/	drunk /drʌŋk/
drive /draɪv/	drove /drəʊv/	driven /ˈdrɪvn/
eat /iːt/	ate /eɪt/	eaten /ˈiːtn/
fall /fɔːl/	fell /fel/	fallen /ˈfɔːlən/
feel /fiːl/	felt /felt/	felt
find /faɪnd/	found /faʊnd/	found
fly /flaɪ/	flew /fluː/	flown /fləʊn/
forget /fəˈget/	forgot /fəˈgɒt/	forgotten /fəˈgɒtn/
get /get/	got /gɒt/	got
give /gɪv/	gave /geɪv/	given /ˈgɪvn/
go /gəʊ/	went /went/	gone /gɒn/
grow /grəʊ/	grew /gruː/	grown /grəʊn/
have /hæv/	had /hæd/	had
hear /hɪə/	heard /hɜːd/	heard
hit /hɪt/	hit	hit
keep /kiːp/	kept /kept/	kept
know /nəʊ/	knew /njuː/	known /nəʊn/
learn /lɜːn/	learnt /lɜːnt/	learnt
leave /liːv/	left /left/	left
lend /lend/	lent /lent/	lent
let /let/	let	let
lose /luːz/	lost /lɒst/	lost
make /meɪk/	made /meɪd/	made
meet /miːt/	met /met/	met
pay /peɪ/	paid /peɪd/	paid
put /pʊt/	put	put
read /riːd/	read /red/	read /red/
ring /rɪŋ/	rang /ræŋ/	rung /rʌŋ/
run /rʌn/	ran /ræn/	run
say /seɪ/	said /sed/	said
see /siː/	saw /sɔː/	seen /siːn/
sell /sel/	sold /səʊld/	sold
send /send/	sent /sent/	sent
shut /ʃʌt/	shut	shut
sing /sɪŋ/	sang /sæŋ/	sung /sʌŋ/
sit /sɪt/	sat /sæt/	sat
sleep /sliːp/	slept /slept/	slept
speak /spiːk/	spoke /spəʊk/	spoken /ˈspəʊkən/
spend /spend/	spent /spent/	spent
stand /stænd/	stood /stʊd/	stood
steal /stiːl/	stole /stəʊl/	stolen /ˈstəʊlən/
swim /swɪm/	swam /swæm/	swum /swʌm/
take /teɪk/	took /tʊk/	taken /ˈteɪkən/
teach /tiːtʃ/	taught /tɔːt/	taught
tell /tel/	told /təʊld/	told
think /θɪŋk/	thought /θɔːt/	thought
throw /θrəʊ/	threw /θruː/	thrown /θrəʊn/
understand /ʌndəˈstænd/	understood /ʌndəˈstʊd/	understood
wake /weɪk/	woke /wəʊk/	woken /ˈwəʊkən/
wear /weə/	wore /wɔː/	worn /wɔːn/
win /wɪn/	won /wʌn/	won
write /raɪt/	wrote /rəʊt/	written /ˈrɪtn/

Appendix

have got

I've got a brother and two sisters. **3 45))**
I haven't got any pets.
She's got a beautiful house.
He hasn't got many friends.
Have they got any children? No, they haven't.
Has the hotel got a swimming pool? Yes, it has.

full form	contraction	negative	
I have got	I've got	I haven't got	
You have got	You've got	You haven't got	
He / She / It has got	He / She / It's got	He / She / It hasn't got	a car.
We have got	We've got	We haven't got	
You have got	You've got	You haven't got	
They have got	They've got	They haven't got	

?		✓		✗	
Have I got		I have.		I haven't.	
Have you got		you have.		you haven't.	
Has he / he / it got	a car? Yes,	he / she / it has.	No,	he / she / it hasn't.	
Have we got		we have.		we haven't.	
Have you got		you have.		you haven't.	
Have they got		they have.		they haven't.	

- You can use *have got* instead of *have* for possession in the present.
  I've got a bike. = **I have** a bike.
  Have you got a car? = **Do you have** a car?
- We also use *have got* to talk about family and illnesses, and to describe people.
  I've got two sisters. **He's got** a cold.
  She's got long brown hair.
- *have got* is not used in the past. For past possession use *had*.
  I **had** a pet cat when I was a child.
  Did you have a pet?
- *I've got… / Have you got…?* is common in the UK especially in conversation, but *I have… / Do you have…?* is also common.

a Write +, –, and ? sentences with the correct form of *have got*.

   they / big house +   *They've got a big house.*

1. she / any brothers –
2. you / big flat ?
3. we / a lot of work today –
4. your sister / a boyfriend ?
5. Roger and Val / a beautiful garden +
6. I / a really good teacher +
7. My brother / a job at the moment –
8. they / the same colour eyes +
9. we / a meeting today ?
10. he / many friends at work –

b Complete the sentences with the right form of *have got*.

   They love animals. They*'ve got* two dogs and five cats.

1. I hope it doesn't rain – I _____ my umbrella today.
2. _____ your phone _____ a good camera?
3. I _____ a new iPad. Do you want to see it?
4. Sorry kids, I _____ enough money to buy sweets.
5. Jane _____ 50 pairs of shoes – can you believe it?
6. I can't call him now – I _____ a signal on my phone.
7. _____ you _____ your keys? I can't find mine.
8. Maria's so lucky – she _____ lovely curly hair.
9. One more question, Mr Jones. _____ you _____ any qualifications?
10. We might have problems getting there because we _____ satnav in our car.

◀ p.59

Appendix 165

Vowel sounds

SOUND BANK

	usual spelling		! but also
fish	i	thin slim history kiss if since	English women busy decide repeat gym
tree	ee ea e	feel sheep teach mean she we	people machine key niece receipt
cat	a	cap hat back catch carry match	
car	ar a	far large scarf fast pass after	aunt laugh heart
clock	o	top lost socks wrong hot box	what wash want because
horse	or al aw	boring north walk ball awful saw	water auction bought thought abroad warm
bull	u oo	pull push football book look good	would should woman
boot	oo u★ ew	school choose use polluted few knew	do suit juice shoe lose through
computer	Many different spellings. /ə/ is always unstressed. clever nervous arrive police inventor agree		
bird	er ir ur	person verb dirty shirt curly turn	earn work world worse
egg	e	spell lend west send very red	friendly weather sweater any said

	usual spelling		! but also
up	u	sunny mustn't funny run lucky cut	come does someone enough young touch
train	a★ ai ay	change wake trainers fail away pay	break steak great overweight they grey
phone	o★ oa	open hope won't so coat goal	snow throw although
bike	i★ y igh	quiet item shy why might sights	buy eyes height
owl	ou ow	trousers round account blouse crowded down	
boy	oi oy	coin noisy point toy enjoy	
ear	eer ere ear	beer engineer here we're beard earrings	really idea
chair	air are	airport stairs pair hair square careful	their there wear bear
tourist	A very unusual sound. Europe furious sure plural		
/i/	A sound between /ɪ/ and /iː/. Consonant + y at the end of words is pronounced /i/. happy angry thirsty		
/u/	An unusual sound. education usually situation		

★ especially before consonant + e

○ short vowels   ○ long vowels   ○ diphthongs

Consonant sounds

SOUND BANK

		usual spelling	! but also
parrot	p pp	promise possible copy flip-flops opposite appearance	
bag	b bb	belt body probably job cab rabbit rubbish	
key	c k ck	camping across skirt kind checkout pick	chemist's stomach mosquito account
girl	g gg	grow goat forget begin foggy leggings	
flower	f ph ff	find afraid safe elephant nephew off different	enough laugh
vase	v	video visit lovely invent over river	of
tie	t tt	try tell start late better sitting	walked dressed
dog	d dd	did dead hard told address middle	loved tired
snake	s ss ci/ce	stops faster miss message place circle	science
zebra	z s	zoo lazy freezing reason lose has toes	
shower	sh ti (+ vowel) ci+a	shut shoes washing finish patient information special musician	sugar sure machine moustache
television	An unusual sound. revision decision confusion usually garage		

		usual spelling	! but also
thumb	th	thing throw healthy south maths both	
mother	th	neither the clothes sunbathe that with	
chess	ch tch t (+ure)	chicken child beach catch match picture future	
jazz	j dge	jacket just journey enjoy bridge judge	generous teenager giraffe age
leg	l ll	little less plan incredible will trolley	
right	r rr	really rest practice try borrow married	written wrong
witch	w wh	website twins worried win why which whale	one once
yacht	y before u	yet year young yoga useful uniform	
monkey	m mm	mountain modern remember email summer swimming	
nose	n nn	need necklace none any funny dinner	know knock
singer	ng	angry ring along thing bring going	think thank
house	h	hat hate ahead perhaps hire helpful	who whose whole

○ voiced ○ unvoiced

OXFORD
UNIVERSITY PRESS

Great Clarendon Street, Oxford, OX2 6DP,
United Kingdom

Oxford University Press is a department of the
University of Oxford. It furthers the University's
objective of excellence in research, scholarship,
and education by publishing worldwide. Oxford
is a registered trade mark of Oxford University
Press in the UK and in certain other countries

© Oxford University Press 2013

The moral rights of the author have been asserted

First published in 2013

2017
10 9 8 7 6 5 4

No unauthorized photocopying

All rights reserved. No part of this publication
may be reproduced, stored in a retrieval system,
or transmitted, in any form or by any means,
without the prior permission in writing of Oxford
University Press, or as expressly permitted by
law, by licence or under terms agreed with the
appropriate reprographics rights organization.
Enquiries concerning reproduction outside the
scope of the above should be sent to the ELT
Rights Department, Oxford University Press, at
the address above

You must not circulate this work in any other
form and you must impose this same condition
on any acquirer

Links to third party websites are provided by Oxford
in good faith and for information only. Oxford
disclaims any responsibility for the materials
contained in any third party website referenced in
this work

ISBN: 978 0 19 451795 9

Printed in China

This book is printed on paper from certified
and well-managed sources.

ACKNOWLEDGEMENTS

The authors would like to thank all the teachers and students round the world whose feedback has helped us to shape English File.

The authors would also like to thank: all those at Oxford University Press (both in Oxford and around the world) and the design team who have contributed their talents and ideas to producing this course.

Finally very special thanks from Clive to Maria Angeles, Lucia, and Eric, and from Christina to Cristina, for all their support and encouragement. Christina would also like to thank her children Joaquin, Marco, and Krysia for their constant inspiration.

The publisher and authors would also like to thank the following for their invaluable feedback on the materials: Beatriz Martín, Brian Brennan, Elif Barbaros, Gill Hamilton, Jane Hudson, Joanna Sosnowska, Wayne Rimmer, Urbán Ágnes, Anne Parry, Belén Sáez Hernáez, Edelweis Fernández Elorz, Emilie Řezníčková, Erika Feszl, Imogen Clare Dickens, Jonathan Clarke, Kieran Donaghy, Kinga Belley, Laura Villiger Potts, Manuela Gazzola, Mariusz Mirecki, Paolo Jacomelli, Pavlina Zoss, Rebecca Lennox, Robert Anderson, Sandy Millin, Sophie Rogers, Washington Jorge Mukarzel Filho.

The Publisher and Authors are very grateful to the following who have provided information, personal stories, and/or photographs: Lindka Cierach, p.30 (interview); Sara Mohr-Pietsch, p.86 (interview); Krysia Cogollos, p.112 (photo and description); Elif Barbaros, p.114 (Kayseri)

The authors and publisher are grateful to those who have given permission to reproduce the following extracts and adaptations of copyright material: p.14 Extract from 'The story behind the picture: American Elections 2008' by Tom Pilston, *The Times*, 17 November 2009. Reproduced by permission; p.15 Extract from 'The image that cost a fortune' by Ben Macintyre, *The Times*, 17 November 2009. Reproduced by permission; p.19 Extract from 'These people were at the museum not to admire the art, but to take snaps to prove they were there' by Marcel Berlins, *The Guardian*, 13 May 2009 © Copyright Guardian News & Media Ltd 2009. Reproduced by permission; p.39 Extract from 'Wish you weren't here' by Tim Moore, *The Sunday Times*, 06 July 1998. Reproduced by permission; p.51 Extract from 'Musical wings on my feet' by Warren Pole, *The Times*, 02 October 2009. Reproduced by permission; p.78 Extract from *Could Do Better*, edited by Catherine Hurley © 1997 Simon & Schuster Inc. Reproduced by permission; p.83 Extract from 'Dolphins save swimmers from shark attack', *The Guardian*, 23 November 2004 © Copyright Guardian News & Media Ltd 2004. Reproduced by permission; p.99 Extract from "Astonishing coincidence: Couple meet 20 years after both having same heart operations… in SAME hospital, on SAME day, by SAME surgeon", *Daily Mail*, 29 July 2010. Reproduced by permission.

The publishers would like to thank the following for their kind permission to reproduce photographs: Alamy pp.13 (Nagelestock), 19 (LusoItaly/taking photos), 21 (Imagebroker), 29, 30 (Andrew Twort/shoes), 35 (NM Photo/shoes), 38 (Directphoto.org/Chanel), 52–53 (Universal/Dreamworks/Phillip Caruso), 68 (Photoshot Holdings Ltd/jellyfish, Arco Images GmbH/bee) 73 (Pictorial Press/Julio Iglesias), 76 (mediablitzimages (uk) Limited/hair dryer), 76 (Joe Fox/policeman), 77 (Feng Yu/tin opener), 83 (Martin Strmiska), 86 (Realimage/radio), 100 and 106 (f4foto/Bethany), 114 (Ayhan Altun), 115 (Donald Nausbaun/painting), 150 (nobleIMAGES/girl blue eyes, Catchlight Visual Services/girl red hair), 151 (mediablitzimages (uk) Limited/dress, Creative Control/top) 152 (Robert Stainforth/walking in wood, Tristar Photos/plane coach car, Gregory Wrona/skiing), 154 (Nicosan/shopping, mauritius images GmbH/ironing, Jochen Tack/wash floor, jacky chapman/tidy lego, Photofusion Picture Library/rubbish), 155 (allesalltag/returning garment, David Levenson/checkout) 156 (Jon Arnold Images Ltd/castle) 157 (Marc Hill/pass exam, Jim Cartwright/e-mail, AFP/win match), 158 (Eye Ubiquitous/Eiffel tower), 160 (PCN Photography/win medal, Commercial Megapress Collection/woman in striped t-shirt); Catherine Blackie pp.154 (pick up clothes) 157 (find keys), 160 (photo on phone, men friends, woman with umbrella); Mark Bourdillon Photography p.39 (Tim Moore); Camera Press p.15 (Rapho/Gamma/Jean-Pierre Rey); Sarah Cardenas p.89; Caters News Agency p.99 (family); David Bailey/Vogue ©The Condé Nast Publications Ltd, p.30; Corbis Images pp.54 (Joseph Lindau/girl with fringe), 60 (Hans Neleman), 69 (G.Baden/mouse), 150 (Sherrie Nickol/Citizen Stock/slim man in jeans), 152 (Simon Marcus/passport), 161 (DPA/Wolfgang Kumm/bee); Thomas S England pp.88, 89 (twins); FLPA Images p.69 (Imagebroker/dog); Getty Images pp.7 and 100 and 106 (Alexander/Jena Cumbo, Oliver/James Whitaker), 8 (Nick Harvey), 20 (John Slater/girl with backpack, Tracy Kahn/man in jeans), 29 (phone), 38 (Jochem D Wijnands/Little mermaid, James Strachan/Barcelona), 54 (Brit Erlanson/woman wavy hair), 54 (Dimitri Veryitsiotis/man in blue t-shirt, man in black t-shirt), 61 (B Blue), 68 (Frank Krahmer/bull, Paul Sutherland/shark), 72 Redferns/Bob Marley), 73 (Fabrice Coffrini/Ziggy Marley, Redferns/Enrique Iglesias), 76 (ML Harris/dishwasher, Davies and Starr/zip, Grant Faint/windscreen wiper, Katherine Fawssett/washing machine, 77 (Arsenal/football), 78 (Tim Graham/Princess Diana, Winston Churchill, 79 (Redferns/John Lennon, AFP/Helen Fielding), 84 (tennis, high jump, Peter Cade/ski, Ports Illustrated/basketball, cycling, AFP/handball/rugby), 85 (John McEnroe) 94 (Getty Images/Rob Lang/men gossiping), 100 and 106 (Cultura/Jessica, Michael Malyszko/Hughes, PBNJ Productions/Abigail, 111 (Getty/Image Source), 113 (Thomas Grass), 115 Donald Nausbaum/painting, Jetta Productions/golf); 116 (Jamie McCarthy), 150 (Ray Kachatorian/girl dark straight hair, Brad Wilson/girl wavy hair) 154 (Doug Corrance/exam, Leander Baerenz/noise, Zia Soleil/people running), 157 (runner, Commercial Eye/girl in classroom) 158 (Victoria Blackie/Man with L plate), 160 (Nicki Pardo/girl red hair, Stephen Lovekin/bracelets), 161 (Picavet/bull, Frank Kindersley/bat, WIN-Initiative/giraffe, Paul Souders/whale, Ben Hall/rabbit, Danita Delimont/sheep, Stefan Sollfors/mosquito, John Giustina/lion, Kieran Scott/goat, Mark Horn/camel, Jim Brandenburg/crocodile, Mike Hill/dolphin, Peter Cade/cow, Visuals Unlimite.d,Inc, John Abbott/snake, Suchitra prints/monkey, Paul Oomen/bear, Paul Souders/jellyfish, Kelly Funk/horse, Tim Flach/mouse, Joel Sartore/pig, Jeff Hunter/shark, James Cotier/fly, Tier Und Naturfotografie J&C Sohns/kangaroo); Robert Harding Picture Library p.69 (Age footstock/snake); I&A Photolibrary p.86 (BBC/Adrian Weinbrecht/Sara Mohr-Pietsh); Image Source pp.155 (empty trolley); Oxford University Press Capture Web pp.6 (Getty Images/Christopher Robbins), 12 (Photolibrary/couple, Getty Images/girls in boat, 36 (Getty Images Rene Mansi/street, David Oxberry/girl), 37 (Getty Images/Junos/timer, Karan Kapoor/boat), 39, 54 (Getty Images/Hybrid Images/girl blonde hair, Corbis/man with moustache), 55 (Alamy/Russell Underwood Images/man shower, Andres Rodriguez/girl with microphone), 55 (Getty Images/David de Lossy/girls singing in car), 71, 76 (Getty Images/Comstock/babies), 78 (Alamy/Stephen Mulcahey/Head boy/Head girl, Bele Olmez/pencil, 85 (ball), 86 Getty Images/Creative Crop/cereal), 94 (Corbis Images/Image Source/three women, Alamy/Johner Images/girls gossiping), 100, 106 (Getty/Comstock/Dixon, Sam Edwards/Kelly), 117 (Getty Images/Lazi& Mellenthin), 150 (Alamy/PhotoAlto/very tall man, Getty Images/Image Source/bald man, Getty Images/Jupiter Images/man with beard, Photolibrary/fat man), 151 (Alamy: Hugh Threlfall/shorts, Oleksiy Maksymenko Photography/Coat, Anatoliy Sadovskiystriped t shirt, Peter Jobst/tights), 152 (Alamy/Juice Images/couple with suitcases, family with car, Getty Images/Michael Blann/tourists, Getty Images/A. Inden/greeting people), 154 (Getty Images/Image Source/lay table, washing machine, Corbis/Monalyn Gracia/put clothes away, Alamy/Relaximages/frying), 154 (Getty Images/Noel Hendrickson/computers, phone call,Getty Images/Iris Friedrich/ironing, Getty Images/Photodisc/people chatting, Emely/make sandwich, Photodisc/planning) 155 (receipt, Getty Images/Yellow Dog Productions/customer, Corbis/Stuart O'Sullivan/Changing room, Getty Images/Fuse/girl trying on jeans, shopping basket, shop assistant), 156 (Guggenheim), 157 (Image Source/Fancy/buy house, Image Source/White/TV control, whiteboard, Image Source/Blend Images/miss train, 158 (Image Source/man reading), 160 (Getty Images/Digital Vision/man at bus stop, Image Source/Cultura/watch TV, running for bus, Image Source/John Rowley/shaking hands, Getty Images/Barbara Penoyar/man with flowers, Getty Images/Image source/tell joke, Image Source/Fancy/mother and daughter), 161 (elephant, tiger, butterfly, chicken, spider); Panos pp.14 (Tom Pilston); Photolibrary pp.38 (gondola), 161 (bird); Press Association pp.56–57, 85 (John Howard); Rex Features pp.30 (Kate Middleton, Nils Jorgensen/Royal wedding), 38 (Kevin Foy/pub), 45 (NBCU Photobank), 77 (Bournemouth News/monopoly board), 77 (Action Press/Ken Follet), 152 (Westend 61/camping, Monkey Business Images swimming), 154 (Monkey Business/bed, Burger Phanie/washing up), 160 (Startracks Photo/handbag, Sipa Press/football match); Stefan Svanström p.63; South West News Service p.47; Tate London p.9; Times on Line p.51 (NI Syndication/runner); p.156 Red Ferns/crowd)

The photograph on page 9 is reproduced by kind permission of: David Hockney. 'Mr. and Mrs Clark and Percy' 1970–71 (Acrylic on Canvas, 84 x 120', Copyright David Hockney, Collection: Tate Gallery, London).

Pronunciation chart artwork: by Ellis Nadler.

Illustrations by: Peter Bull Studios pp.63, 74, 101, 107, 156; Annelie Carlstrom/agencyrush pp.6, 28, 46; Mark Duffin p.20 (signs); Adria Fruitos/Good Illustration pp.78, 79; CartoonStock pp.44, 45/Tim Cordell; Alex Green/Folio Art p.21; Atsushi Hara/dutchuncle pp.58, 87, 92, 93, 102, 159, 163; Satoshi Hashimoto/dutchuncle agency pp.153, 162; Chris Kasch/CIA Illustration agency pp.100, 106; Ob!/Private View Agency p.62; Olivier Latyk/Good Illustration Ltd pp.4, 5; Tim Marrs pp.54, 70, 74, 96; Jerome Mirault/Colagene p.31; Cheryl Taylor/Synergy Art pp.8, 16, 17; James Taylor/DebutArt pp.25, 40, 41; Jonathan Krause pp.48, 49, 64, 65, 103, 108.

Commissioned photography by: Gareth Boden pp.20 ('Lily' and 'Matthew'), 30 (Lindka Cierach), 24, 56 (at bar), 76 (Tippex), 80, 81, 151 (jeans, suit, shirt, tracksuit, trousers, all shoes, belt, tie, cap, hat ,socks, earrings, bracelet, ring), 157 (shaking hand). MMStudios pp.56 (signs), 77 (book), 151 (skirt, top, sweater, gloves, scarf, leggings, necklace), 154 (mistake), 157 (push the door), (160 (salary/bring your dictionary).

Practical English stills photography by: Rob Judges, Jacob Hutchings, and Richard Hutchings pp.10, 11, 26, 27, 42, 43, 58, 59, 74, 75, 90, 91.